Masculinity Goes to School

Both Rob and Pam Gilbert are Associate Professors of Education at James Cook University. Pam has written widely on gender and education and is co-author with Sandra Taylor of *Fashioning the Feminine* (Allen & Unwin 1991). Rob is editor of *Studying Society and the Environment* (Macmillan Educational 1996). They are parents of a son.

MASCULINITY GOES TO SCHOOL

Rob Gilbert and Pam Gilbert

London and New York

First published 1998 by Routledge
11 New Fetter Lane, London EC4P 4EE

Simultaneously published in the USA and Canada
by Routledge
29 West 35th Street, New York, NY 10001
© 1998 Rob Gilbert and Pam Gilbert

Typeset in 10.5/12pt Plantin by DOCUPRO, Sydney
Printed and bound in Singapore by KHL Printing Co. Pte Ltd

British Library Cataloging in Publication Data
A catalogue record for this book is available from the British Library

Library of Congress Cataloging in Publication Data
A catalogue record for this book has been requested

ISBN 0-415-19793-7 (hbk)
ISBN 0-415-19794-5 (pbk)

For Michael

Contents

Acknowledgments

Academic colleagues have been more than generous in sharing their ideas, and we have been fortunate to have worked within a rich network of educational researchers. In particular, thanks to Nola Alloway and Bronwyn Davies for their helpful comments on the manuscript, and also to Leanne Dalley, Jeannie Herbert, Barbara Kamler, Dave King, Bob Lingard, Lyn Martinez, Sandra McEwan and Hilary Whitehouse.

Thanks, also, for the research assistance provided by Danny Keenan, Shane Kuhl and Geri Crouch, and for the support given by Garry Chew, Glenn Dickson and the teachers and boys in the schools involved in our research.

And thanks to Anne Diack and Wallace Rennie, who provided a beautiful venue for writing several of these chapters, and a surfeit of good company while we did so.

Nola Alloway has travelled with us on the boys and schooling journey, as we have explored—as parents and as researchers—the raising of sons, the education of boys, and the construction of masculinity. Our lives and our work have been enriched by her wisdom, her company, her generosity and her love.

PART I

Boys and masculinity:
Current debates

What about the boys?

How do we begin a story about boys at school? For many parents, teachers, academics, education advisers and consultants, the issue of how well boys fare *at* school, and how well they are served *by* schools, is a highly contentious and emotional one, because the issue has so often been framed in terms of opposition and blame. Are boys doing less well at school, and if so, is anyone to blame? Do schools fail to provide for boys' needs? And are these even the right questions to ask if we want to know more about boys and schooling?

The stories that boys tell about themselves at school will feature in later chapters of this book. Here we look at other stories that have been told *about* boys—stories from the popular press of opposition and blame; stories from statistical data about achievement and participation at school; stories from social surveys about boys' health, crime, accident rates and death; and stories from teachers and female students about boys' behaviour at school. We want to use the stories not only to build a multi-layered picture of the complexity of the issue this book confronts, but also to construct a framework for working with the question of boys and schooling in ways that are equitable, just, informed and productive.

POOR BOYS: STORIES FROM THE POPULAR PRESS

One of the most familiar and pervasive constructions of the boys and schooling issue is the one offered by the popular press. In many of the stories told by journalists, boys are represented as losing out in both educational and social contexts, as a new super-breed of girls and women takes control of school, of jobs, of relationships, and of their bodies. 'The sex of success' writes one Australian newspaper,[1] or, as a 1995 magazine cover asserts:

> *Superior Sex*
> *Women are smarter, healthier, more honest and live longer.*
> *These days it's the men who need help.*[2]

In the United Kingdom, *The Economist* considers 'The trouble with men', and the *New Scientist* proclaims 'Hard times for Britain's lost boys', as 'Girls are racing ahead in Britain's schools'.[3] And in America, *Men's Health* takes another typically alarmist stance about the scandal of boys in schools:

> *The War on Boys.*
> Wise up, America! Despite what you read in the papers, the nation's schoolboys are in big trouble.[4]

Fuelling much of this concern are the results of competitive examinations, which are widely seen as evidence that boys as a group are falling behind girls. The media depict this through stories of a new poor underclass in the education system, and of the worrying impact of 'the feminists' on schooling.

But how seriously should we take these headlines? Are boys in trouble in schools, and if so, is their situation worse now than it has been before? Is there a sex bias in the education system—are girls advantaged to the detriment of boys? Have affirmative action programs for girls disadvantaged boys—and have there been no programs to support boys? Is there a recognisable and definable crisis for boys at school—and what sort of crisis is it?

The answers to questions like these cannot, unfortunately, be as easily answered as the popular press would have us believe.[5] Undoubtedly many students are not served well by our current schooling structures or curricula, and nowhere has education been able to deliver on its promise of providing social equity and access for all children. However, the debates constructed in the popular press about boys and schooling

4

seldom approach the topic from this angle. They are little interested in issues of educational and social inequality, more often choosing the easier option of constructing opposition and looking for parties to blame.

The usual media stories are those that treat boys (and girls) as single groups—and as opposing groups. The diversity and difference within and among groups of boys is seldom acknowledged or addressed, despite the fact that an impressive array of research literature indicates how schools serve some groups of boys significantly less well than they serve others. Across the three countries mentioned earlier, African-American, immigrant Caribbean and Aboriginal boys, boys living in poverty, boys who live in rural areas, and boys who do not have English as their first language at home, are significantly more at risk of being disadvantaged in our schools than are boys from white affluent areas. The research also suggests that while some boys may be disadvantaged at school and some 'in trouble', there are still many boys who are not, and for whom the competitive processes of schooling work very well indeed. The rewards for many of these boys become obvious in the post-schooling years, in terms of university access, employment and weekly earnings.[6]

News stories about boys' school results seldom contextualise the problems of school assessment and achievement data within the broader picture of boys' engagement and participation in school. Their reliance on indicators like the top scoring results in various state tertiary entrance rankings is particularly unhelpful in unravelling the problems of assessment, or the complexities of school disadvantage. Such indicators provide little information about how the vast majority of boys—or girls—fare at school. This is not their purpose. They were not designed to do so.

And, of course, it is both typical and yet disturbing for the press stories to construct female villains for their tales: to blame female students and teachers as the cause of boys' educational 'disadvantage'. Such an approach draws attention away from a consideration of boys, of boys' cultures, and of schooling cultures, and encourages debates about education to be narrowly and irrelevantly linked to an 'either–or' attitude. If boys are to do well at school, is it to be at the expense of girls? If girls do well at school, is it at the expense of boys?

Such an argument fails to advance understandings about educational equity and dangerously misinterprets the issue.

So what *is* going on in schools that promotes this view of boys and education? Is it all just a media beat-up, or are there serious issues to confront and redress? Should parents and teachers be concerned about how well schools are serving boys? How can we sort through the research and the stories to arrive at understandings of boys and schooling? This introductory chapter will offer a way through these questions. By looking more closely at the evidence in one of the contexts mentioned earlier, that of Australia, we will test the validity of the concerns about boys' education. We will also identify important issues in the boys and schooling debate, and construct a lens through which to consider and evaluate the key questions.

'WHO WINS AT SCHOOL?': STORIES OF SUCCESS AND FAILURE

Who Wins at School? is the title of a recent report produced by Richard Teese and a research team from the University of Melbourne. It is, the Preface warns, a 'reluctant' title for a report on school achievement and participation.

> School is sometimes celebrated as a race, and no more so than by the champions of yesteryear. But in an era of global dependence on success at school, there are better things to do with the curriculum than to run it as a race. Our choice of title recognises that there are winners and losers and that we must make a record of the race if we are to find ways of ending it.[7]

The study of 'the race' is comprehensive and rigorous, providing evidence on boys' achievement not often available. The issues raised are important in addressing questions of boys' education whatever the context.

School retention rates and subject selection

The report initially considers gender differences in an historical perspective, noting the shift in secondary education from 'an elite system catering for a small minority of young people who prepared for university to a mass general system which now serves most young people, whatever their destinations'.[8] The report argues that the traditional picture has changed, so that boys no longer rely upon successful completion of schooling more often than girls. It is now girls—the report argues—who depend upon school and who consistently complete more years of schooling than boys.

This shift is partly indicative of the changing composition of secondary schooling classrooms since the 1950s. The Teese report notes of Queensland data, for instance, that while there were twice as many boys as girls attending secondary school in Queensland in the 1950s, girls have now 'increased their use of school over the post-war period at up to double the rate for boys'.[9] Figures quoted in the Teese report show that by 1975 girls' school retention rates were higher than boys, and that by the 1990s, the gender gap had widened to 10 percentage points.

In part this hints at boys' resistance to school, and their unhappiness and unease in school cultures. However it is also quite clearly a response to vocational necessity. As the Teese report also notes, many traditional female occupations have required higher levels of schooling—and, unlike boys, girls have not had easy access to accredited vocational training in the workplace. However the figures indicate that boys are now making less use of senior schooling than are girls, and—significantly—the use they are making of schooling is narrow. Boys' subject choices are a clear indicator of the vocational—and 'masculinist'—lens through which many boys view schooling. Across all states, it is the subjects considered to have high vocational potential and 'masculine' status that attract boys. Boys stay away from subjects that are often historically cast as feminised. Languages, the arts, and the humanities, for instance, have poor male representation, and boys avoid language and literature subjects when given the choice.

This sexist stereotyping of subject selection was made obvious in a recent study of gender and school education led by Cherry Collins.[10] The research group asked secondary students whether traditional gender associations of a subject still mattered when they chose subjects, and the results indicate that subject selection is still a central issue to address in terms of boys and schooling. The researchers concluded from their data that:

> . . . boys shy away from subjects with a feminine past more than girls shy away from subjects with a masculine past. We can also conclude that the influence of the past is still surprisingly strong, at this point in history, in the consciousness of both sexes and that boys particularly try to put others off crossing gender boundaries . . .[11]

And it would seem as if schools have to accept more responsibility here if this narrowness of subject choice is to change. Within the Collins et al. study students claimed that they received little teacher support to take up non-traditional subjects, and that boys felt this more than girls did.

> Forty-eight per cent [of the students in the study], less than half, affirmed that students got teacher support. And again, there was a highly significant difference between the sexes of 14 points, with only 39 per cent of male respondents compared with 53 per cent of female respondents perceiving teachers to give a lot of support.[12]

And as other educationists argue, there is no question that boys (and girls) lose from the curriculum imbalance that inevitably results.[13]

> Personal development through the arts is in practice much less accessible to them as is language development through the study of modern languages. Their ability to communicate both with themselves, as individuals, and with others is handicapped. Their knowledge of ideas and institutions has fewer opportunities to grow through the active efforts that the discipline of a school subject imposes. . . . a potentially heavy price is paid by the highly vocational nature of boys' subject selections.[14]

Some boys suffer more than others through this vocational narrowness. The clustering of boys into subjects like higher level mathematics and physics, for instance, means that those who do well are able to enjoy the benefits that high scores in these prestigious subjects still convey. And certainly more boys than girls are able to benefit from this success. However, not all boys do well in higher level mathematics and physics. Boys often occupy the extremes of the performance range in these subjects, producing a 'saucer-shaped' distribution of results which positions many of them as failures.[15] And it is the boys caught at the lowest end of these distributions who are some of the losers in the schooling race. Having chosen subjects which are vested with high masculine status and power, but within which they are unable to succeed, these boys end up not only without high school qualifications, but also with a personal sense of failure within a male domain of achievement.

Differences between groups of boys

But are some groups of boys more likely than others to suffer failure of this kind, as well as a more generalised failure across the board at school? The intersections between socio-economic resources, geographical location, ethnicity and 'race' are critical here, as they demonstrate the groups of boys who are potentially more at risk of school failure. This is particularly noticeable in literacy results, where, although gender remains a key predictor of success, it is clearly affected by a range of other social and cultural factors.

In high migrant density working-class suburbs in western Melbourne, for instance, one in three boys could expect to fail university-accredited English if he chose to take it, compared with an anticipated failure rate for girls of one in five. And yet boys from the wealthy inner east suburbs do better than groups of girls from working-class and rural areas, their results being exceeded only by girls from similar socio-economic backgrounds.[16] This pattern is repeated in other data, where boys from higher socio-economic areas enrol in English as frequently as girls, and, while not matching girls' performance in this same region, are the only group of boys to outperform some groups of girls.[17]

These patterns can also be found in primary schools. Results on a state Year 3 Basic Skills Test for literacy, reported in Alloway and Gilbert,[18] illustrate, for instance, the complexity of the interplay between gender and class. Again, the average scores in literacy are higher for girls than for boys. However the results also indicate that the socio-economic ranking of students' families is strongly associated with children's literacy skills performance. While girls at every step in a ten-point socio-economic scale score higher than boys in the same socio-economic category, boys with the highest socio-economic ranking still fare better at literacy-related tasks than girls up to the first five points of the socio-economic scale. The research also shows how boys with the highest socio-economic ranking of ten still score below the state average for girls, and how boys with the lowest socio-economic rankings score worse than any other group. Alloway and Gilbert conclude that:

> Results of this kind show very clearly that not all girls are doing well at literacy-related tasks, and not all boys are doing equally as poorly as one another. The results suggest a complex elision of gender and class membership. It appears that gender remains a powerful predictor of a child's literacy performance, but that the social and economic resources available to children through their homes and communities impact significantly on their achievement of literacy skills.[19]

Performance graphs in literacy traditionally show girls performing better than boys at all ages, but there are also marked effects of socio-economic privilege, rurality and culture. In Australia, Aboriginal girls still outperform Aboriginal boys, but Aboriginal students achieve lower literacy scores in primary school than other Australian students, and those living in rural and remote areas do less well than those living in urban areas.[20] It is white Anglo girls from high status urban suburbs who cluster near the top of the English/literacy tables, and Aboriginal boys and non-Anglo boys from poor working-class suburbs who cluster near the bottom.

The gender balance changes with mathematics, however, where boys' participation generally exceeds girls' except in high socio-economic status areas. Figures from one Australian state show that the lowest levels of participation in maths are experienced by groups of rural girls and girls from working-class suburbs. For instance, only 1 in 3 girls from outlying working-class suburbs take higher level maths, compared to the statewide level for boys of 44 per cent.[21] However girls' participation in lower level maths subjects is high, and their results are often good. The diversity of mathematics subjects makes gender trends more complex, however, because, unlike English, students can choose from a much broader band of mathematics subjects, both university-accredited and unaccredited. The argument that is subsequently often made is that some groups of girls and boys tend to locate themselves at inappropriate mathematics levels: girls often underestimate their abilities, while boys tend to overestimate theirs.[22]

The severity of gender disadvantage is clearly affected by the socio-economic resources students' families have access to, and this is particularly noticeable in the data available on student outcomes. For example, the Equity Outcomes Project in Victoria[23] demonstrated how such resources are predictors of success in university-approved maths subjects. While girls were more at risk than boys within each socio-economic status category, it was both boys and girls from skilled, unskilled and unemployed backgrounds who were at higher risk of failure than students from professional, managerial and technical backgrounds. Girls from working-class families were the group most at risk of mathematics failure.[24]

Conclusions from such data are complex, but we would argue that English and mathematics still provide evidence that gender disadvantage works against both boys and girls—in different ways. The data presented in the studies discussed here make it clear that gender is still a critical factor in predicting participation and success at English and mathematics—and in predicting subject choice and school retention. Boys' very poor showings in English—and their avoidance of humanities and arts subjects—put them at a clear educational and social disadvantage. However, as we have shown in this chapter, this disadvantage is experienced differently, depending upon geographical location and social and cultural family resources. Some groups of boys are at serious risk of failure in English—as they are of failure in mathematics. Similarly, for girls, it is critical to take account of their locations within networks of resources. All girls are not winners at school and it is critical that we deconstruct the broad gender categories and look more carefully at the intersections between gender and ethnicity, rurality, class and poverty.

It is also critical that we take account of the effect of schooling failure upon the world of work. Recently released data from the Australian Council of Educational Research on reading and numeracy in junior secondary school[25] argued that:

> The consequences of poor literacy include an increased likelihood of leaving school early, relatively poor access to a university education, the prospect of higher levels of longer term unemployment, and a greater chance of being [in] lower paid, less skilled jobs.

The report claims that boys fare worse than girls on literacy and numeracy tests, as do 'students whose main language at home is not English, young people from lower socio-economic backgrounds (measured by parental occupation), and Aboriginal and Torres Strait Islander people'.[26]

However boys' poor performance on literacy tests at age fourteen does not necessarily translate into poor earning capacity at age nineteen. One telling set of figures included in the ACER report shows how good literacy skills provide a clear earnings advantage for nineteen-year-olds in employment.[27] However the earning advantage is predominantly experienced by men rather than women. Nineteen-year-old women with very high literacy skills (measured at age fourteen) could expect to earn $335 per week—a wage that was $60 *less* per week than the wage nineteen-year-old men with the same skills could expect. In fact, young men designated as having low and very low literacy levels were still able to earn more than young women who had very high levels of literacy achievement. It would seem that, as much feminist research has argued for many years, school success does not automatically translate into economic advantage for girls: school achievement is only one part of the picture in deciding 'who wins at school'. It would also seem that the links between literacy (and numeracy) achievement at school, and average weekly earnings are not clearcut. Young men with poor literacy and numeracy skills may well find relatively well-paid work in labouring and skilled manual work—work that is not as easily available to young women. However such work is often more dangerous and less secure than the white-collar work available to young men (and young women) with high literacy and numeracy skills.

BAD BOYS: STORIES OF VIOLENCE AND AGGRESSION

While there are important stories to be told of achievement and performance at school, and of the pathways that extend from the school to the workplace, there are also other stories to tell about boys and schooling which are critical in the boys and education debate. We have considered how issues associated with boys' views of maleness and masculinity influence their subject choice, participation and achievement at school. Boys' views on masculinity also affect their behaviour at school, both in and out of the classroom—as well as their health and their safety in a range of cultural contexts.

Unquestionably the behaviour at school of some boys makes life difficult for many boys, for most girls, and for many teachers, and we address this in more detail in chapters 5 and 7. Schools are forced to spend considerable time, energy and resources on managing 'bad boys', on developing programs and strategies to handle disruptive behaviour, and on repairing the damage done by some groups of boys to schools and school property. The 'doing' of aggressive and violent forms of masculinity in and around the school has become a feature of school life.

A submission prepared for the Australian government on boys' education strategies highlighted this issue as one that had to be addressed more effectively.[28] Academic achievement issues, it suggested, were not the only issues that needed to be addressed in the boys and schooling debate. The submission suggested that surveys were needed from a range of primary and secondary schools to consider the equity of resource allocation between boys and girls in relation to welfare and discipline strategies. The submission argued that the time and funding allocated to disruptive students and classroom management programs was high, but that time and funding provided for these programs was inequitable, in that it almost always was allocated to boys. In other words, an important and costly aspect of contemporary schooling is the cost incurred in the battle to control and regulate a small group of boys.

The claim implicit in the submission was that any analysis of boys and schooling needed to take account of the very considerable time and energy exercised by teachers and educational administrators in the task of boys' behaviour management. This argument is also made by Lyn Martinez who considered the significance of these costs to schools. She claims that 'the commonly reported 80% of administrators' and teachers' time which is devoted to managing boys' behaviour is time lost to curriculum leadership, organising supportive school environments, community liaison and parent support'.[29] She also notes that costs can be expressed in other ways: the cost of teacher stress and time out, which teachers attribute primarily to student behavioural problems; and the cost of vandalism, fire and theft of school equipment. For instance Martinez claims that 'a recent Victorian report estimates that 97% of young firebugs are male, and that the cost of fires to Victorian schools in the past three years has been $30 million'.[30]

In similar vein, the New South Wales Inquiry into Boys' Education notes from its submissions that:

> Boys represent the majority of behaviour problem students. Like girls, boys who do behave and want to learn suffer because of the poor behaviour of other boys. A typical primary school reported that 90 per cent of their detentions are boys. Of the 73 students in special units for behaviour disturbed students in NSW, 62 are boys.[31]

However the report also goes on to show how this 'bad boys' story extends beyond the boundaries of the school. It draws attention to the links between boys and danger, boys and crime, and boys and violence in a variety of contexts.

Boys and danger

Boys are, for instance, far more likely to harm themselves or to be involved in accidental death than are girls. Richard Fletcher cites Australian evidence that boys or men make up 61 per cent of child road deaths, 67 per cent of pedestrian deaths, 86 per cent of bicycle deaths, and 98 per cent of all motorcycle deaths. Male drivers are also far more likely to be involved in truck crashes (99 per cent of such drivers are male), or single vehicle crashes (83 per cent of these drivers are male).[32]

Young men are also almost seven times more likely to die through suicide than are young women, and the dramatic difference between male and female suicide rates has been steadily increasing over the past 35 years. In 1960, 50 young Australian men (6.8 per 100 000) and fourteen young women (2 per 100 000) killed themselves. However by 1994, male suicide deaths numbered 374 (27 per 100 000) and female deaths 57 (4 per 100 000),[33] making Australian youth suicide rates some of the highest in the world.

The high rate of male suicide is often cited as an indicator of the difficulties faced by many young men in contemporary Australia, yet the figures may not tell the whole story of youth suicide. It is difficult, for instance, to know how many fatal car accidents featuring single male drivers might have been suicidal in purpose, or how many young women's deaths through eating disorder illnesses are actually suicidal in intent. A 1995 report[34] points out that there is actually little gender difference in the rates of *attempted* suicide: similar numbers of young men and young women try to kill themselves, although often in different ways. It is suggested, for example, that for every actual suicide there may be 100 times as many would-be suicides.[35] Young men, however, achieve their objective more frequently than do young women; greater male access to weapons may be partly responsible. High rates of suicide in rural Australian areas, for instance, are often linked with high gun ownership rates, and claims have also been made that reductions in suicide rates occur when gun ownership is restricted.[36]

However, boys are not all equally at risk of suicide: some groups of young men are significantly *more* at risk than are others. A report on youth suicide indicates that males from Aboriginal or Torres Strait Islander backgrounds, or non-indigenous males from rural or remote areas, are particularly at risk.[37] Claims are also made that gay men constitute one-third of all male suicides, and that suicide has become a recourse for young men unable to deal with the clash between a predominantly heterosexual world and their own 'different' sexuality.[38]

Boys and crime: boys and violence

Boys are far more likely than are girls to be imprisoned for criminal offences and to be at risk of criminal violence. Men and boys are also at a much greater risk of suffering a violent death, from whatever cause, than are women, and more likely also to be the victims of violence perpetrated by other people. Over 80 per cent of all homicide offenders, and well in excess of 90 per cent of those charged with serious assault, robbery, rape and sexual assault, are men. And while victims of rape, sexual assault and domestic violence are overwhelmingly female, males comprise approximately two-thirds of Australian homicide victims, and 75 per cent of the victims of serious assault recorded by police. They also comprise approximately 80 per cent of assault victims treated in public hospitals.[39]

But, again, this violence is experienced differently. Different groups of men are more vulnerable to homicide and violence. Frequency of homicide victims, for instance, appears to vary inversely with occupational status, with those from the most prestigious occupations having the lowest homicide death rates.[40] The Australian National Committee on Violence (NCV) report notes the particular vulnerability of what are described as 'marginal' members of society—the undereducated and unemployed—whose lifestyles place them at greater risk of becoming both victims and offenders. This is of particular concern for young men who drop out of school and become closely aligned with strongly masculinist street cultures that endorse and expect violent and dangerous patterns of social behaviour.

The rates of homicide also vary with geographical location. Homicide rates for the Northern Territory of Australia, for instance, are consistently more than five times greater than the comparable rates for the rest of the country. The NCV explains this in terms of the unique demographic composition of the Territory: the 'relative youth of the population, the high proportion of males, many of them transient, and the high Aboriginal population'.[41] Aboriginality is a key indicator of likely death by homicide, with homicide rates for Aboriginal Australians as high as ten times those for the general population.

Increasingly, constructions of masculinity are seen to be significant in understanding links between violence and crime. Unlike the narratives of random murder and crime popularised through the electronic media, two-thirds of all homicides are committed by offenders who are family, family friends, or close acquaintances of the victims. For example, the NCV refers to a Victorian study which analysed 117 homicides occurring in the state in 1985–86. Over half of these (60 cases) were described as 'intimate' homicides—between lovers, friends, relatives or former friends—while another 25 cases were described as 'confrontational' homicides, usually resulting from a dispute between males in or around drinking places. Of these, the report notes:

> The vast majority of homicides which take place within the framework of relationships which are of a sexually intimate character appear to result from possessiveness, often jealous possessiveness on the part of males. The confrontational homicides are exclusively male, and imply the existence of a set of norms regarding 'honour' or 'face' which are acted upon in such a way as to lead down an interactional path to homicide.[42]

The NCV report notes that violence has become integrally associated with masculinity and with desirable masculine behaviour, and that society now needs to confront this link.

> . . . an examination of the material on violent crime indicates that to reduce this form of crime in particular we will have to address not only economic inequalities but also gender stratification and male power. Most apparent is the need to confront our construction of masculinity.[43]

MASCULINITY AND SCHOOLING

Given such arguments about boys' problems and the links between school participation and success, and danger, crime and violence, it would seem critical to use the school arena to foreground discussion about masculinity. And yet, as Richard Fletcher argues, this seldom occurs. Fletcher argues that boys suffer many disadvantages in life 'because of the way society (including education) encourages certain types of "maleness"'.[44] Much of the danger to boys' and men's lives is, he claims, associated with masculinism and materialism, and that when combined they 'limit the options for boys thus

17

directly contributing to their poor schooling outcomes'.[45] Current schooling practice, by failing to address the effects of a masculinist, materialist culture on boys, fails—in Fletcher's view—to account for the needs of male students.

Fletcher suggests that boys' location within this masculinist, materialist culture directly affects their academic achievement at school, their participation and retention rates, and their school behaviour. He argues that the most serious educational deficiencies for boys are:

- their underparticipation in all subjects with a non-technology focus and the complete lack of subjects in some crucial areas e.g. parenting;
- their failure to consider family, friendship and community aspects of preparing for a career;
- their dependency for self-esteem on traditional estimations of masculinity, such as sporting or fighting skills, superiority over females, and job status.[46]

However, Fletcher also alludes to the ambivalent way in which these deficiencies are viewed within schools. In school cultures that value 'work over home, paid work over voluntary work, production over health and welfare, rationality over emotionality and competition over cooperation', [47] it is obviously difficult to persuade boys to take non-technology subjects, to value interpersonal skills, or to critique the competitive and aggressive features of male sport. In fact it is not difficult to see the tensions and contradictions within schooling patterns that endorse and sustain masculinist culture through the valorisation of male competitive sport and sporting heroes, through the reinforcement of maths and physical sciences as the most institutionally prestigious of schooling subjects,[48] and through the structure of the teaching workforce, within which key authority and power is embodied in men.

Girls in schools have often been only too well aware of these tensions and contradictions—and recognised the dangers they imposed for their own learning. As we discuss in chapter 3, projects documenting girls' views of schooling frequently produce claims about the unfairness of sport coverage and sport funding within schools, for instance, and about the valorisation of male sporting prowess within the discourses of schooling.[49]

And while male sport serves as a representation of the brute power and physical strength of the male body loosed on the playing fields, mathematics and physical sciences serve as a representation of the rational power and mental strength of the male mind that dominates in the classroom. It is mathematics and physical sciences which still enjoy high institutional prestige, and which are still frequently prescribed and recommended by university course authorities. And it is mathematics which still shows marked differences in participation between boys and girls. While girls participate and perform in mathematics in significantly higher numbers and at significantly higher levels than before, they often choose maths options which are below the level of their abilities. As we have previously argued, this is less likely to happen to boys, who tend to over-enrol in specialist maths and then pay the price for their gendered selection.

The valorisation of the masculine at school thus embraces both sport and mathematics—and key institutional power in schools is still most commonly presented through male bodies. While women dominate at the teaching level, men clearly dominate at the administrative level in schools. The O'Doherty Report in New South Wales, for instance, noted that 81.1 per cent of primary classroom teachers were women, yet more than 67 per cent of non-teaching executive staff were males.[50] Fletcher also comments on the frequent overrepresentation of males in positions of authority and discipline, and their underrepresentation 'in roles emphasising nurturance and support (welfare, canteen, cleaning, teaching aids, counselling)'.[51] He also points out how the male staff's ability to be forceful or even intimidating is the basis of the school's authority.

These issues will be taken up in chapter 5. However, boys' academic achievement and participation at school needs constantly to be framed within its social context: the masculine ethos that dominates and pervades so many aspects of school life.

A FRAMEWORK FOR ACTION: TRAPS FOR THE UNWARY

Just as a number of different stories can be told of boys at school, a range of different strategies has been proposed for responding to boys' issues. However, as we will argue in this book, strategies grow out of differing theoretical positions and conceptualisations about masculinity, schooling and culture, and out of those familiar and readily available schooling practices or technologies that make some approaches more acceptable and 'do-able' than others. Many of these strategies have jostled for prominence and consideration in debates about boys and schooling—but given the complexity of the interplay between boys and schooling, there are inherent dangers.

At the centre of this struggle is the question of how masculinity is defined. Is masculinity to be understood as the destiny of biology, as singular and monolithic, as an essentially different and separate form of psychological development? Or is it to be constructed within the context of unequal gender relations, of multiple and plural human experience and cultural understanding, and of social and semiotic construction? We look more closely at this issue in the next chapter.

And how will boys be understood? Will they be considered as individuals—perhaps 'naughty' and 'dangerous' individuals who need to be changed? Or will their families, their cultures and their social contexts be recognised as part of the way boys take up the practices they do? Chapters 3 through to 8 look closely at this. How will programs for boys justify funding and priority? At the expense of girls or of targeted equity groups like Aboriginal students, or rural students, or working-class groups? Or within a more broadly based approach to social justice and gender relations? We address this at the end of the book. However, initially, we argue here that there are undoubted dangers for boys' programs unless the theoretical and conceptual focus of boys and schooling is carefully approached.

LESSONS FROM THE GIRLS: GENDER AND CURRICULUM REFORM

Many of these dangers are ones that teachers who have worked on girls' education issues have confronted, and there is much that can be learnt from the substantial feminist research already available from this field. While the boys and education issue poses new and different questions—not least because masculinity cannot just be considered a mirror-image of femininity—it also poses some similar questions, because boys and girls, and masculinity and femininity, need to be understood in relation to each other. Increasingly within girls' education agendas, studies have considered the impact for both girls and boys of gendered teaching practice, classroom talk, curriculum construction, school culture, subject participation, and, of course, academic achievement.

Broadly speaking, it is possible to cluster educational reform for girls within three phases or periods of focus,[52] and by considering each of these, and their interrelationships, it is possible to hypothesise a framework that might be effective for boys' needs. Initially, work on girls and education was concerned with a struggle to achieve equity and access to orders of power and privilege. This was soon followed by a concerted effort to value women's knowledge and experiences, to integrate them into the curriculum, and to draw attention to the silences about girls' and women's lives and achievements within what had come to be seen as a masculinist curriculum.

However, this position was broadened in the third phase of reform, as educators realised how different and diverse were experiences of femininity, and how critical to schooling reform was an understanding of social and cultural constructions of gender, gender relations, and gendered subjectivities or personalities. These three shifts through equity and access, to the valuation of women's knowledges and experience, to a more broadly based understanding of gender and gender relations, could be seen to be somewhat chronological—or at least conceptually to build upon each other.

WHAT ABOUT THE BOYS? A POSSIBLE REFORM AGENDA

The appropriation of this three-stage program for boys is clearly worth investigating, although there are some immediate and obvious differences in the boys' agenda. The first issue of access and equity has clear differences for boys and girls. While there are obviously legitimate concerns about boys' access to a full range of secondary school subjects, their access to literacy skills and English studies, or their access to participation and engagement in schools' arts programs and activities, most boys do not lose out financially or vocationally because of this limited access. On the contrary. Unlike girls, boys' choices, as Fletcher maintains, 'have meant that boys have had unequal access to many types of benefits'[53]—social, economic and political. Why would boys want to change?

While we might deplore the narrowness of focus in boys' curricula choices, we recognise the vocational imperative driving their selections. We could easily argue that boys should have access to home science, to parenting classes, to humanities subjects, to English literature, to the arts, if they are to develop appropriate knowledge and experience for a life that is only partially (if, indeed for some boys, at all), located in the world of public 'masculine' work. We could also argue that, given the stories described earlier about boys' health, boys' crime, boys' violence and boys' aggression, access to school subjects that provide other ways of 'being' male and human is critical. But how is this view to be presented to boys and their families?

While girls could be shown the financial and professional advantages of moving into masculinist subject areas, boys can be shown little financial or social advantage in shifting from the powerful, prestigious male domains of mathematics, physical sciences and sport. There may be unequal access for boys to the full subject range of the secondary school curriculum— but for most of them there is certainly not financial or social inequality as a result of such inequitable access. And, unlike girls, boys are not deprived of fair access to teachers' time, linguistic space in the classroom, playground and sport facilities, or funded programs. Boys, as a whole group, receive more than is fair in these ways, and, as Lemaire and Martinez[54] argue, if the funding that has been spent on classroom management programs, special behaviour modification strategies, and reading remediation schemes is included, boys have had a lion's share of school resources.

Significantly, boys also do not have the same difficulties as girls do in terms of gender imbalance in the construction of knowledge or selection of curricula resources. For many years girls sat through endless 'boy's own' type adventure stories, or male adolescent rites of passage novels, or canonised male authors' versions of human relationships, without being able to study novels focused on girls' experiences, girls' interests, or women's readings of society—for fear that the latter would be too dull for boys, who would then cause havoc in the English classroom.[55] It would seem that not a great deal has changed in this regard. While more novels are included that address girls' interests, the English curriculum is still favourably disposed to material depicting male protagonists and male experience.[56]

The same could be said for humanities subjects, science subjects, mathematics, sport, and sex education. Much of the school curriculum could still be labelled 'men's studies': studies of great men of history, of science, of exploration, of the arts, and masculinist readings of these fields. This need not be seen as a deliberate attempt to exclude girls, but rather as evidence of the historical construction of subject disciplines and curricula content. However, the effect is important. Girls were excluded from most of these stories—as were many boys whose cultural backgrounds were different from those of the 'great men' of western civilisation. The versions of 'maleness' on offer in these traditional curricula came predominantly from a narrow range of ways of defining and describing masculinity. Of course, from an essentialist perspective, and in terms of the dominant tradition of what it means to be a man, they can hardly be faulted.

Much of the work that needed to be done for girls in the reform process is therefore unnecessary for many boys. Boys are not necessarily disadvantaged in terms of the construction of the school curriculum if access to male subjects, male stories and male constructions of knowledge counts as a key criterion. And most boys are also not marginalised or silenced by pedagogical practices at school. Studies in classrooms of who talks, for how long, and about what, still show how groups of boys dominate the linguistic space of the school—albeit in traditionally masculinist and aggressive ways.[57] However, it is critical to see how only some groups of boys benefit here. Many boys are observers only: innocent (though perhaps acquiescent) bystanders to the disruption caused by a few— although it is not always the same 'few' as we consider in chapter 5. And some groups of boys—notably indigenous boys, boys from various ethnic backgrounds, and homosexual boys— will not wish or be able to identify with the 'maleness' on

23

offer, or to see textual or visual representation of their experiences in the classroom.[58]

However, when curriculum reform considers the third stage of redress—notably how gender and gender relations are constructed, and how narrow readings of masculinity and femininity impact upon the construction of students' lives, expectations and relationships—then the situation changes rapidly. It is at this level that the major difficulty for boys at school emerges. Narrow and stereotypical versions of masculinity clearly influence boys' lives, affecting how they take up school curriculum options, how they read and make sense of 'men's studies', how they participate as learners in the school environment, and how they can imagine lives as men outside of the school.

Boys' insertion into dominant stories of masculinity and maleness predisposes them to reject and resist literacy and humanities subjects in favour of numeracy and vocational learning; to dominate and compete in classroom and playground arenas for space, time and attention; to valorise sport and physical prowess; to devalue qualities of nurturing, caring, sharing and loving. And many institutional and educational practices implicitly endorse and reinforce boys' choices. The devaluation of English as a prestige subject for university entrance, the glamour awarded to the sciences over history or sociology, the hero status given to sporting figures and sporting teams, the entrenchment of competitive and individualistic teaching and learning styles, the marginalising of discussions of sexuality, parenting, human relationships and nurturing—all of these practices can be read by boys as endorsing and confirming their choices of a narrow version of traditionally masculine school experiences and practices.

CONCLUSION

This chapter has argued that there are many different stories to tell about boys and schooling. However, its key argument is that stories that do not take account of masculinity and cultural issues in an analysis of boys' lives at school are limited in their potential to effect change. The boys and education agenda must include a critical reassessment of masculinity and masculinist cultures in schools if it can begin to redress issues of boys' participation and engagement in schools, issues of boys' poorer scholastic results in schools, and issues of boys' disruptive, resistant and violent behaviour in schooling and other cultural contexts. Such a critical reassessment cannot dodge how masculinity will be played out in diverse ways—as it is experienced differently by boys from different locations, families and communities, and through different sexual, cultural and class orientations. The starting point for boys' work, however, must be through a critical assessment of lived masculinity—and through a thoughtful and informed consideration of how schooling and masculinity intersect.

Heroes and villains: Theories of masculinity and the schooling of boys

How is it that the boys' agenda has become such a priority? Why now? And why has the problem been framed in the way it has? To answer these questions we need to understand how educational aims and programs are constructed in terms of a broader set of social issues. Recent concerns about literacy have been accentuated because of the problem of unemployment. Concerns about a breakdown in school discipline are accentuated because of the community's fears of crime. In similar fashion, debates about the schooling of boys are related to concerns about the social position of men. Chapter 1 showed how the popular press has sewn these two issues together, creating a picture of a common set of forces which threaten men at work and in the family, and boys in schools.

In one sense, this is as it should be, for educational aims need to be formed with an eye to social change, and the changing social and individual needs and entitlements which go with it. In the case of the education of boys, ideas of what boys need are constructed along with notions of the changing role of men in society and of the nature of masculinity itself.

However, while social analysis must always be part of curriculum development and teaching, education policy and practice needs to be protected against the dangers of fads, obsessions and moral panics. To distinguish the important social and educational changes, which we would want to respond to, from the unwarranted crisis rhetoric and hysteria of some of the debates, we need to take a broader perspective on these changes. Equally, to understand the needs of boys and how they may be changing, we need to look carefully at the social context in which they are forming their futures and their understanding of themselves.

MASCULINITY AND MORAL PANIC

If the popular press is any guide, it seems that men as a group are facing an identity crisis, and that boys will have difficulty in seeing a future which is personally attractive and socially valued. Typical of this kind of popular analysis is a feature article published in the Australian weekend press. The piece, 'Homeless in the heart' by Alan Close,[1] is accompanied by a large colour photograph of a man in shirt sleeves, carrying coat and briefcase, and walking with bowed head away from the camera and down a featureless and slightly out of focus road. Dispirited, directionless, neglected, resigned and disillusioned are the feelings the image suggests. And the story completes the picture.

> Looking around, my generation seems to be riddled with blokes . . . who, if not actually car-domiciled, are emotionally so. Homeless in the heart . . . It's an epidemic, a great hollow-eyed army of stunned-mullet men, meandering in aimless circles across the blasted tundra of the industrialised world going, 'Is this all? Is this life? I don't get it.'

The cause of this crisis lies in a kind of 'paradise lost' argument—the passing of a golden age where 'natural' human development was for boys to bond early with their mothers, and then gradually be 'pulled away' into the world of men by their fathers and other men in the community. However, industrialisation has taken men out of the home for lengthy periods each day.

> They are not part of the parenting process and boys miss out on the vital sense of identity provided by male bonding. We are cut adrift from a male lineage. We don't feel ourselves

27

to be part of a tradition, a community—or, usually, a place
. . . We have not learned how to be men. And it is the lack
of male bonding that makes men unable to form meaningful
and lasting relationships with women.

The article argues that men's social position and sense
of identity are in tatters, and the cause, earlier attributed to
industrialisation, is the change in gender roles which occurred
during the 1970s. These changes are caricatured, typically
for such pieces, as women in overalls and men wearing
lipstick(!), and the loss of traditionally male leisure pursuits,
including competition, sport, career, money, beer, cars, muscles, 'even possession of a penis'. Close had become 'literally
ashamed for being a man, convinced that I was responsible
for any number of heinous crimes against womanhood and
the world simply because I was born with two balls and a
dick!'[2]

These guilt-ridden men, so the story goes, retreated into
meditation to explore their feminine sides. But while they were
getting soft, the women have been moving into positions of
power and influence. These 'femocrats' and 'career women',
with their suits and briefcases, have become 'the men of our
generation', while the men have become women, learning to
bake, wash and care for the kids.

We could dismiss this as a trivial piece of popular journalism, but unfortunately it encapsulates many of the terms
in which the popular discussion of men and masculinity take
place. The combative yet self-pitying style, the caricature of
feminism (mixed with claims of support for women's libera-
tion), and the mystical origins of masculinity woven into a
history with no base in evidence—these are the hallmarks of
strands of the populist men's movement propaganda. It is
regrettable but not surprising that such views fit neatly with
the need for sensationalism among the gatekeepers of the
media.

The news feature also illustrates some important elements
of the current concern for boys and their links with the analysis
of masculinity. First, Close is strongly of the view that men
have lost a sense of shared identity because they do not bond
with each other to form close supportive relationships. This
is ironic in an Australian culture which has been criticised for

its sexually exclusive cultural traditions of mateship, segregated clubs and bars, dominant male sports, and which still has one of the most sexually segregated workforces of the world's advanced economies.

A further concern is how the argument defines masculinity over and against femininity, leading to the conclusion that men need to 'pull away' from women in order to become men. This has something of the Garden of Eden about it, as if women will corrupt the natural growth of virtuous manhood. It parallels arguments that men will lose their masculinity if they take on women's work, or that the discipline of the military will be lost if women are allowed to join. In a more positive form, it can be seen in suggestions that women can have a 'civilising' effect on men. All these views present a picture of men as a homogeneous group, whose essence is distinctive to them and at risk of being lost if it is not kept pure and separate. Such a picture denies the differences among men themselves, and the wide range of attributes which could simply be called human, and which are shared by both men and women.

Another aspect of the argument is that particular activities are naturally masculine, and if men are discouraged from engaging in them, then they will lose their masculinity. In this argument, the distinctive character of men survives only so long as they participate in particular kinds of activities (e.g. sport, cars, making money, competing, etc.). But it is not clear whether these are seen to be masculine pursuits in themselves, or only when done in a masculine (say, aggressive or combative) way. Again, given the wide range of men's interests, and of women's, the argument that to be masculine means being involved in particular kinds of activities can only narrow rather than expand men's opportunities to be human.

This news piece nicely captures a range of myths about present-day masculinity. In combination, they construct a belief in a crisis in men's development, with what are seen to be damaging consequences for boys. However, to understand how this crisis has been constructed, and how to combat it, we need to look more closely at its constituent parts. What follows is a discussion of some key arguments about the current crisis in masculinity, and its relation to raising boys.

THE LOSS OF THE ESSENTIAL MAN

An important feature of much of the crisis rhetoric is the idea that there is a central essence to being male, and that modern men, for a variety of reasons, depending on who is putting the argument, have lost it. The result is that boys have no adult models of this essential male to follow, so they too are lost.

A key source of this kind of thinking has been Robert Bly and his book *Iron John*.[3] A typical example of Bly's influence can be found in the work of one leading Australian men's advocate, Steve Biddulph, in his book *Manhood: A Book About Setting Men Free*.[4] Biddulph argues that modern men suffer from a lack of role models who express their inner feelings, and are left having to choose between the 'phony toughness' of the he-man and the 'phony niceness' of the new age guy.[5] Biddulph's solution is to find a 'deep masculinity' latent in young men which, if nurtured, can be learned. Biddulph believes that we need to honour these unique qualities of boys, such as their 'high-energy creativity', as, he claims, pre-industrial societies once did.

> In nature, all development follows a laid-down sequence. In a man's developing, the sequence has been forgotten and the process largely left to chance. If we look at older cultures we see immense and focused efforts going into the raising of boys—rituals, teachings and processes which have only feeble equivalents in our culture . . . The Sioux hunter, the Zulu warrior, the Aboriginal elder and the Mediaeval craftsman lived glorious lives and cared for and protected their people and their world. Why should modern man be any less a man than his ancestors?[6]

This passage shows the confusion of much of the essentialist literature. For instance, from the opening reference to nature following a 'laid-down sequence' (perhaps genetically?), the argument suddenly moves to a cultural practice, which is clearly not natural. However, if the sequence is so natural, as Biddulph claims, how can it be forgotten? Not only does the argument equate a surprising diversity of cultures, but it involves a selective and romantic caricature of history and culture. On the one hand, Biddulph praises the rituals of the past for the security they gave to men. On the other hand, he argues that 'Progress [in dealing with sexism and the oppression of women] lies not in women fighting men but in women and men together fighting the ancient stupidities that have been bequeathed to them'.[7] So the ancients are founts of both wisdom and stupidity.

The interesting question here is how to distinguish them: whether, for instance, the rituals of manhood and their public celebration of being male were signs of wisdom, or a part of this 'stupid' system of oppression in their exclusion of women. Masculinity rites in traditional male-dominated societies imposed conformity and control, and involved misogynist myths, the exclusion of women, deference to hierarchical authority, and fear, violence and pain.[8] How such rituals would improve men's lot in modern society is not clear. These issues are not raised in this romantic view of the past.

Essentialist arguments hold the view that there is a core personality and character which defines masculinity, and which all men actually or potentially share. If the arguments are correct, they have important implications for boys and school-ing. For if we could identify an essence in masculinity, we would clearly be in a better position to develop curricula and learning experiences which would connect with it. However, there are variants of the essentialist argument, and each form has different educational implications. What is interesting about the differences among these arguments is how they specify the nature and origins of this essence.

First, there is the argument discussed above which sees the essence of masculinity as part of cultural memory. In this view, the problems of the present crisis lie in the fact that this essence is lost in history, constrained by aspects of the modern world, or overwhelmed by strong women, especially feminists. The essence is a set of personality characteristics and values which make the ideal man, as illustrated in Biddulph's praise for the Xervante people of the Brazilian rainforest, whom he describes as 'strong and tender, brave and compassionate'.[9] Much of this argument rests on cultural memory or a repressed personality, what we will call here psychic essentialism.

Probably the most widespread beliefs about the essence of masculinity are those which look to biology as the source. In this form of argument, masculine behaviour has natural origins, though the theories again vary. They range across emphases on direct genetic inheritance, chemical theories such as the effects of testosterone, sociobiological arguments about species survival, and inferences drawn from the structure and functions of the brain. Work in contemporary biomedical science has touched on a number of these issues, and the popular press regularly announces some new discovery which is read as confirming one prejudice or another.

Many popular writers on masculinity combine these various forms of essentialism, drawing on those that suit their particular purposes, and overlooking the contradictions that arise.

> To understand what boys are 'made of', we must consider what shapes them: the powerful forces of biology, the uniquely masculine psychological tasks, and the moist, dark, mysterious call of the masculine soul.[10]

The broad sweep of these kinds of arguments makes them difficult to address, for such statements have little regard for evidence or theoretical consistency. Their very simplicity makes them attractive as explanations of gender relations, when in fact a more sophisticated analysis would produce quite different conclusions. Another danger lies in the ease with which they can be used to justify rather than explain behaviour. If masculinity has an unchanging essence, then there is little point in questioning a natural order. This rhetoric functions as an argument for resisting steps to reform gender relations as going against some law of nature, and is oppressive to both men and women. For these reasons, we need to look closely at the chief forms of essentialism.

MYTHS AND THE MALE PSYCHE

Psychic essentialism sees masculinity as a psychological force which governs the state of the male psyche, and which specifies the content of the masculine personality. The exact nature of this psyche varies from one writer to another. One currently popular version is that the key to men's problems lies in a spiritual lack, that men, driven by such things as competitiveness and a repression of feeling, have lost touch with the spiritual dimension of life. The problem with the argument is not a concern for spirit in itself, but the singular vision of what men's spirit is said to be like.

For Biddulph,[11] men's problems lie in the fact that we have denied 'all the varied dark and shadowy forces that whirl around like demons in the male psyche'. In order to be admired by others, men have denied the natural feelings which the crisis in masculinity would evoke, which Biddulph identifies as anger, aggression, grief, feelings of abandonment and rejection, rage and confusion.

This denial sets up a tension or a split in the male psyche which must be resolved through some form of harmony or unity. Biddulph believes that one source of this tension occurs when men reject their fathers, for 'if you are at war with him in your head, you are at war with masculinity itself', and therefore 'you are hopelessly divided against yourself'.[12]

Formaini, in her evocatively titled book *Men: The Darker Continent*, also emphasises men's 'state of isolation from themselves' and a 'split which lasts throughout life'.[13] She explains that:

> In being divided against themselves, men face many personal and collective difficulties. Most important of all, men get cut off from direct contact with the 'essential self' and this then means that great problems arise which inhibit the kind of psychological development leading to maturity.[14]

But where has this essential self come from, and how can we identify it if it has been so long repressed or forgotten? Biddulph finds men's spirit in an inheritance from Cro-Magnon man, who 'lives somewhere deep inside our hearts and minds and calls to us'. Cro-Magnon man represents 'what is best in the spirit of manhood':

> Indomitable and invincible and wild, ready to protect and defend and compete, his instinct and perceptions necessary to ensure the survival of the human race, this primitive man at the center of our psyches must be allowed room to live

and breathe and express himself. If this rudimentary part of us dies, male identity dies.[15]

Elsewhere Biddulph describes Cro-Magnon man as 'wise, tough, skilful, nurturing, courageous and in touch with the forces of the universe', and argues that men can move forward only if they can retrieve this repressed memory.[16] We might wonder how Biddulph developed such insights into the character of these men, how he came by this unique access to prehistory. The reality of course is that this image is Biddulph's creation of the kind of man he admires. The attempt to found it in some long-lost history is a fiction, a cross between the primitivism of *Planet of the Apes* and the anachronism of *The Flintstones*. Discussions of prehistory based on actual evidence give a much more varied picture of the cultural construction of gender relations and what was involved in being male.[17]

The fiction of a golden age for men is fed by a rejection of contemporary society, for Biddulph believes that modern culture has repressed this natural masculinity. The solution to the problems of modern men, we are told, lies in a return to nature. In advising men on how to free their 'wild spirit', he argues that:

> The god of men does not dwell in the suburbs or the office towers . . . You will need to find a spiritual basis for your inner life that is specifically masculine and *based in nature*, which connects you to the earth you live on. As you grow older this will be your source of strength and harmony, freeing you from fear and dependency on others.[18]

This theory, when applied to the situation of boys, constructs a picture of boys riven by conflict, plagued by images from ancient cultures, and corrupted from a natural development by modern civilisation. Formaini says that boys are damaged very early on in life by the society's requirement 'to work and be profitable and to uphold the male systems which have been in place for what must be thousands of years', with the result that 'half of its members are damaged to the extent where they are split from their essential selves'.[19]

The arguments of psychic essentialism raise important questions about the pressures that boys face as they construct their understanding of themselves. It is for this reason that such arguments have a strong appeal to those who sympathise with the challenges boys face. Ideas about masculinity are important to boys as they try to identify an image of manhood to which they might aspire.

However, on closer inspection, the psychic essentialist analysis is not helpful, because it is based on a series of false premises. First, it starts with the assumption that conflicting pressures are unnatural. Yet both boys and girls, and adults as well, are constantly faced with complex choices, conflicting loyalties, perplexing dilemmas about preferred futures and the kinds of people they want to be. To suggest that this is some historical aberration which we can abolish is to create a false hope. What we must do is understand that complexity, diversity, change and conflict are an inevitable part of life, and that we need a flexible, open and responsive approach to it. This is quite the reverse of psychic essentialism, with its promotion of a unified and unchanging harmony.

Second, psychic essentialism suggests that there is only one true way for men, and that to depart from it is to reject the only model of humanity that men can aspire to. To reduce masculinity to a singular unvarying essence is to deny men the capacity to re-create themselves in new, diverse and imaginative ways. Rather than lament a split in men's psyche, as if the solution was some universal unity, we need to promote different ways of being men.

Third, the implication of the essentialist argument is that all men, from the modern industrial worker to the Brazilian hunter-gatherer to their prehistoric ancestors, face similar problems, and that there is a common solution in a universal masculinity. This reduces historical change and social and cultural diversity to an irrelevance. If the possibilities for men are to be recognised, we need to value the diversity of human cultures which sustains these possibilities, rather than neglect them for some historical fiction. Whatever the merits of arguments about the nature of masculinity in small-scale pre-industrial societies, it is surely naive to suggest that this should be a model for boys' upbringing in the complexity of the modern (or postmodern) world.

This is not to say that the traditions of masculinity are not important. As Connell argues, there are positive aspects of the images of masculinity which dominate our culture:

> This includes hero stories from the *Ramayana* and the *Iliad* to the *Twilight of the Gods*; participatory pleasures such as neighbourhood baseball; abstract beauty in fields such as pure mathematics; ethics of sacrifice on behalf of others. That is a heritage worth having, for girls and women as well as boys and men. (As the rich heritage of feminine culture is worth having, for boys and men as well as girls and women.)[20]

While the discourse of the hero has been appropriated by men in violent and individualistic ways, heroic storylines can be opened up to more varied and positive masculinities. A genuine valuing of the traditions of masculinity will not try to narrow these to some singular concept imposed on history and culture, and proposed as a core of all men's psyches. The challenges boys face will be made more difficult by such an exclusive model. They will be better understood and responded to if we recognise the possibilities for men which lie in the real diversity of human experience.

BODIES, BRAINS AND BIOLOGY

Some of the most dogmatic claims about men's natures come from writers who draw on natural science and biologically oriented psychology. There has been quite an explosion in this work in recent years, so much so that any attempt to address issues in the education of boys can hardly afford to ignore it. For if boys' 'nature', predispositions and abilities are biologically given, as some of the more simplistic biological arguments would have it, then the possibilities for boys and their education are immediately constrained.

The 'boys will be boys' myth neglects the real diversity of boys and narrows the possibilities for them. It can excuse failure and unacceptable behaviour, or propose superficial explanations of problems in boys' education. What follows is an overview of biological essentialist positions, in which we identify some of the flaws and dangers of biological determinist arguments.

Boys and their brains

One of the most publicised of recent attempts to attribute sex differences and hence masculinity to biological causes has been based on studies of the structure and functioning of the brain. The argument is that male and female brains are structured differently, that this means that they are organised differently in their operation on tasks, and that the different processing leads to different outcomes, so that men do better on tasks that suit their brain structures, while women do better on tasks that suit theirs.

One of the most widely known of these arguments is Moir and Jessel's book *Brainsex*.[21] The authors, in dogmatic style typical of much of the populist application of natural science to social questions, make strong claims that the sexes are different because 'The brain, the chief administrative and emotional organ of life, is differently constructed in men and in women; it processes information in a different way, which results in different perceptions, priorities and behaviour'.[22] They further claim that this is known 'beyond speculation, beyond prejudice, and beyond reasonable doubt'.[23] Another book makes similar claims that differences in the brain structures of girls and boys account for differences in 'memory, imagination, and control of bodily movement, and in how men and women think, feel, act, and perceive things'.[24]

Here again we see the simple shift from a difference in biological make-up, which can be investigated with the tools of the natural scientist, to what is described as 'male behaviour', which can't. This is a crucial step in the biological essentialist argument, and one of its chief weaknesses. However, the scientific evidence itself simply does not warrant these claims.

Brain research does point to differences in features like brain size and structure in male and female brains, though it is conflicting and based on surprisingly small samples. There is also evidence that when men and women complete particular tasks, there are sex differences in the areas of the brain involved.[25] However, some quite large studies have found no significant sex differences in size,[26] and some parts of the brain are larger in men and some larger in women. Some early claims about sex differences in brain structures have not been confirmed by later research.[27] Further, it is misleading to refer to the brain as being connected in a particular way, as if brains operate in a similar manner to hardwired electronic devices.[28] This denies the flexibility and interactiveness of the brain revealed for instance in the fact that particular functions can involve different parts of the brain at different times.[29] The conclusion must be that our understanding of brain structure and function is far too elementary to justify the confident claims of direct cause of personality and behaviour.

However, popular belief has been very receptive to claims that the left and right hemispheres of the brain are different in men and women, and that this accounts for behavioural differences. For instance, Moir and Jessel claim:

> Man keeps his emotions in their place; and that place is on the right side of his brain, while the power to express his feelings in speech lies over on the other side. Because the two halves of the brain are connected by a smaller number of fibres than a woman's, the flow of information between one side of the brain and the other is more restricted. It is then often more difficult for a man to express his emotions because the information is flowing less easily to the verbal, left side of his brain.[30]

A similar picture is given by Ridley in his bestselling book on evolution and sex:

> The two hemispheres of the brain become more different and more specialized in boys. The corpus callosum, which connects the two, grows larger in girls. It is as if testosterone has begun to isolate the boy's right hemisphere from the colonization by verbal skills from the left.[31]

This deceptively simple scheme sounds logical enough, and its clear dichotomy of male and female supports commonsense assumptions and beliefs about sex differences. One recent magazine article called it 'visible proof of the existence of female intuition'.[32] However, these claims are a combination of unwarranted generalisation and gross oversimplification. There are conflicting studies on the size of the corpus callosum (the neural system connecting the two hemispheres), with some showing men's to be larger and others women's. Peters' review of the evidence on this point concludes 'The absolute size of the corpus callosum appears similar for the sexes, and this suggests a comparative level of interconnectivity'.[33]

Hoptman and Davidson also point out that sex differences in corpus callosum (CC) anatomy have been found only inconsistently. They do refer to findings that there is one part of the corpus callosum, the isthmus, which seems to be larger in consistently right-handed women than consistently right-handed men. However, studies which measure interhemispheric interaction suggest that women's reaction times are slower than men's, so the larger CC did not produce greater connectivity between the two hemispheres.[34] In other words, on this evidence, difference in CC size, the most remarked upon of the alleged structural sex differences in the brain, seems to be unrelated to the function it is claimed to explain.

So what populists like Moir and Jessel and Ridley claim is a powerful distinguishing feature of male–female brain differences turns out to be quite unproven. Hoptman and Davidson conclude that there is a 'lack of consistent evidence of sex or handedness differences in interhemispheric interaction',[35] and Kimura concludes that the evidence for differences in brain asymmetry between men and women is 'meager and conflicting'.[36]

More stridently, British neuroscientist Steven Rose comments on these 'myths about the almost mystical implications of lateralization in the human brain', including 'views on left-brain cognitive masculinity versus right-brain affective femininity'. Rose describes the work, which originated in the nineteenth century, as 'an entire speculative apparatus about how functional brain asymmetry was a uniquely human characteristic, and how adults, males and whites showed much greater such asymmetry than children, females and blacks. Then and now, such stories are generally little more than ideological fantasies.'[37]

The point of these rather involved considerations is to demonstrate the very complex and unresolved state of research into brain organisation and structure, but also to show how ready the popular imagination is to draw unwarranted conclusions from it. These unwarranted conclusions are usually in the direction of confirming rigid gender dichotomies and the inequalities that go with them, though some schools of feminism have also succumbed to them.[38] If the biological structures and functions, on which differences in performance and predisposition are said to be based, are themselves unproven, how can it possibly be claimed that differences in masculinity and femininity can be attributed to them?

The testosterone beast

Another aspect of this debate is the role of testosterone in producing sex differences of various kinds. While there is strong evidence of the role of testosterone in reproductive sex differences, effects on non-reproductive aspects of the behaviour of men and women are unproven. Again, however, the popular translation seems unconcerned about such qualifications. Take the following claim by Elium and Elium:

> Boys are biologically driven via a drug-like hormone that is one of the most powerful manipulators of behavior the world has ever known. It is this force that pushes boys to be aggressive and inspires them to win at all costs. . . [It] turns a playful nine-year-old human into a fourteen-year-old 'Incredible Hulk'. From conception to manhood, this force triggers the human male body and brain to take a masculine form. It is the hormone testosterone.[39]

We see here the same rhetorical ploy as with brain structure: take a highly specific aspect of biological sex difference, exaggerate its impact, and attribute to it a powerful and apparently unlimited effect on people. If we test these claims against the research, the evidence is simply not there to suggest such strong links between testosterone and difference in behaviour. For instance, Kimura quotes research on the relationship between testosterone and performance on a spatial ability test which indicated that men with low testosterone scored more highly than men with high testosterone, while women with high testosterone scored more highly than women with low levels.[40]

British biologist Ben Greenstein also discusses theories that certain learning and perception problems result from the action of testosterone, but asserts that there is 'no evidence for this elaborate theory'. Greenstein discusses the role of testosterone in producing organisational changes in the developing brains of various species, and shows that effects found in species such as rats are not found in humans or primates. Of the more flexible and adaptable capacities of humans, Greenstein concludes: 'It seems that humans and the other primates have to a great extent been liberated from the chemical straitjacket imposed by the sex hormones on lower orders'.[41]

Man the aggressor?

One area of behaviour frequently referred to as having a biological base is human aggression. For parents and educators this is an important issue, because concerns about the raising of boys, and difficulties in educating them, are often attributed to the problem of disciplining a natural inclination to disruptive behaviour. In fact, some proponents of the biological theory of masculinity see natural aggression as the key male characteristic:

> The biggest behavioural difference between men and women is the natural, innate aggression of men, which explains to a large degree their historical dominance of the species. Men didn't learn aggression as one of the tactics of the sex war. We do not teach our boy children to be aggressive—indeed, we vainly try to unteach it. Even researchers most hostile to the acknowledgement of sex differences agree that this is a male feature, and one which cannot be explained by social conditioning.[42]

Observers of the desperate exhortations of parents and coaches at weekend football matches may find it difficult to believe that boys are naturally aggressive and do not need to be taught. More importantly, the evidence from biology simply does not support this sensational claim.

Popular beliefs about aggression are remarkably consistent. Goldstein summarises the commonly held view that:

- aggression is instinctive, and violence occurs because in some individuals the aggressive drive is abnormally strong;
- failure to express anger results in stress. It is healthy to

express anger, and children should be allowed to get it out of their system;

- the aggressive instinct can be controlled through providing other outlets like football or violent movies;
- extreme acts of violence are a sign of mental illness.[43]

Goldstein reviews the biological argument, based on experimental electrical stimulation of the brains of laboratory animals, that aggression results from a physiological process of activation of the hypothalamus. He concludes that these are more likely to be the result of cognitive and environmental factors that are themselves responsible for the stimulation in the first instance.

A recent meta-analysis of largely experimental studies of sex differences in aggression showed greater aggressiveness among men than women, but the effect size was so small that in most studies it would be considered unimportant.[44] Even this small difference was reduced when only moderate forms of provocation were taken into account. The authors speculate that the small difference in unprovoked aggression could be associated with gender factors which make men more ready to interpret situations as provocative.

Also, if aggression were caused mainly by hormonal change, we would expect that aggressive behaviour and interpersonal conflict would show some sudden shifts in adolescence, but, in their review of this matter, Laursen and Collins found that the evidence did not support this. Conflict was more continuous than discontinuous, and it varied considerably across settings and relationships in ways that the biological theories would seem unable to explain.[45]

Turner[46] points out that testosterone levels and fighting are sometimes associated during the mating season in mammals, but that in primate species the two are not associated. The correlation between testosterone levels and aggressive behaviour in pubertal boys was weak but positive, but since being aggressive or experiencing aggression raises testosterone levels, it is impossible to say which is the cause and which is the effect.

In his review of the relation between sexual aggression and a range of hormonal and other biochemical substances and processes, Prentky concluded that 'A neurochemical theory can neither substitute for, nor account for, the critical role of social learning'.[47] Turner concludes that 'There are clearly no simple genetic or hormonal factors that can explain the variation in aggressive and antisocial behaviour between individuals or the difference in such behaviour between males and females'.[48] Other studies have found no evidence that the tendency to violent crime is inherited.[49]

Finally, biological explanations of violence tend to overlook how varied are the motivations, provocations, expressions and contexts of its different forms:

> Multiple masculinities are implicated in the gendered patterning of violence. Men's violence toward men involves a masculinity of status competition and bravado among peers . . . Men's rape and assault of women reflect a masculinity of domination, control, humiliation, and degradation of women . . . Other types of harm involve a shameless masculinity or a masculinity of unconnectedness and unconcern for others.[50]

After close scrutiny of the evidence and arguments for the beast within and its biological nature, Klama concludes that aggression is not a natural category of analysis; that it cannot be parcelled out to nature and nurture, or to a biological core with a cultural overlay of modifiers or constraints; that it is not located in particular genes, hormones or brain centres; and that it is not unalterable. Rather, 'various kinds of aggressive behaviour are the developmental consequences in specific environments of multiple and diverse interactions within and between social animals or humans'. It is 'one of the most flexible and widely varying aspects of the social lives of animals and people'.[51]

Biology and masculinity

It seems clear from this review of biological essentialism that to see brain structure, genes or chemistry as the cause of some overriding masculine personality type, with constant and unalterable characteristics, is simply unfounded. However, the essentialist argument continues to assert that biology is basic and therefore privileged in this complex system of human behaviour, in that it determines the limits to individual capacity, the patterns of differentiation among groups, and often the originative force for what people do. The picture is more realistically seen as a complex interaction of biological potential, developmental experience and social context, where biological sex is only one of a huge number of possible influencing factors. The situation is nicely captured in Rose's description of the indeterminacy of the relation between the brain and behaviour:

> . . . brains and the organisms they inhabit, above all human brains and human beings, are not closed systems, like the molecules of a gas inside a sealed jar. Instead they are open systems, formed by their own past history and continually in interaction with the natural and social worlds outside, both changing them and being changed in their turn.[52]

When the focus moves from the biological capacity to actual performance, the claims for essential differences are even less successful. There is much less difference between men and women and between boys and girls than the essentialist arguments claim, and what differences there are are not fixed. The constant finding of psychological research into this issue is that 'sex differences are small, their origins unclear, and the variation within each sex far outweighs any differences between the sexes'.[53] This allows us 'to predict very little about a specific individual's performance on the basis of sex alone'.[54] Perhaps the most significant point here is the wide variety amongst men and women, which should focus attention on their potential for variability rather than the reductionist search for a single dominant form.

The natural science project is driven by preconceptions of necessity; education looks for possibility. Science assumes determination; education embraces potential. To this extent, biological essentialism is, by and large, anti-educational, and educators must challenge at every turn constraining deterministic views of science. The fascination with natural science as a solution to all our problems is part of the current technological age, and we will always be susceptible to claims of one spectacular finding or other. We should remember, however, British geneticist Steve Jones' caution about the readiness of science and the popular media to accept claims of genetic causes for behaviour: 'There have been announcements of the discovery of single genes for manic depression, schizophrenia and alcoholism. All have been withdrawn.'[55]

There is evidence that even the most respected of scientific journals can favour work which confirms the deterministic view,[56] and many of us are predisposed to see deterministic explanations as tough-minded and authoritative. (This can make them particularly appealing to men.) To counter this we need a healthy skepticism where biological explanations of human behaviour are concerned. We have seen that quite unfounded claims can be widely accepted in the popular imagination, diverting attention away from positive action and towards a resigned conformity.

This popularity is so great that some authors find these biological claims irresistible, despite realising how simplistic they are. Biddulph's recent book is a classic example. The book is a litany of exaggerated populist accounts of biological sex differences. Yet, while accepting a strong biological determinist argument, Biddulph tries to acknowledge its limitations, but ultimately fails to avoid quite gross generalisations. For instance, after counselling that biological differences among men and women are slight, that they are only tendencies which don't apply to everyone, and that we need not accept them as limitations, he proceeds to claim that 'The right side of the brain handles both feelings and actions, so men are more likely to take action while women tend to mull over something to the point of paralysis!'.[57] Such stark stereotypes may appear so extreme that they do not warrant comment, but, unfortunately, they are the currency of much public debate in the area.

And yet, in calling for more attention to a critical approach to gender differences, and to diversity and possibility for men and boys, we would be foolish to ignore the role that the physical experience of masculinity can play in this. As Connell observes:

> Masculine gender is (among other things) a certain feel to the skin, certain muscular shapes and tensions, certain postures and ways of moving certain possibilities in sex. Bodily experience is often central in memories of our own

lives, and thus in our understanding of who and what we are.[58]

We need to understand how these experiences are created in the contexts in which men live and how they have learned to respond to them. Part of this derives from reproductive difference, since 'Gender is, in the broadest terms, the way in which the reproductive capacities and sexual differences of human bodies are drawn into social practice and made part of the historical process'.[59] But we should also remember that 'The physiology of orgasm and penile erection no more explain a culture's sexual schema than the auditory range of the human ear explains its music'.[60] The connection between reproductive physiology and behaviour is overlaid by the powerful forces of history and cultural differences. To acknowledge this, we need to turn the biological argument on its head, and focus our attention on how 'the social relations of gender are experienced in the body (as sexual arousals and turn-offs, as muscular tensions and posture, as comfort and discomfort) and are themselves constituted in bodily action (in sexuality, in sport, in labour)'.[61]

To increase rather than constrain the possibilities for boys, we need to broaden our view way beyond the biological. As Connell points out, 'Masculinity is not a biological entity that exists prior to society; rather, masculinities are ways that societies interpret and employ male bodies'.[62] Accordingly, we need to focus on the social practices in which boys come to understand themselves, and how these practices engage their relations with their bodies and with other people. This requires that we understand how boys are constructed as social beings in their everyday lives.

FROM ESSENTIALISM TO POSSIBILITY

Becoming a man is a matter of constructing oneself in and being constructed by the available ways of being male in a particular society. It is a matter of negotiating the various discourses of femininity and masculinity available in our culture, those powerful sets of meanings and practices which we must draw on to participate in our culture and to establish who we are. Understanding boys is primarily about understanding how these discourses operate, and recognising a number of key points which have previously been omitted or not sufficiently emphasised in discussions of masculinity.

First, being masculine is an accomplishment which boys and men must constantly achieve in every situation they enter, a project by which they construct their life histories in particular social and institutional contexts.[63] Butler refers to gender as a performance, 'a reenactment and a reexperiencing of a set of meanings already socially established'.[64] It is 'the repeated stylization of the body, a set of repeated acts within a highly rigid regulatory frame that congeal over time to produce the appearance of substance, of a natural sort of being'.[65]

Seeing masculinity as a performance is an important check on the tendency to attribute to men some underlying internal unity which is the source and cause of masculine behaviour. This is strategically important, because a search for some internal origin and cause can distract us from the real focus— what boys and men actually do. 'Instead of wondering whether they should change their behaviour, men "wrestle with the meaning of masculinity"'.[66]

Masculinity as a performance, rather than some internal essence, also means that we cannot try to degender boys and men as if we could somehow rid them of hegemonic masculinity and discover some universal person underneath. This would be a mistake, for not only is gender too important a part of people's experience and their investment in their sense of self, but this would also risk abolishing the positive as well as the negative aspects of masculine culture, an important problem as we saw in the last section. Connell suggests a kind of 'gender multiculturalism' which would open up the possibilities of gender to all people. Seeing masculinity as performance demonstrates that this is not simply a matter of changing attitudes. It also requires a focus on material inequalities and power relations, and how these operate in everyday practices.

Second, we need to avoid seeing everything about people as being primarily differentiated by their sex, as this would blind us to the importance of 'race', class, ethnicity and other dimensions of human experience. It would also blind us to the simple experience of being human which men and women hold in common, with all that that implies about identifying and achieving a desirable way of life for all people. However, being human always involves being human in a particular way, and gender is a necessary part of that.

These intersections highlight a third aspect of masculinity—its relational character. Conventional masculinity is constructed along with, but in contrast to femininity, so neither can be studied independently of the other. The discourse of hegemonic masculinity has most often been analysed as a series of dichotomous relations between opposing ways of being, with the two sets of dichotomous terms distinguishing stereotypical masculinity from stereotypical femininity.[67] Seen in these terms, masculinity is more rational than emotional, more callous than empathetic, more competitive than cooperative, more aggressive than submissive, more individualistic than collectivist, etc. These implicit assumptions guide our view of what is natural, and 'construct men's thought and action in ways which often feel normative and compelling, rather than being simply one of a potential myriad of choices'.[68] The obsessive exaggeration of these distinctions is one cause of the extremes of violent, misogynist and generally anti-social practices of some men.

While this analysis may be useful in identifying a range of elements associated with the dominant image of masculinity in our culture over recent times, it cannot be used simply as a description of an actually existing form of masculine practice. To do so is to produce just another essentialist theory. Such a simple model can hardly comprehend the real complexity of how men think and act. For instance, the individual dichotomies cannot be simply added to each other to form some overall dichotomy, so that men are seen to be rational, callous, competitive, aggressive, individualistic, while women are emotional, empathetic, cooperative, submissive and collectivist. A person can be emotionally committed to achieving power over others, or rationally committed to collectivity. In fact, it is more likely that people are both rational and emotional at different times in different contexts. Further, if masculinity is associated with individualism, how do we explain the traditions of collective masculine ethos in unions, sports and the military?

This acknowledgment of the complexity and conflict that characterises the experience of masculinity is the fourth key point. We have seen the problems of arguments which seek an overriding biological source of men's behaviour, but sociological theories can also neglect the complexity of the construction of masculinity. A widely espoused view is that boys and girls internalise beliefs and values of conventional sex roles through a process of socialisation. But such a theory implies that there is a general social consensus about gender roles which guides this socialising process. It also suggests that there are normal male and female characters on which children are said to model themselves. Sex-role theory ignores the complex and even contradictory nature of gender in our society.

There is no single consensual model for children to internalise, but rather a competitive and conflicting variety of styles of masculinity which are waxing and waning and combining and dividing as ways of being male change over time and place.[69] Becoming masculine or feminine is not a continuous process of developing an ever clearer and more refined internalised model which then expresses itself through or is applied to behaviour. Rather masculinity is constructed, negotiated and struggled over as we participate in the practices of everyday life. This accounts for the difficulty boys have in finding a place within the competing ways of being male, despite the fact that being male gives boys access to certain privileges. As Segal explains, 'men, although the favoured sex, with higher levels of self-confidence and self-esteem, may nevertheless experience a lack of certainty over their "masculinity", rather than a lack of satisfaction with it'.[70]

Recognising this complexity brings us to the fifth point, the idea of multiple masculinities. Masculinity is not a unified discourse, though the hegemonic form of masculinity, like most dominant discourses, will usually be represented as coherent, rational and obvious. But in fact, masculinity is diverse, dynamic and changing, and we need to think of multiple masculinities rather than some singular discourse. When we talk about 'multiple masculinities' rather than 'masculinity' we do not mean that boys and men simply inhabit one of these and remain untouched by the others. Multiple masculinities are, rather, multiple possibilities opened up in our culture which expand rather than constrain the opportunities for men to live rewarding lives for themselves and others. Most boys and men will take up a variety of these possibilities at different times and in different contexts, but this diversity will always be constructed within the discursive frames of the culture, and some of these will be more powerful, pervasive and insistent in the pressures they create. These regulatory discursive frames produce and are reproduced in the symbols, stories and practices which embody our understanding of ourselves and others, in the institutions through which our society operates, and in the practices of the people we meet in our everyday lives.

Take as an example boys' involvement in video game culture, an important part of the lives of many boys, and one which will be discussed later in this book. The production of video games is an industry driven by the need to attract potential buyers. Advertisers of these games must project an image which appeals to the readers' and viewers' sense of who they are and how they would like to be. To do this they produce and reproduce images, ideas and practices which make certain ways of being male attractive, heroic, daring, while disparaging other ways. The marketing process must tie the games to this image of desirable embodied masculinity.

In responding to these advertisements, consumers are invited to see themselves as certain kinds of people and to make sense of their lives in certain ways. As Dawson puts it, 'Masculine identities are lived out in the flesh but fashioned in the imagination'.[71] Buying and using the magazines in which the advertisements appear, and the video games themselves, engage boys in a specific social practice and establish relationships to other boys. Even when they play the games as a solitary pursuit, they are entering an imaginative world which they will later discuss and share with their friends. The result is a social and cultural practice constructed around game culture, but one which becomes inextricably linked, as we will see in chapter 3, to a very specific discourse of masculinity. The video games position boys in an ideology, a social practice, a set of social relationships, and an embodied sense of self, all involving what they see as normal and desirable ways of being male, and how they see themselves to be.

The processes of the social construction of masculinity outlined in this example are replicated to varying degrees in every aspect of boys' lives—in school, the family, sport and a host of other daily activities. No one of these practices is all-powerful in itself. Boys will respond to them in active, selective and even oppositional ways, so the effect of any discourse on the construction of masculinity is contingent, tentative and unpredictable. However, if these practices are structured by a dominant view of what it is to be masculine, their combined effect will narrow the possibilities for boys rather than expand them. To construct and maintain a sense of who they are, boys must draw on the available terms, categories and ways of thinking, acting and interacting which these various contexts provide, including the specific forms of masculinity associated with them. The fact that these available forms of masculinity are complex, diverse and contradictory makes this a difficult task, but this very difficulty may make the strongest and most conspicuous form even more attractive for the security it may seem to offer.

It is for this reason that one of the key problems boys face in becoming male is that of dealing with the dominant image of what it means to be 'a man'—the discourse of hegemonic masculinity. Some commentators have questioned whether there is a single dominant form of masculinity which warrants the label hegemonic, preferring to describe the stereotyped popular image as a culturally exalted rather than a dominant form.[72] In our view, it is reasonable to speak of a pervasive and powerful form of masculinity which is exalted *and* practised across discourses and social contexts, which regulates thought and action, and which therefore can be called hegemonic. We have seen in the analysis of essentialism some examples of this dominant discourse, and this book deals with other aspects of it in society and school. This does not, of course, imply that this form is always dominant, that it is uncontested or that it is uniform in nature.

We believe that the problems of masculinity are best understood as the performance of a set of gender relations in a context where one set of storylines and repertoires of action is culturally dominant and socially powerful. This performance is always complex and precarious, as it combines with other dimensions of social experience and division, like 'race' and class. The competitive and aggressive elements of masculinity turn back on it, so that difference is seen as a threat, and attempts to moderate it become attacks on its integrity. In this way, the exaltation of dominant masculinity heightens the fear of failure and hostile rejection of alternatives, increasing misogynistic, homophobic and self-destructive behaviours.

The defensiveness of the essentialist men's movement, and the crisis rhetoric we saw earlier in this chapter, fail to come to terms with these aspects of masculinity. Rather than focus on the challenges to hegemonic masculinity as a threat to men, we need to see them as opportunities to expand the human possibilities for men and how they can contribute to a just and rewarding world for all men and women. Education has a crucial role to play in this. But to proceed in this direction we need to see how boys experience masculinities in our culture, and particularly the hegemonic forms which define dominant views of what it means to be a man. The following chapters review a range of aspects of these issues with a view to recommending a way ahead.

PART II

Boys and contemporary cultures

3

Playing the game

The last chapter reviewed two theories about the origins of masculinity—psychic and biological essentialism—and concluded that neither was able to account for the way boys and men respond to the issues surrounding masculinity. These theories are too rigid, unitary and simplistic (and sometimes fanciful) to explain the complexity, variety and change in the masculinities which boys and men live out in their daily lives. The chief reason for this is that neither approach looks at masculinity in context, for each is based on assumptions that masculinity is fixed in biology or the distant past. Consequently, the theories neglect the cultural variations in masculinities, how they change over time, and how boys and men at any particular time and place are negotiating a diverse and conflicting range of ways of being masculine. No adequate understanding of masculinity, or of how boys are confronted by and come to terms with it, can ignore the contexts in which masculinities are constructed, sustained, challenged and changed.

This chapter reviews a number of public sites in contemporary society which are central to how issues of masculinity are played out. The choice of 'play' as the key metaphor in the chapter is deliberate. In one sense, 'play' directs our attention to sport and recreation as an important site in which boys meet institutionalised forms of masculinity. In another meaning, play also suggests that, while sport and recreation are for boys an authentic and normal part of their lives, much of their leisure activity can be seen as a kind of rehearsal or practice for the lives they will lead in the future as men: boys 'play at' masculinity, trying on various forms and modes. Yet another meaning of 'play' hints at the naturalisation of these practices—at the almost automatic way in which many of these practices 'play' or run in sites like sport and recreation. Dominant masculinity can be seen as a persistent discourse playing in the background to the actions of boys, with those actions then frequently read and interpreted in terms of the background agenda.

Boys' lives are lived out primarily in institutions—family, school, sporting and other recreational clubs—and the discourses of masculinity play through all of them. To see how boys are positioned as masculine, we need to understand these discourses: how they position people so that certain ways of thinking and acting become naturalised, how they appeal to boys' developing desires, how they exert power which boys feel they must respond to in some way. Even in the less regulated time of informal group and even solitary play, boys are still immersed in the discourses of masculinity through the products of the leisure industries—the toys, movies, magazines, video games and television images that create so much of their culture. Masculinity is played out constantly through these multimedia fields of pleasure, and, as we will argue in this chapter, the forms of masculinity on offer through these fields, and the reading/playing positions they make available, are narrow.

Family relationships are discussed in chapter 4. Here we consider sport and the various electronic media as contexts in which masculinity is produced, and examine their ideologies, bodily practices and discursive effects. Boys spend considerable time 'practising' masculinity through their participation in sport and boys' leisure cultures, and a particular feature of both sport and boys' cultural activities is their highly structured, rule-based ordering. In this chapter, we look at how boys understand themselves and their social world, and how they come to engage in it through bodily movements and styles of dress which sustain images and satisfy desires of particular forms of masculinity. It is important also to see how these discourses work across a range of contexts. Interpretations constructed in one context are evoked, taken up and given new significance in others, in what has come to be called the intertextual character of meaning making. And the commercial manipulation of the images of popular culture results in the construction of stories, or ways to 'do' masculinity, that are dauntingly common across a range of media sites.

PROFITABLE PLAY: MARKETING MASCULINITY

A good example of this intertextual creation of meaning is in the marketing campaigns of the leisure industry. The same masculine superheroes, for instance, are syndicated across film, television, electronic games, toys, and clothing, in some of the slickest marketing campaigns of the retail world, and it is these commercial considerations that have had a major impact on the saturation of masculine storylines in children's culture. Huge profits are at stake in children's play, as Kline[1] describes in a discussion of Disney's mega-hit *Aladdin*. He records that for a production and promotion cost of $50 million, the income from ticket sales, video cassette sales and product licensing alone will exceed $950 million. Of this, toy licensing on its own is estimated to be in excess of $250 million, while the Nintendo video game from *Aladdin* is expected to produce $250 million.

With these sorts of profits in mind, it is hardly surprising that the private commercial needs of marketers far outweigh the social or educational needs of children in relation to the type of television, electronic games, toys, movies and magazines that are produced. United States children's television, for example, is often little more than a creative outlet for toy manufacturers, and is strongly dominated by marketing criteria. Most of the programs (over 60 per cent according to a study by Kline) feature a genre identified as 'action teams': a genre targeted at boys, and typically featuring a superhero who is part of a structured team 'always in mortal conflict with a rigid hierarchy led by a megalomaniac'.[2] Action team heroes feature well-known boy's 'action toys' as lead characters. They typically battle a great deal, speak little, convey almost no emotion, and have a vast battery of weapons and vehicles (all of which can be purchased). They are confident, aggressive and mean, and live in hierarchical worlds where the struggle is on a grand and cosmic scale between good and evil.

Boys can purchase the merchandise that accompanies these programs and play independently or with other boys in games that rely predominantly upon beat-'em-up, knock-'em-down strategies requiring little verbal exchange other than a repertoire of battle cries, weaponry noises, and collision effects. Masculinity is here being played out not only in the backdrop of flickering televisual images, but also in the overflow of promotional play equipment that goes with these images: the toys, electronic games, clothing and household items marketed at children. And, as Davies, Thorne and Alloway demonstrate, the gender 'play' of boys shows them taking up positions within this discursive site.[3] Boys play within the storylines made natural and desirable through the discourses of popular culture.

Important here is the overflow into the home and into children's family spaces of the gendered world of children's toys and games, and the intermingling of discourses from various institutional sites. The masculinities on offer, not only through promotional animation programs, but also through popular film, game machines, magazines, clothing and music, are now part of the material culture of the home. Boys can not only watch the movie or the television show: they can also own the game, the toy, the magazine, the shirt, the cap, the stickers. They can eat the pizzas and chips. They can sleep under quilt covers and behind curtains printed with action heroes. Indeed, with the increasing home ownership of multiple video recorders and television sets—and parents' increasing fear of allowing children to play outside or on the streets— many children's bedrooms become the playgrounds for the promotional toys of the electronic age.

This increase in bedroom play, as well as the new range of technologies the new playground demands, has meant that much of children's play takes place beyond the adult gaze, beyond adult participation, and therefore beyond surveillance and criticism. Like most children's play, both now and in the past, these are worlds which many adults see only from a distance. However, unlike much of children's play in the past, rapid technological change has meant that many adults have little understanding or experience with electronic leisure pursuits. Some adults tend to disapprove and patronise; some grudgingly admire and even enjoy its sophisticated technique; some find pleasure in entering a world of such apparently simple storylines. Whatever our response, it is important that we do not presume too readily to know what children take from these stories: to presume that the positions boys take up within these storylines of action and aggression are always the same, that they do not 'play' within the parameters of possibility. Given what we have said about the complexity of the discourses of masculinity, we need to remind ourselves that children read stories differently and in ways which we cannot know in advance. In interpreting the messages of popular culture, we need to acknowledge the multiple meanings that can be drawn from them, and the diverse uses these cultural practices can serve for their participants.

Despite this diversity, our current interest is in how these discourses affect boys by constructing and excluding particular forms of masculinity. For the institutionalised nature of these processes, and their base in the mode of production of the media society, produce a form of masculinity which we recognise as establishing a hegemonic dominance across many sites. As discussed in the previous chapter, hegemonic masculinity is, by its very ubiquity, the most powerful form in generating particular understandings and ways of acting. It is the most readily available set of ideas and exemplars, and its interpretations are the most familiar and the most easily assumed.

We saw in the previous chapter the key themes which inform our understanding of the operation of masculinity—its differentiation from and privileging over femininity, the body as a key signifier of how we understand ourselves as gendered, and the performative nature of masculinity. Other important issues are played out across the cultural sites and practices which we discuss in the present chapter. Violence is never far from view in any discussion of masculinity, and runs through all the sites visited here. As Connell[4] points out:

> Televised sports, Hollywood action movies, superhero comics, airport-rack novels, violent video games and children's plastic toy sets relentlessly insist on the bodily superiority of men and their mastery of technology and violence.

The silenced masculinities experienced by marginalised groups, the most obvious being gay masculinities, are part of the dichotomised construction of masculinity. And the problem of difference is inevitably an issue, as we try to acknowledge the effects of 'race', class, disability and the diverse masculinities which go with them.

GOOD SPORTS

If some of our key signifiers are the male–female dichotomy, violence, and men's bodies, we need hardly look further than organised sport for evidence of the formation of hegemonic masculinity. In many respects, men's sport is the archetype of institutionalised masculinity, and the images of men which dominate its ideology are the quintessential manifestation of the masculinist ethos.

However, like all social institutions, sport is complex, diverse and changing, and it is no simple matter to sort out the values of sport which we would want to promote from the negative elements which might need to be revised. Engaging in sport is for many boys and men (and girls and women), one of the most enjoyable pursuits of everyday life. This pleasure has been interpreted in various ways.

A survey of thirteen- to eighteen-year-old Australians identified very strong feelings that sport was good because it keeps you fit, is fun, and brings you friends.[5] The most important attractions of sport were clearly the social aspects, but many of these young people also valued the possibility of pursuing their own standards of excellence in ways they felt they had some control over.

> For many, playing sport was in a sense losing oneself into the sport completely. For that time, all needs were being satisfied; physical, mental, social and emotional. All other problems and life pressures ceased to exist; being blocked out by this total involvement with sport. There was a great sense of urgency and need to have this escape. It is an escape which they feel frees them to be truly themselves, and at their best.[6]

The connection with sport is of course an important factor in the way many boys construct a desirable sense of self. When asked about the importance of sport in their school lives, the boys interviewed for the present study were unanimous in seeing it as a key part of their experiences.[7] Sport is a social context unlike any other, a world in which boys compete with each other relatively free of the supervision of parents or teachers, where the rules are simple and the rewards immediate. While the sports field is their own territory, with parents and teachers banished to the sidelines, they also know that if they perform and excel in this context they can attract the kudos which they have witnessed a thousand times in televised sports, school assemblies and dinner table conversations.

For many boys, sport provides entry to a world of men. Coaches, older players, club supporters, school 'old boys' and other men will look approvingly on their success, welcoming them into a world of recognition and status. Angus has shown this world in his study of a Catholic boys' school, where it was a powerful connection to men and the wider world of business and work.[8] It is also central to many boys' relationships with their fathers, and boys get some of their most conspicuous attention and appreciation from their fathers by participating in sport.

This valorisation of sport is active among boys themselves. In interviews conducted for the present study, boys commented that sport is valued because 'it makes you fit', 'relaxes your mind and gets your mind off school', and 'makes you more popular'. However, there are signs also of a more adult sports ideology, foreshadowed in the comment that 'when you want to get a job you'll look more professional and look like you can make a difference'. While one boy observed that schoolwork can discipline boys in ways useful for sport, another commented that sport feeds back into study:

> I reckon it could help you in your studies. I don't know why. I like sport. I think of it as a guy's game really. It'd make you coordinated, make your brain work a bit more. Like when you play football you always have to think one step ahead of what you're doing to start with. It's the same with basketball. You have to plan your tactics and plan your

moves. If you can do that in football you can do it in school. I've never experienced it though. It sort of passed me by.

While boys seemed here to be echoing the view that sport can 'make a man of you', the connection between sport and socialising was the most conspicuous aspect of the group discussions:

It's active—you get to do something—it's better than sitting around at home watching TV—you get out and do something, make friends and that. Boys with a lot of friends like sport—people who are good at socialising are good at sport.

The people who don't play sport they're not going to make as many friends. People think that to prefer to come down to the library and read a book rather than go and play sport is not cool.

Shane explains that there is an element of necessity in this.

You've got to be good at sport to get along with other people 'cause they play sport and if you don't play sport then you'd be reading a book in the library or something and they don't like doing that. So you've got to play sport that they like to be in a friendship. I think it's good for fitness. I do half of it for getting friends 'cause you know if you're not going to do it you're not going to succeed on friends. And I also do it to get fit and enjoy.

There was also some scepticism about sport. Eric, a cricket player whose main interest seems to be computer games, criticises the excessive respect for sporting prowess, though he values its social aspect:

To most of the other kids in the school if you get a good shot in basketball you're supposedly the most popular boy in school until someone else does a better shot. I don't find that just playing good at sport [is important]. It only means you can do stuff physical. It doesn't mean you're mentally powerful if all you can do is play sport. I only play cricket on Friday. I only play it with my friends because all my friends are in there. I'm OK at it. You get together with people you don't know just to talk and muck around playing and stuff.

The bonding value of sport makes it for many boys a key indicator of their masculinity. As such, sport has to be clearly distinguished as a male pursuit. While some girls do play sport, the boys interviewed did not believe that sport dominates girls' time or priorities as it does for boys. One secondary boy's explanation of this difference in interest was ironic, in that, while he believed girls' interest in sport was motivated by gender relations and a concern for the opposite sex, there was no similar interpretation for boys.

> I've never really heard a girl sitting there and talking about how she did this at a basketball game or anything. It's pretty much just the guys who do that. The girls don't sit around and say how many points they scored at the football game or anything. I don't think the girls are into it as much. They just play to keep their bodies fit. [If a girl's] got a really good body all the guys will want her.

Boys' greater interest in sport has its costs, as noted in one group discussion:

> [Girls] do more work than we do because they don't have to go to sport training. They've got more time. Boys' parents push them to do really well in sport, but girls' parents push them to do really well in school. Boys don't have enough time to learn because they always want to get out and play.

Sport is such an important dimension of boys' lives that it is a constant touchstone for many of their interpretations and judgments about other aspects of their experience. For instance, sport figures strongly in what it means to be cool, and it is crucial to their need to be part of a social group. Unfortunately, this image of the cool sociable sportsman is constantly set against the picture of the boy whose interests might be to read a book, a practice most often associated with girls.[9] In this respect, sport is one of a number of masculine pursuits which run counter to a commitment to school learning.

The social value of sport for boys is problematic to the extent that it separates boys and girls, and competes with their commitment to school. However, the pleasure to be gained from it surely warrants continued support for participation in sport as long as this is not socially destructive. Yet there are strong elements of the practice and ideologies of sport which are just that. For instance, the evidence is that the infusion of sport with the ideology of hegemonic masculinity is an important factor militating against positive and continuing participation in and enjoyment of sport for young people. It also has other deleterious effects on those who do participate.

While boys may be introduced to the idea and rudimentary experience of sport by parents, especially fathers, the fun of social contact with a range of others is the chief reason why sport continues to be played. Winning is then learned as a value along the way. By the ages of nine or ten, boys begin to recognise themselves as good or incompetent in sports. Those for whom sport is a positive experience, that is, those who are respected or even admired by peers or praised by parents and coaches, commit themselves to it even more firmly. Those who see their abilities surpassed by increasing numbers of peers, or for whom the sporting experience is in other ways largely negative, are likely to conclude that sport is not for them.[10]

As boys get older, this dichotomy is accentuated by the increasing hold on organised sport of the 'will to win' ideology and its association with hegemonic masculinity. For the world of organised sport, and especially its public version in the media, is constructed as a hegemonically masculine activity, to the detriment of many boys and girls. As sport is seen as a key site for the development of masculinity, in ways and to an extent not applying to the development of femininity for girls, pressures and demands are imposed on boys which change and even supplant those of enjoyment and social contact. Increasingly, the criteria for judging successful involvement in sport become those of 'being a man', but the image of manhood created is increasingly narrowly defined as being tough, competitive and dominant.

The sexually exclusive nature of many male sports is one of the biggest problems for the creation of positive masculinities in sport. Since sport is for many parents and participants a 'masculinising project',[11] its very purpose could be seen to be subverted if this exclusivity were challenged. In his interview study of men and sport, Messner[12] illustrates its importance to men as a means of setting them apart from women.

Referring to the experience of being tackled by a feared professional football player, this comment from a white professional man gives a fascinating insight into sport as a bastion of the remnants of male power:

> A woman can do the same job as I can do—maybe even be my boss. But I'll be *damned* if she can go out on the football field and take a hit from Ronnie Lott.

The social bonding of male sport is one of its most powerful effects, but its exclusion of women is also one of its greatest social costs. Putdowns of women in the sporting arena range from the derogatory use of language, where calling a man 'wimp', 'wuss', 'weakling' or 'girl' means the same thing, to the crude and even brutal references to women and sex in the shower room songs.[13] From an early age, boys learn this attitude from fathers, brothers and peers to the extent that it becomes a natural part of many male sports. It is also a rehearsal for and an endorsement of domination in male–female relationships.

However, while the sociality of play is one of the main attractions of sport, there is no reason to believe that this has to be sexually exclusive. It is difficult to see how the widely observed misogynist nature of locker room culture can be challenged unless there is much greater integration of men and women in sport. Related to this is the unequal provision of sports and sporting facilities which supports this institutionalised sexism (compare the leading football, cricket and men's basketball stadiums in every Australian capital with their female equivalents). By giving men the most exciting opportunities, preaching that the virtues of sport are inherently masculine, and segregating women out, sports confirm the prejudice of men as a superior breed.

While sport is therefore a key context in the differentiation and privileging of men over women, an equally important contribution to masculinism lies in its bodily practice and the relation with violence. The dominant representation of men's sport is based on an ideology and a practice which are crucially connected with the most anti-social aspects of masculinity. Whannel's study of televised sport illustrates the problem here, in that:

> . . . while there is a wide range of qualities invoked—toughness, aggression, commitment, power, courage, ability to withstand pressure, and also balance, poise, judgement, timing, dexterity, speed, accuracy, concentration, flair, imagination—there is a tendency to evaluate more highly the first six of these. In turn these qualities conform closely to conventional constructions of masculinity.[14]

An important aspect of the masculinity in sport is a commitment to what the Cambridge journalist quoted above called 'superiority to physical suffering'. In Australia in 1990, it was reported that a million people, most of them males, are affected by sports injuries each year, resulting in an annual cost of approximately \$1 billion.[15] Sabo, reflecting on his own experiences in American football, refers to the 'pain principle', in which:

> We learn to ignore personal hurts and injuries because they interfere with the 'efficiency' and 'goals' of the 'team'. We become adept at taking the feelings that boil up inside us—feelings of insecurity and stress from striving so hard for success—and channelling them in a bundle of rage which is directed at opponents and enemies.[16]

Sabo argues that the need to justify pain, to take it without complaint, and to see it as character-building, leads to the view that pain as punishment (as meted, for instance, by father to son) is acceptable. This acceptance of pain is a dangerous mix when combined with the need in the dominant discourse of masculinity to sense physical power. To learn to be a man involves learning 'to project a physical presence that speaks of latent power' through practised combinations of force and skill, and boys see as an important task the development of bodily appearance and body language that suggest this power.[17]

While to be able physically to overpower opponents is central to the game, Schact's study of rugby union suggests that the scars (of battle?) are more often discussed than the injury inflicted on one's opponents. The explanation may be that, while not all players will be able to inflict injury on opponents, all can at least bear the pain of injury in silence. Boys don't cry, and being able to withstand pain is seen as a universally available test of one's developing manhood.

The danger here is that, if a boy is taught to be oblivious to pain, to suffer it in silence and give it no heed, then to inflict pain on others will be seen as no serious offence, for they also will be expected to respond in this way. If to register pain is contemptible, then those who do register it are also contemptible, and deserve what they get. This rather simple logic can lead to the view that to hurt others is acceptable. It would also suggest that there is little reason to sympathise with those who are hurt, since they are expected to conform to the same stoic ethos. If they do not, they may be seen as unworthy of sympathy; the practice of masculinity may then encourage a neglect of the pain of others. Carried to these conclusions, the view that pain is to be accepted with equanimity is a very dangerous element of masculinity. The fact that it thrives in male sports is a cause for concern.

To exert bodily power is to some extent a necessary element of every sport. However, we need to distinguish here between the kind of power and control which one can have over one's body in the challenge of playing golf, surfing waves or climbing mountains, and the power and control over other people which is a requirement of many confrontational competitive sports, especially those involving body contact. Confrontational contact sport is where the will to win involves physically dominating others, and determination to succeed can easily lead to hostile aggression. In the Australian context, the most popular examples of this kind of sport are the two codes of rugby football—league and union—the archetypes, along with boxing, of aggressive masculinity in sporting practice and its representation.

In the introduction to this chapter we mentioned the importance of intertextuality as meanings from one context are transferred to another, transforming how it is understood, emphasising some aspects of the situation over others, importing ways of doing things. Sport and aggressive sport in particular are excellent examples of this. We have seen how the boys interviewed for this study saw sport as a disciplining practice which might prepare them for success in school and later life. A more common example is the representation of sport as a form of war, illustrated in a press report of a football trainer describing one player's concern for an injured opponent: 'He showed a lot of compassion for "Plathy". In the heat of battle, it was wonderful to see . . . I was proud of him the way he stood over Plathy and looked after him until I arrived. It was real men-in-combat stuff.'[18]

The war metaphor is played up by coaches, players and especially the media as a way of promoting the spectacle of the game, and the public fame and personal status of the heroes who play it. A key target for this promotion are the boys who will aspire to such fame themselves, take the message home to their parents, and pass it on to their own children in later years.

> Patriarchy's mythos of heroism and its morality of power-worship implant visions of ecstasy and masculine excellence in the minds of the boys who ultimately will defend its inequities and ridicule its victims.[19]

The connection between sport and war is sustained by the culture of violence. Without this the war metaphor would refer only to winning and losing, in the sense that political language also uses the military analogy of strategies, campaigns, wars and battles. But physical sport goes further than this, as it actually embodies violent practices which mimic those of war. This is not a necessary connection, as the practice of body contact sport could equally be seen as a development of rough-and-tumble play rather than military conflict. However, rough-and-tumble play is a childish pursuit: war is much more glorious; and play does not arouse the vicarious fear of violence: war clearly does. This infusion of the ethos of war is achieved through the language of battle, and to play sport becomes a warrior act:

> In a recent *Rugby League Week* (6 July 1994) the individual players are lauded as ruthless, flashy, legends, villains, killers, assassins, dynamos; groups of players are called killer packs, contenders, marathon men, a murderous mix, who are involved in payback, rampage, and murder in the first degree (Manly 60 v St George 0).[20]

Is such a discourse necessary? Clearly not from the players' perspectives. While they may enjoy their gladiatorial image, players in the more violent sports (rugby in Australia, ice hockey and American football in the US) do not generally support the levels of violence in their games.[21] However, the discourse does reflect the common understanding of what the games are about and how to play them. For instance, in an Australian survey of violence in sport, 80 per cent of rugby league players reported that punching, an illegal tactic according to the laws of the game, occurred often. In fact, the survey found that the worst violence occurs below the elite level, where the checks of disciplinary committees and televised evidence are not available.

It is this level that boys experience, and the problem of violence is no less great in school sport. In fact, recent examples of violent incidents in school rugby league provide revealing evidence of the connections among sport, violence and masculinity. In April 1997, an Australian bank withdrew its sponsorship of a national schoolboy rugby league competition because of a series of violent incidents, including one all-in brawl.[22] Yet in criticising the bank's decision, a league administrator praised the way that playing the game exposed individuals 'to the principles and disciplines that build men'.[23] Dealing with violence in these sports is overdue. While such extreme episodes may be rare, violence itself is not, and the close association of contact sports with violence and an accepting, even celebratory, attitude to pain makes them unsuitable for school level sports. If they are to avoid such condemnation, the onus is on such sports to change their rules so that they do not promote violence among competitors. However, other confrontational competitive sports (basketball, soccer and the like) are only contingently related in their forms of play to hostile aggression. While they can be played in this way, it is also possible to frame in a different way the competition on which they are based. Wolf-Light describes the pleasures he finds in testing his abilities in sport, in the 'intensity of purpose' and heightened awareness of his physical senses, emotions and intellect. Competitive sport can become a joint celebration of the pleasure of bodily exertion. In offering the opportunity to stretch themselves, opponents can value each other's contributions to the game without the vindictiveness of the gloating victor or the shame of the ridiculed loser.[24]

Sexually segregated sports are still seen to be necessary across a wide range of social situations. Sometimes this is pure prejudice, when girls are prevented from playing in men's teams despite their ability to win a place (and vice versa). At other times it is justified by different levels of physical size, strength or skill. This latter is a difficult matter. There are certainly sports where physical differences are such that integration could result in unequal contests, but there is no reason why this needs to be prevented by legislation by sporting bodies, rather than the process of selection on performance. Of course, the provision of segregated sports can protect all sorts of group differences, as seen in sports segregated into levels by age, sex and ability, but this need not prevent open competition as well. The problem here is that girls and women will not be able to develop ability comparable to men if they are not given the opportunity. The history of sporting achievements, such as the rate at which women's records have been catching up with men's in Olympic events,[25] suggests that we simply cannot say what the outcome of such opportunities might be in the long term. For the moment, we can say that exclusivity in sport is harmful to gender equity.

Sport can be an arena for the promotion of values of independence, pride, resilience, self-control, fitness and strength. In an abstract sense, and combined when appropriate with values of empathy, modesty or compassion, these ideals are desirable qualities which all boys and girls should be encouraged to practise and experience. However, values are not experienced in the abstract. They are lived in relation to other people and in particular social situations, where they are combined with other goals and adapted to other demands. In the case of sport, independence can become an exclusive concern for one's own success; pride can become the will to dominate or even injure; self-control can become a disdain for compassion and sensitivity to others; and strength can be interpreted as aggressiveness and the ability to exert power over others. If sport is to be a positive experience for all, both participants and non-participants, then it needs to rid itself of these anti-social tendencies.

To rid competitive sport of its violence, physical aggressiveness, misogyny and the will to dominate and harm other people, we will need to change and possibly abolish many of the present forms of sport. Some will see this as a loss of a glorious tradition and a challenge to masculinity. But this ignores history, for dangerous aspects of sport have always been the subject of debate and reform, from the outlawing of hacking in nineteenth-century rugby[26] to the continuing attempt to control violence in contemporary football codes. It is impossible to predict how far this will have to go before these aspects of the games disappear, but go they must if sport is to be open to all in ways that are not threatening and harmful.

Schools need to be part of this effort, for they have a responsibility to ensure that activities sponsored by them are available to all without risk of harm or offence. This means promoting sports and physical education programs that are positive in their effects on boys and girls and the relations among them.[27] To identify what this means, we need to know what it is that boys and girls value about sport, what kinds of programs they want, and how these might be offered in ways that are non-sexist, maximising the possibilities for boys and girls.

In 1991, the Australian Sports Commission sponsored a study to ascertain ways of increasing participation in sport among young people. The study provides fascinating evidence of the need to change the emphasis on competitive 'win at all cost' approaches to sport. Sport to the young people surveyed was a means to fitness, fun and friends, but underlying these were more complex feelings that sport developed self-reliance, offered social networks and a sense of belonging, and recognition and approval from others.

The young people rejected power and the sense of control that characterise the sports of hegemonic masculinity, because of their emphasis on 'fierce competition, domination/failure and egoism'.[28] They also rejected suggestions that sport should be valued because it developed guts, but when this was recast to the idea of determination, both boys and girls felt it was important and a valuable quality in sport. Similarly, while they currently experienced the 'win at all costs' ethos, they did not desire or approve of it, and felt that it was imposed on them from above by coaches and others. However, as they were not able to challenge this ethos, the most common response was to drop out of sport. The report concludes that 'It cannot be stressed too strongly that the "win at all costs" values are alienating potential sports players and are losing current players'.[29] That the ethos of dominant masculinity is excluding

71

large numbers of boys and girls from the potential pleasures of sport is, together with its other negative aspects, surely sufficient reason to reform its operation in schools.

PLAYING WITH MASCULINITY THROUGH ELECTRONIC GAME CULTURE

Just as sport provides a critical nexus for masculinity, linking the male–female dichotomy, the male body and violence, electronic game culture performs a similar function. The multimillion-dollar video game culture cannot simply be passed off as apolitical entertainment, any more than can mass market romantic novel culture. Like other forms of entertainment, it implicitly speaks a politics of gender: a politics, in this case, that aligns masculinity with power and aggression, with victory and winning, with superiority and strength, and with violence and misogyny. A politics, too, that embraces the physical and involves the body in its practice. Video game culture simultaneously speaks pleasure and power. It positions and privileges boys within a multimedia field of embodied fun and entertainment, while at the same time offering access to potentially powerful literate and technological practice, and to socially dominant ways of 'being' as a person. And it does this under the guise of 'entertainment', asking to be read as practice that is beyond criticism and beyond social scrutiny.

Electronic game culture produces a variety of responses from parents, teachers and politicians, partly indicative, as we have argued earlier, of the different access that many adults have to the technologies associated with game playing and boys' electronic toys. Many adults are obviously unworried by this new set of cultural practices, perhaps because of a general nostalgia for romanticised childhood pursuits or simply because they have little actual knowledge of gaming culture. The pleasure speaks loudest: boys are entertained and having fun. Other adults feel nervous, expressing concern about the time children spend playing video games, about the violence and aggression in the games, and about the possible links between screen violence and social violence.[30]

It is this latter aspect that has become of major concern, supporting public debate and research on the effects of violence in electronic media and televisual texts. The inquiry of the Australian National Committee on Violence observed that 'it is generally conceded that viewing television violence may produce attitude change, provide justification for violence and suggest that problems can be solved through aggressive behaviour'.[31]

However, as Patricia Edgar noted of an inquiry into TV violence in Australia, 'the body of research on the subject provides no clear direction for a regulator to take'.[32] Community members have different understandings of, and different levels of tolerance to violence, and research studies are (understandably) unable to make strong links between violent and aggressive behaviour and TV viewing habits or electronic game playing.

Boys only

Surprisingly, however, as Alloway and Gilbert argue in a paper on video game culture, 'very few research studies of computer gaming and its effects on young people have started with what seems to be one clear feature of this culture, its maleness, and how maleness and violence may be linked'.[33] Although some girls do play and enjoy electronic games,[34] electronic gaming is constructed predominantly as a male activity and a male field of pleasure. Just as the 'Barbie' culture constructs a highly gendered representational field targeted at girls, the 'Game Boy' world of video games offers much the same to boys and young men. Through participation in the multimedia practices associated with electronic gaming, boys and young men enter into a discursive field in which constructions of hegemonic masculinity dominate, and within which they can practise and play at masculinity, and at what it comes to represent.

As David Buckingham and Julian Sefton-Greene noted of their studies with British teenagers:

> Despite the fact that many girls played computer games and possessed their own systems . . . there was little doubt that this was perceived as a primarily male domain.[35]

Other research supports this. Video games have been noted to have far more masculine themes, male figures and male voices on screen than television does,[36] and the public video game arcades are frequented far more often by boys than girls.[37] Game arcade parlours have become not unlike the pool hall or the public hotel bar as arenas for the display of competitive, aggressive and sometimes violent masculinity, while the newer and more expensive cyberspace cafes offer the opportunity to display and play a different 'yuppified' version of masculinity which is off the street and performed less publicly.

In recent Australian research by Alloway and Gilbert,[38] game-playing teenage boys in a provincial city were quite convinced that game playing and game arcades were predominantly male spaces and male pursuits.

> . . . it's sort of like a boys' thing. Like girls have like knitting and riding horses . . . I think computer games are more of a guy thing.

> . . . it's definitely male dominated, you know.

Several other boys also described how girls would 'tag along' and watch. 'They're not really here to play' said Danny, although two of the boys thought that girls who did play probably did so because they were 'tomboys'. Generally, the girls' observer-status presence provided a backdrop to the boys' action, just as in other male sporting venues. Most of the boys knew little about the girls who were in the arcades, had obviously not noticed too much about what the girls did, and assumed that if girls were there they must have come in with their boyfriends. When Danny was asked about what sort of girls came to the arcades, he was obviously stuck for an answer: 'I don't know. Just girls. I don't know. Girls are girls.' The space was clearly designated as male, for male pursuits, a social site for boys. 'It's definitely social. There's all kids your age and that. There's not that many places around to go.' Almost all of the boys went with male friends or met up with male friends at the arcades.

As Alloway and Gilbert document, the maleness of this culture is made very clear in the texts that advertise, promote or review video games, and almost invariably targets a young male market. Game playing, Alloway and Gilbert claim, becomes linked with a particular type of masculinity. They demonstrate, for instance, how phallic symbolism and locker room humour in the texts ask us to identify the game, the game machine, and the game player as masculine: as phallic, as powerful, as physical, as 'body'. For example, they refer to an advertisement for a Fighter Stick (an input device for game machines) in which a young man straddles a crocodile which raises its erect head between the boy's legs. 'Never loan out your stick' is the text. And, in another example, they describe a double-page spread advertisement for a new control pad which features a huge roll of soft pink toilet paper on a plain dark background: 'It's what the Streetfighters will need if you get your hands on a Score Master'.

Gender relationships

While boys and men are clearly identified as the major potential consumers of the video gaming culture, and maleness is associated with aggression, power and physicality, electronic game culture articulates a politics of gender: 'a politics that constitutes gender as asymmetrical relations of power'.[39] These sexual politics are usually patriarchal, sometimes misogynist, and intrinsically homophobic, and frequently marginalise and demean activities or attitudes associated with the feminine or with non-violent masculinities, positioning them as 'other' to hegemonic male characters. Strategies range from narratives that attribute male characters with dominant status, to mild expressions of contempt for that which represents the 'other', to outright misogyny and homophobia.

While many print-based texts have been analysed over the past two decades for sexist representations, gaming texts seem to have escaped scrutiny. Women in game narratives are often 'damsels in distress' needing to be rescued by male combat figures, or sexualised and eroticised women warriors who can give the kiss of death, slice off heads with a fan, or use their long hair to imprison and destroy. Electronic game narratives aimed at the slightly older young male adult audience are more explicitly violent, legitimising rape and sexual and physical domination of women through the narratives and game strategies.

However, as Alloway and Gilbert note, hegemonic masculinity is not only marked out in relations of power with women. It is also identified in relation to subordinated masculinities. Games advertisements and reviews, and the games themselves, combine to mark the parameters of hegemonic male status, often by asking readers to identify with a masculinity like this:

> *No Cops*
> *No Laws*
> *No Wimps*
> *Are you a Girlie-Man or a Megaracer?*[40]

The 'megaracer' in this advertisement is visually represented by a scarred, aggressive and threatening male punk figure, constructed as oppositional to control, to the law and to less violent masculinities, as well as to femininity.

Violence

One of the most disturbing features of images like these is the way that they so powerfully and seductively coalesce images of masculinity and violence. The violence evoked is often what Giroux would call 'ritualistic violence':

> . . . utterly banal, predictable, and often stereotypically masculine . . . Audiences connect with such depictions viscerally, yet they are not edifying . . . offering few insights into the complex range of human behaviour and struggles.[41]

Giroux argues that one of the pedagogical consequences of the use of such violence in the cinema is that 'it contributes to the commonsensical assumption that Hollywood film is strictly about entertainment and need not be judged for its political and pedagogical implications'.[42] The same could be said of the violence in video game texts. The violence and strident hegemonic masculinity are masked under the guise of leisure and pleasure.

Helen Cunningham suggests that there are six identifiable narrative genres in computer games: platformers (where characters have to leap from platform to platform, as in *Super Mario Brothers*); shoot 'em ups (hi-tech military games like

Doom); beat 'em ups (hand-to-hand combat like *Streetfighter*); sports (like *NBA Jam*); strategy (role-playing and strategy games, like *Zelda*); and puzzlers (like *Lemmings*).[43] Like most genres, these are certainly not discrete forms, and the conventions of both platformers and strategy games frequently occur in the more violent genres as well as in sports games. A review of the video game version of *True Lies*, for example, describes it as a 'rough, tough, grit-your-teeth-and-party shoot 'em up/platformer with enough action to quench the most blood-thirsty of appetites!' And sports games similarly interweave generic conventions, particularly in the way in which violence can become integral to the genre. A review of *Speedball 2* claims that it 'mixes soccer and senseless violence', with a 'liberal sprinkling of extreme violence and tactical gameplay'.[44]

Violence, as Alloway and Gilbert argue, becomes one of the key pleasure features of electronic game culture, inviting players to 'engage viscerally with the action' and to 'take pleasure in the vicarious experience of gratuitous violence'.[45] Violence also offers an important oppositional position to take up in relation to femininity: a way for boys to 'know' that they are taking up an acceptable and recognisable form of maleness; a way to associate themselves with the world of men rather than the world of women—to be 'megaracers' rather than 'girlie-men'. In the Australian study referred to earlier,[46] many of the boys commented on how much girls and women hated violence. They claimed that it was the violence of electronic games that prevented many girls from playing and that encouraged their mothers to criticise the games.

> She hates them. She really hates computer games . . . Too violent.

> Like my mum has seen me play *Doom* and she despises that game. She just really does not like it at all. It's like 'What do you do in this game? Just kill things? Yeah. Yeah. That's all right son, see the therapist.'

Ironically, adult opposition to violence serves to cement its position as integral to a 'real' and successful version of masculinity: 'no cops, no laws, no wimps'. The more girls, women and adult censors protest, the more boys may be convinced that this is a critical aspect of masculinity to embrace and 'do'. This seemed to account, in this study, for the boys' attitudes to letting younger brothers play violent games—allowing them entry as apprentices into masculinist culture. When asked whether young boys should be allowed to play these games, the majority of the boys were non-censorious. They saw few problems with younger boys playing the more violent games like *Mortal Kombat* and *Virtual Cop*.

Violence is obviously not just a feature of video game culture. Violence is—as one fifteen-year-old male game player commented—'everywhere. You can't avoid it.' Boys and young men can plug into violence on television, popular film, the internet, radio, advertisements, brochures, magazines, newspapers, novels, theatre, MTV . . . The video game site is but one site within a complex set of sites. Video game playing is situated within a complex interplay of discursive and social practices that similarly construct violence, aggression, gender relations, ethnicity and power. The violent narratives common to video game texts are only 'readable' and recognisable because they repeat narratives written elsewhere. Because they dovetail so easily into these other meaning-making regimes, video games and video gaming then become easily 'naturalised' in cultural practice.

Playing the body

A distinguishing feature of video gaming is its interactivity and overt involvement of the body. As Alloway and Gilbert argue, gaming texts eagerly promote the idea of 'full sensory, embodied experience', and they quote software advertisements, for instance, which boast that players would 'have to ride bareback on a screaming bullet' to be connected any faster to the heart of the game.[47]

Increasingly, electronic games offer a virtual reality which boys find exciting.

> It's good, it's fun, it's realistic. You can slide and crash and stuff like that . . . You're actually in the driver's seat.

> You can use your hands and you get to use your eyes and targeting and they're running past . . .

It's really realistic. You've got different viewpoints to view the car from and the wall fights you when you go around a corner . . . You can't get that sort of realism anywhere else really . . . In the arcades you actually sit in the seat with the pedals and the steering wheel.

. . . you're actually in the driver's seat . . .

When I'm playing the game, I'm there . . . and you get like demented. Like . . . I can't switch off. Like I mean like when I go for a block in the game I actually physically jump up in the air. It's really quite annoying . . . It's just, I don't know, maybe your brain short circuits or something. You feel like you're there.[48]

And, again, as Alloway and Gilbert demonstrate, game manufacturers feed directly into this desire for an embodied game-playing pleasure, by producing a range of products that link boys' bodies to game narratives. Players can 'shoot' at the screen, strap on vests or use joysticks that vibrate to the action of the game played.

In many ways, however, game playing is still only a practice for a 'real' masculinity, as it might be performed and played out in the sporting field. Game playing is often a solitary, passive and even (in some games) intellectual problem-solving exercise: all features not normally regarded as masculine. However, the multibillion-dollar gaming industry buys into the potential tension of passivity and activity by selling gaming merchandise through masculinist discourses of power, control, risk taking and violence.

The gaming industry offers boys of all ages the opportunities to 'play' masculinity at home. And, as we argued at the beginning of this chapter, the 'play' metaphor is useful. Electronic games and sport both provide playgrounds for boys: they offer pleasure and enjoyment and fun. They both also provide boys with space with which to play at masculinity, and to practise the embodied, competitive and aggressive features of dominant forms of masculinity. And in both sites, masculinity 'plays' as soon as the games begin. Both sets of 'games' are strongly rules-based and tightly structured: there is little space for 'free play' or playing differently. Both are about learning to do masculinity from within dominant and hegemonic discourses.

CONCLUSION

It is important to recognise that popular cultural practices like those associated with sport and electronic gaming—whether by intent or by default—produce and market a politics of gender under the guise of apolitical pleasure and entertainment. It is equally important to recognise that many boys and young men may have little understanding of how they are positioned through such play; how gendered subjectivity, pleasure and desire are deeply implicated in the game playing; and how they may come to know and to desire themselves in the terms of the practices they engage in.

In such a situation, the motivation to change is hard to find. We must keep in mind that boys' leisure pursuits often deal not only in knowledge about what it means to be and to relate to others as a gendered subject—but in pleasure and desire and subjective experience. The difficulty with sport and gaming texts, as with other aspects of boys' culture, is that they frequently compound understandings of masculinity and gender with violence and pleasure. And this is the challenge for those who would like to offer boys other ways of being men and doing masculinity.

Another challenge is to fully explore the implications of these forms of leisure. For instance, both sport and electronic game playing share common features. Both are highly structured and rely upon externally provided rules and regulations; both offer limited opportunity for expression in other than bodily movement and dexterity; both provide key topics of conversation and shared cultural experience for boys; both require a considerable investment of time; and both are legitimised and endorsed through a broad range of intertextual links with other respected 'male' cultural practices.

To what extent these features are related to, and reinforce, rigid and narrow readings of 'masculinity', and press boys to conform to restricted codes of dress, speech and behaviour, is uncertain. However, boys' participation in cultural practices which are so carefully controlled and structured does suggest we consider this question carefully. Working with boys in this context, therefore, does not simply involve identifying the politics of the texts. The issue is about critical and reflective analysis of cultural practice; about enabling students to read the processes wherein they take up personal, relational and cultural meanings; about mobilising boys' desire to do their gender otherwise. It seems particularly important that boys and young men have the opportunity to understand and to contest a masculinity that is not only rigidly constructed, but also expressed in terms of domination and control of others; gratuitous violence and institutionalised warfare; and competitiveness at any cost.

4

Sons and lovers

Within the realm of human relationships—boys' lives in their families, with girls and with women, and with their peers at work and at play—the impact of unproblematised masculinity is keenly evidenced. As we argued in chapter 3, the cultural construction of 'masculinity' is powerful in Australian culture. It pervades all areas of boys' lives in subtle and not-so-subtle ways. It affects the way they dress, the way they talk, the way they choose leisure pursuits, the way they interact with friends, family, school friends and workmates. It affects the way they take themselves up in the world as 'men'. And of course these constructions of masculinity are not lost upon women and girls as mothers, lovers and friends to boys—nor upon adult men as they struggle to identify their roles as fathers, as teachers, as friends, as employers of the boys of the 1990s.

The globalisation of culture, and the intrusion of television, film and commercial marketing into so many spheres of life, mean that cultural constructions of masculinity paraded by Nintendo, by Hollywood, or by cable TV are accessible to all. And as we argued in chapter 3, there is little celebration of difference in these readings of masculinity—little heroism associated with standing outside conventional paradigms. While many girls learn how to recognise resistance to traditional modes of femininity as courageous and independent, there is limited support for boys to make similar readings against masculinity.

In many areas of life, masculinity has changed little— accommodating only the peripheral demands of a new feminist world and altering itself in merely superficial ways. And this is particularly noticeable in terms of family life and sexuality. Angela Phillips argues that, unlike girls, most boys have men around them now who are not radically different from the men whom their fathers would have seen.

> They still expect to hold authority in the family, they still expect to be the main earners and to determine how the family economy will be managed, they still do little housework and spend far less time with their children than their wives do.[1]

While girls have been reshaping their lives as daughters, as mothers, as lovers and as friends, there has been little similar encouragement or support for boys to refashion their lives in similar ways. Ironically, adult men—and to some extent, girls and women—often seem complicit in supporting and maintaining forms of masculinity that position their sons and brothers for adult lives as men that are headed for emotional loneliness and violent injury or death. Any analysis of the statistics for youth suicide, criminal charges, sexual offences, jail sentences, domestic violence or family breakdown, for instance, shows us that boys and young men are in trouble. The links between violence and masculinity will be examined more carefully in chapter 7, but in this chapter we will consider how discourses on parenting and on male sexuality contribute to these links by positioning boys to reject their mothers, to romanticise their fathers, and to fear emotional intimacy.

PARENTING THE BOYS AND MEN OF THE FUTURE

In chapter 3 we considered the intrusion into the home of electronic media, and the blurring of boundaries between home and public society through the commercial marketing of boys' culture. The masculinity on offer through popular film, television shows, game machines, children's books, gaming magazines, toys, clothing and music now has physical manifestations in the home as T-shirts, mugs, stickers, pencils, schoolbags, curtains, placemats and caps offer constant repetition and reinforcement of masculine narratives. Australian homes cannot be seen in isolation from the social and cultural constructions of masculinity (and femininity) at large in the community.

The home thus becomes another site within which boys have the opportunity to 'practise' gender: to practise appropriate performances of masculinity. It also becomes an important site within which boys learn about gender difference and learn to construct themselves in opposition to girls and femininity. As this chapter will argue, many of the naturalised practices of the family and of parenting are based on oppositional readings of femininity and masculinity. Boys' and girls' behaviour is first interpreted in terms of gender difference—in terms of what would be the expected behaviour, speech, play, dress, action of a boy, as opposed, say, to a girl. As Deborah Cameron[2] argues, 'gender difference' is so naturalised in our culture that it has become a 'cultural script' through which we give meaning to patterns of behaviour.

Cameron argues that such a cultural script can lead towards an assumption that 'feminine' and 'masculine' are what we *are* or traits we *have*, rather than 'effects we produce by way of particular things we *do*'.[3] She draws upon Judith Butler's assertion that 'gender is the repeated stylization of the body, a set of repeated acts within a rigid regulatory frame which congeal over time to produce the appearance of substance, of a "natural" kind of being'.[4] Cameron's claim—in support of Butler—is that:

> becoming a woman (or a man) is not something you accomplish once and for all at an early stage of life. Gender has constantly to be reaffirmed and publicly displayed by repeatedly performing particular acts in accordance with the cultural norms (themselves historically and socially constructed, and consequently variable) which define 'masculinity' and 'femininity'.[5]

The family arena is a key space within which gender is constantly reaffirmed. It not only provides a space within which children can practise and perform gender and have their performances rejected or reaffirmed. It also provides a space within which they can observe adult gender practices and performances. The numerable studies of the language practices of families and of children provide clear indication of this. As Cameron claims, 'people are who they are because of (among other things) the way they talk',[6] and certainly analysis of speech practices between adults and children, and between groups of children, is an interesting indicator of how adults fashion appropriate gender behaviour in children, and how children then perform gendered talk in their families and peer groups.

Jennifer Coates suggests that an analysis of the considerable research material on children's language acquisition indicates that there are six ways in which children learn 'gender-appropriate' language:

1   through explicit comment on certain aspects of linguistic behaviour (e.g. swearing, taboo language, verbosity, politeness);
2   through adults providing different linguistic models for children to identify with;
3   through adults talking to children differently depending on the sex of the child (e.g. adults are more likely to interrupt girls, and lisp more when talking to little girls);
4   through adults having different preconceptions of male and female children (e.g. adults expect female infants to be more verbally able than male infants);
5   through adults responding differently to girls and boys using the same linguistic strategy (e.g. boys arguing or talking assertively are more likely to get a positive response than girls);
6   perhaps most importantly, through children's participation in gender-specific subcultures which create and maintain distinct male and female styles of interaction.[7]

The home is obviously a key site within which children practise, perform and learn about femininity and masculinity, and a key site within which adults practise and perform the gendered roles of 'mother' and 'father'. Commonly available parenting discourses are obviously important to consider in this discussion of boys in their families, for women and men are likely to practise and perform as 'parents' from within the range of options available to them through cultural readings of appropriate and effective parenting. Such discourses can be read through a range of cultural texts: television programs like *The Simpsons* or *Neighbours,* and popular magazines like *The Women's Weekly* or *Family Circle.* But they can also be read through the prolific production of print-based parenting guides.

Guides for raising sons—as distinct from general guides on parenting—have become popular in the 1990s, and come in a variety of forms, and from a number of different positions on masculinity. Some pick up explicitly on the challenge that feminism offers to parents of sons.[8] Some aim to untie the knot of masculinity and loosen its parameters.[9] Some examine the complex, poignant relationship between mother and son.[10] Some document the usually unheard voices of fathers as they talk about caring for and loving children.[11] And some tell a tale of lost boys drowning in a sea of femininity, desperately searching for manhood and the 'moist, dark, mysterious call of the masculine soul'.[12]

Themes that emerge from these texts are on the whole clustered around two central positions. One looks to reassess and revalue the role of mothers: the bond mothers have with sons; the responsibility they are seen to carry to produce 'real' men who can take their place in a masculinist, heterosexual world; and the pain they feel at the almost inevitable separation of the son from this relationship. Many of these books examine the cult of 'mother-blaming' and the inevitable effects this has had upon women's relationships with their sons. Books of this type also look at the difficulties mothers have in breaking out of old patterns and in building new ones that might loosen the ties between masculinity and violence, and offer support for boys to explore and interrogate masculinity.[13]

On the other hand, a second focus in parenting guides is a focus on the role of masculinity and manhood in the raising of sons. Many of these texts argue that boys cannot become healthy and successful men unless they separate from their mothers, become closely aligned with fathers or father figures—and are guided towards finding and tapping into an essentialist male psyche.[14] Such texts often argue for the restoration of male narratives of heroism and courage,[15] and for the power of biology in predetermining male behaviour.[16]

Other texts are more interested in exploring social changes to masculinity: in documenting different ways of fathering—and different ways of being a man with children.[17]

Blaming mother: patriarchal parenting practices

Women constantly find themselves inserted into traditional storylines about mothering and motherhood popularised and naturalised through folk tale, women's magazines, contemporary film. Motherhood as an institution, and as a set of powerful social discourses, largely figures unproblematised in the talk and actions of everyday life. And 'mothering sons' introduces a special set of social practices. Mothers of sons are expected to humour the rascals, 'mere males' and wild ones of masculine storylines: to love them, sacrifice for them and—most importantly—know when to let them go. Nothing is worse than the mother who clings. The mother who overprotects. The mother who feminises her son. Or the mother who neglects her son to enjoy a career. Whether through object-relations theory, Freudian psychology, or Dr Spock truisms, the awesome responsibility for producing a healthy, 'masculine' son is seen to lie initially with the mother, and the mother's relationship with her son.

The result of this construction of mothering is that it then makes it possible to see women as responsible if a son fails to become a successful 'male' person. If men choose homosexuality, or if they are heterosexually impotent, perhaps it was because their mothers 'emasculated' them? If men are paedophiles, if they are rapists, did they have a failed relationship with their mothers? Perhaps their mothers worked outside of the home and didn't care for their needs as infants? And women are also often blamed for male violence and crime. As Betty Frieden sarcastically comments on the post-war scenario in America:

> It was suddenly discovered that the mother could be blamed for almost everything. In every case history of a troubled child; alcoholic, suicidal, schizophrenic, psychopathic, neurotic adult; impotent, homosexual male; frigid, promiscuous female; ulcerous, asthmatic and otherwise disturbed American, could be found a mother. A frustrated, repressed, disturbed,

martyred, never satisfied, unhappy woman. A demanding, nagging, shrewish wife. A rejecting, overprotecting, dominating mother.[18]

Mother-blaming, according to Silverstein and Rashbaum, began in earnest during and after World War II, with popular social commentaries like Philip Wylie's *Generation of Vipers*—a book that hit such a popular nerve in the USA that it was reprinted twenty times. Silverstein and Rashbaum argue that books like Wylie's constructed 'mom' as a site of neurotic tension, as the emasculator of sons and husbands, and as a threat to the fabric of the nation. Certainly popular culture has traditionally defined mothers as being 'the problem' in boys' lives, and as Babette Smith argues in her contemporary study of *Mothers and Sons*: '. . . Western culture abounds with the theme of sons "coping" with their mothers, "escaping" from them, or rejecting them in order to be a "real" man'.[19]

Silverstein and Rashbaum trace the development within masculinist culture of a strong anti-mother, anti-woman stance, through discussions of such wide-ranging cultural stories as *Hansel and Gretel, Jack and the Beanstalk, Boyz N the Hood, Home Alone* and *Hook*. They look at how, in stories like these, mothers and older women are frequently constructed negatively and oppressively in relation to young men, and at how common it is for women to be seen as unable to provide appropriate parenting for their sons in a female household. Mothers are inadequate: boys need a father—or so the stories go. Mothers will stand in the way of a boy's independence: boys need their own space and freedom.

This theme is very similar, for instance, to the populist position advocated by Don and Jeanne Elium in their discussion of *Raising a Son*.[20] According to the Eliums, boys *must* escape from their mothers: it is their biological destiny. To not escape is to fail to achieve the potential of manhood. Boys must journey over the bridge 'from mother to father', leaving mother and the 'feminine' behind, and travelling onwards to a real masculine identity with the father. This journey is not, according to the Eliums, a conscious choice made by sons. It is 'the inner urge of the male plan of development'. The boy cannot help himself: he is nudged out of the nest by biology, and when he is so nudged, 'mom' becomes a figure to abuse.

As the Eliums suggest, 'mom' is soon seen as stupid: an adult woman with whom a nine-year-old boy can justifiably be angry.

> By nine years of age the son questions Mom's authority in earnest. He is slow to dress and dawdles over any small task. Easily angered, he often considers his mother stupid . . .[21]

By comparison, fathers, claim the Eliums, are 'like gods to their sons'.[22] They can do little wrong, and words from them are precious and treasured. Given the weight of these popular stories—and the seriousness with which many of them have been received in psychology and child development—it is hardly surprising that many mothers of sons feel confused and trapped by discourses of mothering and care. Not only does mothering position women as key targets for criticism and blame if boys stray from the paths of righteousness, but it also places them in an invidious social and economic position. If they love too much they can destroy their sons' burgeoning sense of masculinity; if they don't love enough, they can cripple a boy's future emotional life. And caring for their sons' material, social and physical needs requires a significant input of labour and sacrifice that is predominantly to be borne by mothers.

This becomes especially critical in relation to school involvement, where mothers overwhelmingly carry the burden of supervising schoolwork and dealing with school personnel. As Annette Lareau notes in her analysis of gender differences in parent involvement in schooling, both working-class and upper middle-class fathers were predominantly absent from schoolwork.[23] Lareau notes that, mirroring studies of housework, 'working-class women and men appear to engage in a clear division of responsibility by gender', and that there is little difference with upper middle-class families.

> Although fathers do have important authoritative roles, particularly in upper-middle-class families, the labor of managing children's school careers . . . follows other aspects of childcare. . . . . mothers rather than fathers are overwhelmingly responsible for caretaking, including shaping their children's school careers.[24]

The significance of this for boys' engagement with early literacy is obvious,[25] and in chapter 8 we consider the educational fall-out associated with the gender segregation of parental involvement in schooling.

While the absentee father is still a clear feature of most family life,[26] fathers are generally absent in only one sense. The patriarchal presence of 'the father' is felt in the family even when the embodied 'father' isn't home. Fathers still feel ownership of their children (and their wives) even when they are separated, and the tragic and destructive stories of estranged fathers who track down and murder children or wives who leave them occurs with frightening regularity. As John Stoltenberg observes, 'male ownership of children has always been separate and distinct from the labour of human custodianship'.[27] Women are the custodians: men are the owners. And such an unequal distribution of power and labour in childcare and child-raising has had inevitable effects upon children's growing sense of understanding of women and men, and of femininity and masculinity.

The danger associated with this exclusive linking of the labour of childcare to women has been the object of much feminist work over several decades. Over twenty years ago, for instance, Dorothy Dinnerstein[28] maintained that female-dominated childcare guaranteed antagonism towards women by children of both sexes, because attitudes towards women are rooted in the attitudes developed towards early parental figures. Similarly Nancy Chodorow[29] argued that exclusive female mothering was a major factor in both the creation and perpetration of male domination. She suggested that men developed a neurotic form of masculinity: one that was defined negatively as that which is not feminine. By inverting their earlier identification with the mother into a fear and abhorrence of femininity, boys repressed those qualities they took to be feminine inside themselves, and rejected and devalued women and whatever they considered to be feminine in the social world.

As Lyn Segal notes in her discussion of mothering, this position has often been used to explain 'the prevalence of male violence and of men's profound inability to sustain equal and caring relationships with women'.[30] The devaluation of the institution of mothering—and the slippage, then, to the devaluation of women as mothers—operates within a naturalised set of violent patriarchal practices.

Feminist challenges to patriarchy in the home

For many feminist women, the question of how to raise sons, and how to approach child-raising so that boys and men do not take up patriarchal and distanced relationships from women, has been exceedingly challenging. A recent edition of the journal *Feminism and Psychology*, for example, was completely devoted to the question of 'mothering sons', and a series of feminist women wrote of the dilemmas of bearing and caring for male children.[31] In their introduction to the edition, Rowland and Thomas examine the tension for feminist mothers of putting feminist principles into practice. ' . . . it is one thing to analyse "the patriarchy" in the lecture hall or on paper; quite another to confront the possibility that the toddler in the living room is already busy rehearsing its rules and practising for membership right there in your own home'.[32]

The journal asks the question: 'how is it that loving and innocent boy children metamorphose into patriarchal men?' And it is this question which has preoccupied much of the literature exploring the mother–son relationship. What is the role for women in this challenge? How can mothers reflect upon and construct mothering practices that will position men differently and yet allow them spaces and opportunities to live their lives within the constraints of masculinity cultures? How can feminism influence the mother–son relationship?

In a powerful and provocative analysis of research on the mother–son relationship, Babette Smith[33] argues strongly that there is much more work to do here. She claims that 'feminism has failed the mothers of sons': that the mother–son relationship has remained '[q]uarantined from feminist influence'. While feminism has brought about significant changes in the mothering of daughters, it has brought about negligible change in the mothering of sons, argues Smith. She describes with alarm her experiences of seeing mothers time and again 'being told what to do, where to go and indeed, where to get off by their young sons'.[34] In her Australian study, women frequently settled for the role of 'audience to a hero', accepting inequality between the sexes, and endorsing constructions of masculinity and femininity that relied upon a dominant male and a submissive female. Smith suggests that there is both a disjunction between the way contemporary boys and girls are raised, and a danger that the possibilities wrought by feminism 'might perpetuate the gap between the sexes rather than bridge them'.[35]

This argument is supported by research on family and unpaid work, and on the changing roles for men and women in the home. An Australian study of how families use their time[36] makes it clear that there is serious inequality in the family world of work. Many boys experience regularly the lived reality of male authority and domination as it might be demonstrated through domestic violence or patriarchal power in the family home, and they also experience the lived reality of unequal and unfair workloads in domestic labour. Australian women still do about 70 per cent of unpaid work in the family—more than twice the percentage for men. And no matter how many hours women work in the paid workforce, they still do more unpaid work than men do. This unpaid work in the Australian home is also gender segregated, with men spending one-third of their unpaid work hours in outdoor tasks like maintaining the car, the pool and the yard, while women are indoors with cooking, cleaning and childcare.

The absentee father is a reality for many boys. At no time in their lives do children have as much access to their fathers as they do to their mothers, and fathers are far less involved than are mothers in the routine 'work' of day-to-day living— cooking, cleaning, laundry, childcare. Sons eventually take up roles not unlike those of their fathers. In the Australian study referred to above, teenage sons living at home do less unpaid work around the family than their sisters—and most of it is done outdoors. Childcare, and the unpaid work of the family, are still very much a responsibility for women, despite the shifts in gender relations over the past twenty years.

Most of the parenting guides give scant attention to the links between gender, class and culture in the raising of boys,[37] and seem often to be written in a social vacuum with a generic male child positioned at the centre. Little is written in Australia, for instance, about the parenting of Aboriginal boys, or of parenting strategies for parents struggling with unemployment and poverty. Similarly the Eliums' American guide to parenting practices implicitly assumes a monocultural, unclassed population—as does the Hawley account of how boys can become men.[38]

Even the social construction of gender is treated lightly, if at all, and, in terms of understanding how better to relate to sons and their appropriation of masculinity, this is a critical omission. As Smith argues in her Australian study:

> Until I wrote this book, I had no idea how little I knew about masculinity. My ignorance was not unique. It was typical. I was the 'typical' mother of a son. More than anything else, writing this book has taught me how fundamental it is that women who mother boys develop a realistic understanding of the socialisation process which creates what is called 'masculinity'. It has made me realise that it is a woman's ignorance of 'masculinity' that is her downfall in her relationship with her boys. We blunder through lack of knowledge.[39]

'Male culture', says Smith, has defined women as 'the problem' in boys' lives, whereas in reality, the real problem for boys is masculinist culture. Until mothers make it their business to learn about and understand masculinity, they will sell their sons short. Women need to use their knowledge of gender to work sensitively and emotionally with their sons as they struggle to insert themselves into social and cultural practices; they need to support and encourage their sons to interrogate and explore masculinity and its effects upon their lives; and they need to insist on equality and justice in family work and responsibility.

This endorsement of a role for mothers that is stronger and more socially courageous is also advocated by Silverstein and Rashbaum in *The Courage to Raise Good Men*. Silverstein and Rashbaum take up the issue of whether or not women should pull back from loving their sons for fear of 'emasculating' them, and emphatically argue the importance for women and men of *not* pulling back. Like Smith and Phillips, they see masculinist culture as being dangerous for boys and young men. The role for mothers (for parents?) is—from the perspective of these women—to make visible the problems associated with masculinity; to maintain a close and loving relationship with their sons; and—as many of the writers argue—to refuse to play anything other than a major role with their sons as they journey through adolescence and young manhood.

The rejection of the mother: power to the father

> To grow into a healthy man, a boy must develop a close bond with his mother, so he can learn about his own humanity; and then he must be taken by his father to discover what it means to be a man.[40]

These new and courageous feminist approaches to mothering are not easily balanced beside many of the arguments currently advanced about fathering such as the one quoted above. While many feminist texts attempt to restore the rights of women to love and care for their sons with dignity and courage, and to share with them the intelligences and knowledges of women and of the feminine, masculinist texts about parenting sons are far more likely to see little role for women past the very early years of potty-training and nursing. Successful parenting of boys is predominantly regarded as a male task—at least in the 'fun' aspects of parenting like leisure time, holidays and outings.

On the whole, many of the new 'fathering' texts are extremely reactionary. They appear to have developed out of a dissatisfaction with feminist readings of masculinity and of gender relations, and a longing to return to a pre-feminist historical period: a mythological age where men were warriors and gods who 'cared for and protected their people and their world',[41] and where women were owned and enslaved. A period, it would seem, where patriarchy ran unchecked.

Robert Bly's *Iron John*[42] has been instrumental in framing this approach to manhood, but in Australia, Steve Biddulph's *Manhood: A Book About Setting Men Free*[43] is one of the best-known populist guides illustrating what such an approach looks like for parenting and gender relationships. Mothers have little role to play in the raising of sons, according to Biddulph. In fact, 'boys cannot learn to be a man from Mum, however good a mum she is',[44] and the 'mummy's boy' or 'wimp' is derided in his text. Biddulph's views on fathering are similarly extreme and generalised. '. . . boys in our society are horrendously under-fathered'[45] he claims, and are easily diagnosed into two distinct types.

> One type takes on macho-mania . . . This type will usually group in highly competitive and low-quality friendships with other neglected boys or young men.
> The other type is underconfident—a 'Mummy's boy'—and is often depressed. Younger boys of this type often have problems with bedwetting or soiling . . .
> Both these types suffer the same problem—father-hunger.[46]

In Biddulph's text feminist women are caricatured as women who secretly drive past building sites wondering whether to whistle; wives are caricatured as looking 'glowing, relaxed, warm and feminine' when men do the 'hard' things in the house, like 'argue with the builder, battle the kids and make the decisions'; and daughters are caricatured as needing to be flattered and admired.[47] While Biddulph claims to be opposed to violence, violence is implicitly threaded through *Manhood* in the call for a return to the warrior; in the strong case made for floor wrestling with sons; in the statement that men have an 'actual talent for discipline'; in the suggestion that men need to be 'persistent' with their wives to get sex; and in the extraordinarily insensitive assertion that domestic violence is 'as Australian as going to the beach'.[48]

Biddulph's book will appeal to many men (and many women) because it calls for a return to a mythical warrior kingdom where women enjoyed submission and slavery, and men enjoyed huntin' and shootin'. And there is deep-seated longing in men and women of the late twentieth century for a form of femininity and masculinity that looks rather like the world that Biddulph creates: a mythical world of shape and beauty and order. A world that is not fragmented, chaotic and incoherent; a world without economic or social ills; a world without pain and suffering. And a world where the 'natural' gender order is played out in Garden of Eden simplicity. Women are often as complicit in desiring this 'natural' order as are men: women often know their own 'femininity' as it is constructed oppositionally to 'masculinity'. Loosening gender from such a clear and defined paradigm can be frightening for women—just as it is frightening for men.

However, no amount of longing will make such a world happen, and by drawing a picture of such a world, Biddulph's text can offer little in the understanding of contemporary gender relations, or contemporary constructions of masculinity. At its worst, it can, in fact, be read as a deeply conservative and anti-feminist tract, which leaves boys stuck in practices that have been responsible for their estrangement from girls and women and their recourse to violence and aggression. Much as Biddulph's text offers advice for 'setting men free', and for helping them be proud of their maleness, it does so by denying them emotional links with their mothers and other women in their lives, and by advocating a reverence for physical action that slides towards aggression and dangerous risk-taking.

Books such as Don and Jeanne Elium's *Raising a Son*[49] similarly romanticise and glorify the role of a powerful essentialist masculine force in the raising of a 'healthy' son. Ultimately it is fathers who must take charge of their sons, and it is only fathers who can take a boy to manhood. The Eliums argue for the role of biology, of psychology, of the unconscious soul, and of culture in the movement of boys towards manhood—although the cultural argument they use is based on Robert Bly's reading of ancient initiation cultures. Throughout their guide, biological and psychological determination become the driving force for a boy's development. Together these are regarded as responsible for male aggression, risk-taking, rule-breaking, and competitiveness, and they become used as an excuse for boys' rudeness and arrogance to their mothers, for their separation from and rejection of women, and for their reverence for their fathers.

Such an argument seems to assume a certain biological and psychological determinism to boys' and men's health: boys and men can't help dying or being maimed in the ways they are. This is their biological and psychological destiny. Because they are born male, more boys than girls will die from car and road accidents, die at work, die from street violence, die by their own hands—kill others and spend their lives in prisons. However as we have argued in chapter 1, boys and men are not all equally at risk of violence. Some groups of boys and men have much higher risks than others; social and cultural conditions impact upon any genetic, biological potential. Masculinity is lived and played out differently by boys and men from various class and ethnic backgrounds.

Such biological and psychological determinism as proposed by the Eliums seems to accept dangerous and violent lives for boys and men—and for those that they harm. It seems willing to sacrifice boys and young men at the altar of Manhood, as if death, maiming and the taking up of violence as a lifestyle are part of a contemporary boy's initiation ceremony. Fathers, it would seem, need to be willing and complicit partners in this exercise—but because mothers are less likely to support such pain (stupidity?) for their sons, they cannot participate. To become 'wild men', boys must be taken from their mothers. Within this paradigm, women cannot raise 'good men' alone.

Texts like these by Biddulph and the Eliums—and similar texts like those by Hawley[50]—demonstrate little understanding of the complex cultural contexts in which boys and young men now live. They show little concern for the effects that hegemonic discourses of masculinity have had upon children's and women's lives, as well as upon men's lives. In many ways the texts are contemporary arguments for a return to—and need for—patriarchal power and privilege.

Manhood is constructed in a monolithic and singular way, and yet books like Kewley and Lewis's *Fathers*[51] remind us just how multiple and varied is the experience of fathering and masculinity. This book brings together sixteen different fathers talking about the joys of fatherhood, their love for their children, their memories of childhoods that were often authoritarian and traditional, and their commitment to making futures for their children and their families that will be loving, nurturing and fulfilling.

Books like Kewley and Lewis's offer no easy panacea for parenting. However, what they do is remind us that lived experiences of masculinity are rich and diverse; that fathers cannot so easily be stereotyped as 'wild men' or patriarchs or absentee landlords; and that contemporary men can work beside women as equal partners in the parenting process. Discourses about fatherhood that make it possible to problematise patriarchal practices, that support many forms of masculinity, and that are not oppositional to feminism, are more likely to lead to loving and nurturing family contexts within which boys can take up more diverse and less restrictive positions as young men.

TALKING ABOUT SEX . . .

It is this diversity that is important to hold on to in talk about sexuality. The danger of the Manhood-style discourses is the image of male sexuality that they implicitly endorse and value. The 'wild man' constructed through Bly and Biddulph's texts tends to be a lone and remote figure, communing with nature in splendid isolation. Such a man takes up a patriarchal position in his family with his wife and daughters—and has an unease (even dislike) of women more generally. Biddulph actually encourages men to believe that women aren't interested in the 'sensitive new age guy' (SNAG)—that they all, secretly, want a man who'll take the initiative, boss them about, be persistent, and follow 'the wild and free' part of him and 'go for it' when it comes to intercourse. Again: biology gets the blame.

> In sex and loving, much of the time the man has to make the running. This is a matter of biology. Learn to be persistent and courtly. Be protective.[52]

Boys' attitudes to sex

Pseudo-biological arguments like these have often been advanced as an excuse for male sexual violence to women, and to actively encourage such attitudes in books about fathering sons would seem to be particularly inappropriate. Aggressive and dominating attitudes to forced sex need critical reassessment and renegotiation—not endorsement—and the assumption that all women secretly want to be dominated (raped?) has to be rejected. It should come as little surprise that many boys have inappropriate and dangerous attitudes to heterosexual relations, often fuelled by populist discourses such as those Biddulph taps into.

Is it OK for a boy to hold a girl down and force her to have sexual intercourse if:

	No	Yes	Unsure
He spends a lot of money on her	173	6	8
He is so turned on he can't stop	159	10	18
She has had intercourse with other boys	164	10	13
She is stoned or drunk	160	8	18
She lets him touch her above the waist	141	22	24
She says she's going to have sex with him then changes her mind	141	16	30
They have dated a long time	130	28	28
She's led him on	91	61	35
She gets him sexually excited	103	51	33

N = 187

For instance, a Queensland survey of year 9 boys (fourteen-year-olds)—modelled on a Californian survey—found these alarming results. One in three of the 187 boys believed it was 'okay for a boy to hold a girl down and force her to have sexual intercourse if she's led him on'.[53] Another 18 per cent were unsure as to whether or not this was acceptable, with less than half of the boys believing the situation did not justify forced intercourse or rape. When the boys were given a set of reasons as to why a boy might hold a girl down and force her to have sexual intercourse, and asked in each case whether it was OK to rape, there was not one category that did not get an affirmative answer from some boys, or a response of 'unsure' from others.

This survey revealed frightening acceptance of men's rights to women's bodies—particularly sexually active or open women—and of men's expected ownership of women. The survey did not discover if the boys did not know that forced intercourse was actually 'rape' and a chargeable offence. Nonetheless, the attitudes revealed in this survey seem to be borne out in practice in young teenagers' experiences of sex. In an Australian study of girls at risk of dropping out of school, comments like these were common from the thirteen to fifteen-year-old girls interviewed.[54]

> If you don't do it you're a geek or you're just not with the crowd. So a lot of girls, mainly in year 8, got a lot of pressure on them to have sex with guys in years 10, 11 and 12. And, I think it's just really unfair for the girls because they don't really get a chance . . .

> Well, a lot of girls say yes to sex when they don't really mean it, just to make their boyfriends, you know, be with them or something.

> . . . When girls get pressured into sex it's not only by the boyfriend, it's by like his friends and by their friends.

An Australian survey of teenagers' attitudes to sex conducted by *Dolly* magazine found that more than a quarter of the girls claimed that they were pressured into having sex for the first time by their boyfriend,[55] and Liz Kelly presents similar data from the United Kingdom. She cites a British survey of 1244 16–21-year-olds in which over a quarter of the young women stated that they were pressured or forced in their first sexual experience.[56]

Parents seldom have an opportunity to confront teenage boys about attitudes to forced sex—or to help in a possible reconstruction of teenage sexual relations. While 60 per cent of young women in one Australian study identified parents as the preferred source of information on sex education, only 30 per cent of young men did so.[57] While boys nominated fathers more frequently than mothers as the preferred source, only about a quarter of all the boys who responded felt that they could talk to their fathers about sex and sexuality—and almost none of them felt that they could talk to their mothers.

Szirom's study also found that male friends were far more likely to be a source of information for boys about sex than parents were, and that the result was often the sharing of inaccurate and ill-informed advice in the confines of the locker room.[58] As Liz Kelly discovered in the United Kingdom, this then made it more likely that pornographic material, as well as the boys' sex talk, would become resource material for boys on sexuality. Kelly claims that 'more of young people's sexual knowledge comes from coercive experience and/or pornography than from education either at home or in school'.[59]

Kelly refers to Angela Hamblin's survey of 200 readers of *Spare Rib* which drew attention to the increasing role of pornography in teenage sexuality. Pornographic material was here being used not only to legitimise sexual activity, but also to legitimise specific forms of sexual practice. Kelly claims that over three-quarters of the young men and women interviewed in her research reported having seen a pornographic video or magazine, and that titles checked with the Metropolitan Police Obscene Publications Squad revealed that a sizeable minority of these young people had seen 'hard core' and illegal material.[60] Gender differences were marked here. More young men than young women reported that they used pornographic material, and used it more frequently.

Male sexuality: distancing and fear of intimacy

One of the dangers associated with constructions of male sexuality, particularly heterosexuality, is the emotional distance and isolation from women with which it is so often associated. Susan Griffin claims that boys learn from an early age how important it is to crush signs of emotional need and dependency and instead to perform a masculinity that separates them from the feminine and the female. And much of this may be a result of patterns and practices of parenting. According to Stoltenberg, it may be through his father that a son learns to withdraw from the influence of his mother, and hence to withdraw from sensations of feeling and emotional connectedness. Stoltenberg suggests that the legacy of the father–son relationship is that it is usually:

> . . . a boy's first exposure to [the] complex interlock of sexual politics. The lessons he learns in this relationship last a lifetime, and they become the basis of all he ever believes to be true about who he is supposed to be in relation to women and to other men . . . the father–son relationship is an element of culture that replicates and reproduces many of society's most fundamental sexual-political values.[61]

101

The increasing estrangement from their bodies, and distancing from their mothers and from other girls and women, are often identified as key elements of male sexuality as it is traditionally constructed within heterosexual and masculinist paradigms. An explanation of how this estrangement and distancing might have become so central to discourses of male heterosexuality is advanced by Victor Seidler.[62] Seidler argues that masculine identity has been so closely aligned with constructions of 'reason'—a quality women and the feminine are reputed to lack within western oppositional constructs—that rationality, and all that it becomes associated with, 'has become a critical basis for male superiority within social life'.

It affects how men, especially heterosexual men, listen to others and what they are ready to hear. Since rationality is identified with knowledge, it is denied to women. Emotions and feelings are likewise denied as genuine sources of knowledge within the culture. Rather, they are associated predominantly with weakness and femininity, and so as antithetical to the 'strengths' with which boys learn their sense of masculine identity.

Seidler suggests that a significant difference between constructions of female and male heterosexuality is that for women bodily existence has come to be seen as continuous with emotionality. This is not so, he argues, for men, who are positioned oppositionally to emotion and subjectivity.

As men have learnt to identify with their reason, they have also learnt to be estranged from their bodies, to regard them as having no part in their identities or experience. This can place them outside and beyond their own lived experience, as if destined to observe their lives from outside.[63]

However, Seidler notes that within this dominant sense of masculine identity, sexuality remains 'a troubling contradiction', because it demands the very 'surrender and spontaneity which men have grown up to be suspicious of'.[64] To deal with this, men must turn sex into 'performance'—separating it from emotional contact by objectifying the subject of their desire and detaching themselves from intimate involvement.

While femininity and masculinity are both 'performances', the greater competitiveness which is part of masculinity, means that it is in more constant need of being proved. And this can result in a particularly adversarial and irresponsible stance towards heterosexual relations. Pleck, Sonenstein and Ku, for instance, noted the strong connections for teenage males between an acceptance of hegemonic masculinity and performance and arrogance in heterosexual relationships. In their work:

> . . . a male with a more traditional conception of manhood reported more sexual partners in the last year, reported a less intimate relationship at last intercourse with his most recent partner, viewed relationships between women and men as more adversarial . . .[65]

Many men need constantly to demonstrate their masculinity, or to be around other men who do it for them, and Chodorow argues that this is directly related to boys' experiences of early childcare and of later parenting. Because women are predominantly the carers and nurturers of young children, girls and boys have different experiences of sexual identity and of relationships. Girls can stay connected to their mothers, and feminine personality can be defined 'in relation and connection to other people'.[66] However, as we have argued earlier, women are encouraged to separate from their sons— and sons to separate from their mothers—within many of the prevailing discourses on parenting and child development.

The arguments made earlier about changing the role of women and of men in the parenting process seem critical here. Parenting practices which positively value the potential role of mothers and women in boys' lives, and which offer rich and diverse experiences of lived masculinity, go some way towards shifting these hegemonic discourses of male heterosexuality. And it is perhaps important also to return to an argument presented earlier in this chapter by Smith, that mothers (and, we would argue, fathers) need to understand more about the social construction of masculinity in building relationships with their sons. As Smith argues, 'a woman's ignorance of "masculinity" . . . is her downfall in her relationship with her boys. We blunder through lack of knowledge.' The more that all of us know of how masculinity is built and practised in social contexts—particularly in home contexts—the more we might be able to offer boys different contexts, different interactions, and different ways of 'being' masculine.

Learning about sex

· It would be reassuring to report that contemporary sex education programs in schools reflected current theorising about gender and gender relations, but, despite the best intentions of many teachers and school communities, official sex education programs are generally seen to be inadequate and unhelpful.[67] As Szirom argues, sex education in schools is most likely to be reproductive education, or, as Davidson notes, education about the 'facts of life', which usually meant 'someone else's life—a frog's or a rabbit's'.[68] When the 'facts' are applied to human beings, Davidson comments that this is most often done 'in such a way as to fail to indicate that human sex was anything more than a mechanical process on a par with the workings of a steam engine'. The desires and longings that come with sex tend to be ignored.

Yet for many boys, school is one of the only sites—other than the locker room with its pornographic magazines and sex jokes—through which to learn about sexuality. And yet programs designed for boys that go beyond reproduction, that consider how desire and feelings are implicated in sexuality, and how constructions of masculinity affect the way boys take themselves up as sexual subjects, are very thin on the ground. One of the only programs in Australia, for instance, that attempted to address male sex-role stereotypes as a part of considering sexuality, was dropped because it was seen to be potentially controversial.[69]

Sexuality issues traditionally sit on the edges of mainstream curricula—if they exist in the school at all—often being taken up by outsiders or guest speakers. This way they are easily marginalised from the 'real' work of the school, and are not addressed as part and parcel of its everyday practices and purposes. The result is often an increasing neglect of sexuality education, and, as Liz Kelly warns of current experiences in the United Kingdom, an increasing tendency to single out sexuality issues for censorship and silencing.

The failure of mainstream sociologists and educationalists in theory, policy and practice to integrate an understanding of sexuality in their frameworks and the fact that sexuality has been the 'optional extra' in equal opportunities initiatives, resulted in sexuality being a soft target for conservative attack in the media and through legislation.[70]

Many educators argue for sex equity and sexuality to be linked, accepting that 'it is necessary for educators to increase their understanding of ways in which sex education can be sex equitable and ways in which sexuality contributes to sex inequities in general education'.[71] Sex education programs, for example, have to look at the inequitable sexual roles often presumed for women and for men—and at the inequitable positioning of women and men as sexual subjects.

As almost every study of teenage sexuality indicates, girls have to assume responsibility for contraception—and use contraception more frequently than do boys. An Australian report on adolescent health noted, for instance, that only 19 per cent of sexually experienced males in a recent survey reported that they used condoms.[72] In other words, many boys choose not to use condoms, and many girls are not in positions where they can demand that boys do.

> They should have them [condoms] in girls' toilets . . . Because like guys sort of like don't have to feel that there's much responsibility . . . It's not like a girl gets pregnant so it's her fault because she said yes. And like most of them force themselves on her anyway, so what can they say? Not—er—'I think I'm going to get pregnant'. And they say 'oh you're paranoid and . . .'[73]

Pleck, Sonenstein and Ku[74] argue that condom use is associated with a boy's perception of masculinity. Boys with a more traditional conception of manhood, for instance, used condoms less consistently, viewed them more negatively in terms of male sexual pleasure, were less concerned with their partners' urging for contraception, and believed that males were not responsible for contraception.

There is a resounding silence in many sex education programs about female sexuality, particularly in terms of female desire,[75] and a similar silence about homosexuality. Trenchard and Warren[76] surveyed 416 young people (two-thirds male, predominantly white and almost half working class) who had faced hostility and abuse because of their sexuality. Of these, 60 per cent said that homosexuality or lesbianism was never mentioned by any of their teachers, but that if it had been mentioned, it was mentioned in a negative or unhelpful way.

As Trenchard and Warren conclude, gay students are particularly at risk of verbal and physical abuse and are constantly exposed to uninformed and derogatory images of homosexuality and lesbianism through the media, playground talk and anti-homosexual/anti-lesbian jokes. There is clearly, as Debbie Epstein argues,[77] a 'presumption of heterosexuality' within schools, and a resultant homophobia that becomes normalised within school practices. (We address this more in chapter 6.) This heterosexism undoubtedly leads not only to physical abuse and harassment of young men who are unsure of their sexual orientation, but also to a culture of verbal violence and humiliation.

Schools are intensely sexual places where boys learn a great deal about what it means to be a sexual 'male' person. '[S]ex talk, sexual behaviour, sexual relationships, sexual abuse and harassment, sexual identity, sexual divisions and sexual politics are threaded throughout the wharp [sic] and wheft [sic] of interactions between students, staff and students and staff.'[78] And within this sexual arena there are notable silences—and, what Kelly calls, 'uncomfortable' presences.

For instance, until recently the sexual nature of male violence in school contexts was silenced and desexualised, as was the sexual harassment of female teachers and students. As we demonstrate in chapter 7, even pre-school boys are able to use discourses of male sexuality to position their female teacher as sexual object, and male sexual harassment of both female and male students is reported by up to 90 per cent of students. And yet discourses of sexuality are seldom invoked to explain classroom behaviour or discipline difficulties. While boys are positioned within discourses of institutional power as 'student' to more powerful 'teacher', they are also positioned in other discourses as male subjects which can potentially override the teacher–student relationship.

CONCLUSION

The intensely sexual presence of masculinity, femininity and heterosexuality in the school provide for 'uncomfortable' presences. These, again, are often unproblematised through sex education programs, or through the more traditional curricular domains of schooling, or through the naturalised practices of heterosexism within school cultures. If schooling *is* to provide a space within which boys can reflect upon masculinity and their sexual lives, it needs to deliberately consider boys' experiences as sons within their families, and boys as lovers and sexual partners within their communities. It needs to take on board the unpacking of masculine culture and the loosening of the ties between masculinity and violence.

Understanding more about parenting and the ways in which adults are implicated in the gendering of boys, and more about male sexuality, as it has been constructed oppositionally to femininity and the female, will be critical to this task. Mothering must not be devalued here, for the role of women to provide loving and strong support for their sons can be, as we have argued earlier in this chapter, powerful in its implications. Fathering, too, needs to be supported and encouraged, but again, fathering that reinforces misogynist and violent attitudes to women, is not what boys need. The raising of sons requires the love and understanding of adults who are aware of the effect of masculinity on boys, and who are determined to give boys opportunities to live fuller and more diverse lives than rigid and hegemonic approaches to masculinity propose.

PART III

Boys and schooling

Masculinity goes to school

We have seen in previous chapters how boys negotiate masculine identities in a range of social situations. In sport they look for sociality and the expression of power; in popular culture they find images of fantasy and possible futures they might entertain for themselves; in families they experience complicated relationships of generation and gender. Each of these sites entails appropriate ways of being masculine, and each offers boys possibilities for forming views of themselves and relations with others. Yet the meanings generated in each context also carry over to the others. In any situation, boys confront multi-layered complexes of expectations and ways of meeting them, and competing images of how they might see themselves.

In this chapter, we consider the school as a context for the development of masculine identities among boys. The focus is on the images and practices of masculinity in schools and how they place boys in relation to each other, to girls, to teachers and to the curriculum. We see how the school generates gendered experiences for boys, and how the cultures which boys themselves construct are influenced by a range of masculinities. Chapters 7 and 8 focus on two problem areas which are of current concern—disruptive behaviour and violence, and literacy learning.

The research on boys in schools is sporadic, but growing. As we noted in chapter 1, there is considerable work in the

tradition of feminist educational research, and no understanding of boys in schools can succeed without the conceptual
tools for studying gender developed in feminist scholarship
into girls' education. However, and understandably, this research has been driven by a concern for the impact of
masculinity on the experience of girls, often resulting, for
instance, in the relative neglect of the diversity of forms of
masculinity and the gender differences among boys themselves.

Of course, much research into schooling in general has
been dominated by male perspectives, so that there has been
a de facto research into boys for a very long time. This is
evident in the work to be reviewed later on school bullying
and literacy, and is illustrated in Hudson's observation that
'All our images of the adolescent . . . the restless, searching
youth, the Hamlet figure; the sower of wild oats, the tester of
growing powers' are masculine images.[1]

The feminist work on girls has been supplemented by
studies of boys in the youth culture tradition, which has been
a rich source of ideas about boys' school experiences and their
meanings.[2] These studies offer insights into how masculinities
are played out by groups of boys struggling to create a sense
of identity while developing viable social relations with others.
However, this work has not generally been informed by theories
of gender, and has been criticised for taking a romantic view
of its subjects, downplaying the misogyny of boys' culture and
its effects on girls.[3]

The most useful work on boys and gender studies the
construction of gender from a relational perspective, where the
practice of various forms of masculinity is seen to be constantly
constructed along with but in distinction from femininities,[4]
and where the focus is on both boys and girls as participants
in this process. As Mac An Ghaill argues,

> we need to consider not only gender *differences* but also
> *relations between* young men and women and *within* young
> men's peer groups. It is important to see masculinity not
> simply as complementary to femininity, which tends to rein-
> force perceived unitary conceptions and 'natural' binary
> differences.[5]

This chapter draws from all three types of study, and tries to integrate them into a picture of the construction of masculinities in schools. We should note, however, that the amount of research on boys in school, especially young boys, far outweighs that done in other contexts, where the processes of the construction of masculinity may well be different. For instance, Thorne cites her own and other work which suggests that the separation of boys and girls in play and other interactions is greater in American schools than in their neighbourhoods and homes. Jordan observes similar patterns in Australia.[6]

The weight of evidence on boys in schools is at secondary school age levels, and even there usually for older age groups. This has enabled the better studies to acknowledge the imminence of work and the economy as part of the picture in which boys see themselves as men in training. It has also highlighted the importance of sexuality as girls and boys become more sexually active.

However, this emphasis could imply that the development of masculinity is primarily associated with pubertal sexuality or the onset of employment, and that the periods before (and after) this one are somehow less important. Yet the evidence is that, while boys and girls beginning school clearly recognise themselves as boys or girls in terms of the group they play with, they are still not clear on all the characteristics which adults attribute as appropriate to that identity.[7] They still have to learn what it means to be a boy or a girl, and the school is therefore a powerful site for the elaboration of that identity from the earliest years.

How boys and girls respond to the challenges of secondary school, sexuality and impending employment is heavily influenced by the resources they have available to them, including the skills, habits, predispositions and understandings they have developed over a life course which has begun long before. On the other hand, as Johnson points out,

> Masculinity and femininity are not character traits or social roles which are learned during childhood and adolescence, and which are fixed and intransigent in adult life. Instead, they are ongoing social processes dependent upon systematic restatement, a process which is variously referred to as 'performing gender' or 'doing gender work'.[8]

If we neglect the early years of schooling we will limit our understanding of the repertoire on which the performance of masculinity draws. But we need to remember that this repertoire, and the contexts of the performances, will continue to change throughout life. There can be no suggestion that the formation of masculinity in schools is laying down some fixed unchangeable pattern. This is of course why work to promote socially positive forms of masculinity throughout the life course is important and worthwhile.

GENDER CONSTRUCTION IN SCHOOLS

Schools, like all institutions, are thoroughly gendered in their own organisation and practice. In the research focus on the culture, activities and interactions of children and adolescents, there is a danger of seeing the school itself as some neutral background in which students construct gender among themselves. Alternatively, those given to biological theories of gender, or to notions that boys will be boys because of the influences on them from outside school, are likely to believe that there is nothing schools can do to influence how masculinity develops. Accordingly, they are susceptible to the argument that the school has little part in the process.

Such a position shows little understanding of the process of gender construction or of what happens in schools. The school as an institution, with its historically reproduced rules, routines, expectations, relationships and rewards, and its deployment of artefacts, resources and space, actively shapes what happens within it, for all its inhabitants. Gender is pervasively and powerfully implicated in this shaping.[9]

We cannot know just how various students interpret this institutionalised process, but there is no doubt that they are aware of many aspects of it. They can clearly see, for instance, patterns of authority and power among teaching staff, and are very sensitive to how they and other students are treated, as well as how teachers treat each other. They are quick to identify unfairness in the distribution of resources, or rules which they see as unproductive and designed only to regulate them, an important source of disaffection among many students. On the other hand, the origins and nature of much of their school experience may not be evident at all, going unnoticed and being taken for granted as a natural way of doing things.

If we are to understand how masculinities are constructed in schools, we need to see these experiences as part of an articulated set of practices which, perhaps explicitly but often surreptitiously, construct models, ideas, activities and relations which promote particular forms of masculinity. While the significance for gender relations of any particular experience is not predetermined, equally there is no aspect of schooling which is not articulated to some extent to the gendered relations among the school's inhabitants. The ability to see how these experiences are articulated to gender relations is the key to understanding schools as sites for the construction of masculinities.

Accordingly, a key part of our focus is the organisational structure and symbolism of schools and the school management practices which constitute it. We then address the part which teachers play in creating a structure of relations into which students are inserted, and how the curriculum contributes to the construction of gendered experiences for boys. Finally, we discuss the extensive research on boys' school cultures.

THE INSTITUTION OF MASCULINITIES IN SCHOOLS

Researchers are increasingly recognising that the very form of organisational management of a school is a significant part of the gendered nature of the institution. In her study of school power structures, Lyn Davies claims that a 'competitive, point-scoring, over-confident, sporting, career and status conscious' version of masculinity dominated school management.[10] This 'competitive manager typescript' was the most powerful image of masculinity in the schools Davies studied, defining a reality where themes of hierarchy and individuation were prominent. Bronwyn Davies cites literature on managerialism in which total quality management (TQM) is promoted as a weapon in the economic war, where organisations can suffer casualties or be destroyed unless they turn defeat into victory with TQM.[11]

Mac An Ghaill[12] found evidence of a similar ethos among teachers whom he labelled 'new entrepreneurs'. These teachers promoted managerialism and an entrepreneurial approach to schooling and the curriculum, and developed a form of masculinity 'within the political nexus of managerialism, vocationalism and commercialisation, with its values of rationalism, possessive individualism and instrumentalism'.[13] Mac An Ghaill shows how, in the school he studied, this ideology was in the ascendant, producing a sexist division of administrative tasks and status hierarachy, and a valuing of rationalist tasks like testing over emotional ones like counselling.

In neither study was this masculinist management ethos the only form of masculinity, but its compatibility with favoured management theories in the education system made it a dominant form. This is a good example of a form of masculinity being promoted in ways that we must assume are not immediately obvious to all involved, though some of the teachers Mac An Ghaill interviewed did criticise its gendered nature.

Staff relationships other than administrative ones also promote particular forms of masculinity in schools. A range of personal and professional relations among staff are involved in this process, as when male and female teachers distribute such tasks as discipline or organising sports in stereotyped ways. Parental involvement is also often complicit in this. Mothers, as noted in chapter 4, are likely to be more involved in their children's schooling than fathers, through such activities as voluntary assistance at canteens or attendance at parent nights. Fathers may be more involved in more public or higher status activities like parents' organisations, working bees or fund raising.

The most well documented forms of gendered relations in the institution of schooling are the relations between staff and students, and from the earliest feminist research on teachers' interactions with children there has been a constant flow of evidence of this. From the first years of school, teachers distinguish boys and girls in their reference to children. For instance, they use labels of 'big girl' and 'big boy' as terms to praise or admonish children, producing a clear image that to be mature is to be mature in a particularly gendered way. It is no surprise that children themselves then claim these labels as identities to distinguish themselves from babies. In Thorne's study, these particular terms ceased to be used by teachers by fourth grade, but were replaced by terms like 'ladies and gentlemen', continuing the gender distinction as a central element of student identities.[14]

In some respects this discipline strategy comes back to haunt teachers when what it means to be mature is no longer defined in terms of the teachers' ideas of cooperative behaviour, but by notions of independence and rebellion drawn from other sources, especially the aggressively masculine images in the media. If teachers refused to make gender difference such a key aspect of school identity, this might pre-empt some of the less desirable aspects of dominant gender ideologies.

There is a wealth of other research to show how teachers, like parents, treat boys and girls according to gendered assumptions of what is appropriate. In her review of research on gendered interactions in early childhood education, Alloway[15] reports an impressive variety of ways in which teachers' interactions with children conform to sexist stereotypes. In these studies, teachers interacted more with boys than girls when the children were engaged in masculine stereotyped activities such as block construction and climbing, while they gave more attention to girls in such activities as dramatic play. The kinds of questions teachers ask, their responses to children's answers, their practices of rewards for behaviour, and teachers' perceptions of student ability were influenced by assumptions about gender differences. Walkerdine's study, for instance, showed that girls who performed well were more likely to be seen by teachers as working hard, where boys' high achievement was described in terms of their natural wit and brilliance.[16]

In treating children in this way, teachers are doing no more than what parents do. From birth children are treated by parents and other carers according to stereotypical notions of how boys and girls are different.[17] But in schools, where education aims to expand students' repertoires of ideas and skills, to limit learning in this way is simply anti-educational.

This variation of interactions and teaching practices according to the sex of the children does not operate only at the level of the individual teacher–student relation. It also becomes institutionalised in recognisable and often valued teaching styles. Mac An Ghaill reports that, in the school he studied, the more authoritarian male teachers colluded with male students' opposition to the school ethos by, in the words of one female teacher, preferring the 'yobbo footballers, romanticising their aggressive rebellion'.[18] Though they had to confront the macho boys to maintain control, these teachers did so in ways that reflected the same dominant authority forms followed by the boys themselves.

In a recent Australian study, boys describe how male teachers commented on the looks of girls passing outside the classroom ('I'd buy that for a dollar!'), and how male teachers see being 'one of the boys' as a valuable asset in controlling boys.[19] In Mac An Ghaill's study teachers ridiculed boys by saying they were acting like girls, though Wolpe shows that this kind of sexist comment is used not only by men teachers but also by women.[20] This involvement of male teachers in sexist discourse simply served to 'confirm and celebrate a normative macho mode of masculinity that many male teachers identified with, highly valued and amplified'.[21]

Similarly, Beynon's study of a boys' school showed how using physically coercive discipline methods such as shaking, pushing and hitting were part of what it meant to be a good teacher in the eyes of the principal and staff. 'Men and boys were expected to behave in a certain kind of way, put in a certain kind of manly performance, if they were to win the accolade of being a "good teacher" or a "good lad", whether that was a praiseworthy "rough diamond" or "playground hard".'[22] Askew and Ross report that many women teachers feel the pressure to conform to this authoritarian teaching style, and that boys push them to 'teach like a man'.[23]

Sport is another arena in which schools construct gender. Teachers use extra-curricular activities like sport to establish more personal and open relations with students than they believe the formal classroom might allow. However, if classrooms are seen by students as sites for a constraining and bureaucratic regulation, while the sports field is accepted as a place for aggressive forms of physical and other forms of domination, then a student committed to one context will find it all the more difficult to commit to the other. On the other hand, if both contexts promote a competitive ethos where success is always at someone else's expense, then calls for cooperation and respect for rules will be seen as hypocritical.

Baker and Davies have shown that even when teaching is informed by motives to overthrow sexist stereotypes, masculine ideologies and relationships can produce quite the opposite effect.[24] In their analysis of a history lesson aimed at a critical study of sex roles in medieval England, the sexist assumptions of modern stereotypes were projected into the past, producing anachronisms that confirmed limiting gender relations. But in telling and fascinating ways, the gendered nature of the learning experience was not restricted to the content of the lesson, but was implicated also with the relationships through which the lesson was conducted. In identifying, albeit playfully, with the boys against the girls in debates about sex roles, the teacher set up a relationship which gave authority to the boys' sexist views. This is an excellent illustration of how relationships in school are unavoidably and pervasively gendered, and evidence that unless teaching practices are critically scrutinised, they will tend to confirm dominant power relations.

In reviewing such research, Haywood and Mac An Ghaill show that teachers' work embodies ideas of what it means to be a man.[25] In the case of male teachers, their 'identities, ideologies and pedagogical styles demonstrate a particular purchase on certain masculinities. It is a purchase on what kind of men they are.' In this way, male teachers' masculinity is performed and constructed along with that of the boys, and is an important aspect of the gendered nature of schools.

MASCULINITY AND THE CURRICULUM

Curriculum content is the third brick in the wall of the gendered institution of schooling. While management and teaching styles and ideologies are implicated with gender relations, so are institutionalised patterns of knowledge. The research on the gendered nature of knowledge has operated at a number of levels of abstraction. At its most general, the argument is that certain theories of knowledge or epistemologies are in themselves characterised by features that form a binary set of oppositions associated with the binary distinctions of masculine and feminine. More specifically, there are also arguments that particular subjects are more closely related to masculine interests and activities than others. Both arguments have important implications for schooling.

We have seen in chapter 2 how the binary argument presents masculinity as valuing rationalism and universalism as ways of understanding the world. This argument has been elaborated to claim that there are distinctively different ways of knowing which are associated with masculinity and femininity, though we need to avoid the confusion that this means that men and women necessarily think or learn differently.[26] Rather, there are particular attitudes to knowledge that are part of the performance of masculinity; to do masculinity is to take a particular epistemological stance.[27]

The masculine epistemological stance is based on a number of assumptions,[28] and the extent to which boys take it up as the way to be will colour their responses to the range of curriculum experiences schools offer. First, a belief in objectivity holds that direct knowledge of the facts of nature allows us to produce objective accounts of the world unmediated by interpretation or culture. Its belief that we can describe reality as it really is makes it unlikely to favour arguments that problems should be solved through consultation and the consideration of a range of views.

Second, the assumption of essentialism is that we can reduce the complexity of the world down to its basic elements, discovering the true essence of things, also known as reductionism. The reductionism and fragmentation of this world view is a weakness in understanding problems in context, where relationships can be more important than the nature of the parts. For instance, in this assumption, intergroup relations become a matter of following abstract rules rather than considering the relations among the people in the group.

And third, representationalism is the belief that the descriptions we have of the world mirror reality, that language and theory do not mediate reality but give us transparent access to it. Foundationalism ignores the theory-laden nature of knowledge, and how culture and interpretation frame the way theories are constructed and used. This can lead to dogmatism and the rejection of others' perspectives, so that the 'strong leader' becomes a masculine image of someone able to impose his will on others rather than to understand and accommodate their views.

Seidler explains that the valuing of abstract reason and morality quite separate from feelings, emotions and desires has meant that notions of 'objective rightness', an abstract approach to morality, and the fragmentation of reason and feelings have become normalised as masculine. He argues that this fragmentation 'constitutes both a source of the damage that, as men, we do to ourselves, and a facet of our patriarchal power'.[29]

Aspects of these knowledge values clearly relate to the dominant form of masculinity discussed in various sections of this book: the emphasis on technical knowledge, on solutions to problems which are justified in abstract rather than personal terms, on an individual competitive approach to problems rather than a collaborative one. They also offer insights into the kinds of knowledge values which boys come to hold as they construct themselves as masculine. For instance, boys are more likely to have a pragmatic instrumental approach to schooling, in that they see success as a means to an end rather than intrinsically interesting or valuable. One consequence of this is their tendency to do what is needed to succeed in the curriculum as far as their career aspirations require, but to avoid a commitment to learning and involvement in school activities beyond this.

This analysis also parallels the well-known tendency for science, maths and technology to be seen as natural choices for boys, and it is still the case that dominant forms of masculinity are primarily associated with a narrow range of school subjects (when they are associated with subjects at all). As Davies puts it:

> Proper hard, non-subjective subjects like maths, science and technology provide a haven of acceptable (male) knowledges which confirm that true knowledge lies outside oneself and independent of any subjectivities, independent of those emotions which need to be held in check. They are rational, cool, controllable, abstract, distant, and unquestionably hegemonic.[30]

In his review of the gendered polarisation of humanities and maths/science subjects, Martino argues that it derives from the history of gender divisions in the workforce.[31] This is best illustrated in the parallel between feminine/masculine identities and mental/manual labour distinctions in Willis's study of working-class boys.[32] It also points to the gendered nature of the commonsense distinction between the public arena as a predominantly masculine site, while the private domain of family and personal relationships is a feminine preserve.

These divisions have given rise to claims that feminine intuition, emotion and expressivity are naturally associated with the humanities, while maths and science attract boys because of the kind of rationality involved in these subjects. The prejudice that boys are naturally interested or talented in these subjects, and the recognition that these are high status subjects that will give boys access to desirable male careers, has been a factor in the position of power that men have traditionally held in the workforce.

However, while this view has been very profitable for many boys, it has not been so for all. Subject choice should be made in light of a range of factors like personal abilities and economic considerations. Many boys enter these traditionally male subjects because of the myth of success that they promise, but boys whose inclinations and talents lie elsewhere can easily lose out by opting for these subjects. Also, changing employment patterns, such as the rise in the service and financial sectors, mean that career options may be better served by other subject choices.

Mac An Ghaill found that in the school he studied boys still dominated high status technological and commercial subjects like business and computer studies.[33] An Australian survey of subject choice in years 11 and 12 found that economics and business were more likely to be studied by boys from higher than lower socio-economic backgrounds, while for girls the relationship was reversed.[34] The meaning of this is illustrated in the example of senior school enrolments in business subjects in the state of Queensland, where, in a subject entitled Business Organisation and Management, 52 per cent of 1996 enrolments were boys, while in the subject Secretarial Studies, only 6 per cent were boys.[35] So while some boys are opting for a different curriculum orientation, strongly gendered distinctions remain.

The masculine epistemological stance has been influential across the entire curriculum. In chapter 8, we argue that masculine interests have tended to dominate the English curriculum, and there is similar evidence in other subjects like the social sciences, where the selection of curriculum content has reflected a masculine perspective.[36] So while many boys avoid humanities and social sciences because of their departure from traditionally masculine knowledge values, these subjects can also be incorporated into a masculine ethos. In fact, this masculinist tendency across the curriculum is often an attempt by the less masculine subjects to appeal to masculine knowledge values, as when English teachers set action novels and science fiction, or history teachers emphasise the history of war.

But it is not only curriculum content that reflects masculine values. Learning and teaching processes may also be involved. Redman describes his fascination with the study of history when a teacher demonstrated his ability to 'intellectually out-manoeuvre anyone in the room'.[37] Redman was impressed by the 'muscular intellectualness' of the teacher, and his ability to 'push people around intellectually'. This meant that, for Redman, the study of history gave access to a masculinity which, while rare and in some ways subversive of more dominant traditional forms, nonetheless confirmed key aspects of that tradition. This echoes the revealing comment by a boy interviewed in Mac An Ghaill's study, in which the student equated doing well in studies as equivalent to being 'hard' in a street gang because 'it's still about beating other people'.[38]

Masculine knowledge values affect the curriculum in diverse and subtle ways. As with theories of management or styles of teaching, the link with masculinity is not always apparent. However, if we accept that many of the problems boys face at school are the result of an unquestioning acceptance of traditional masculinities, and if we are to open up options for a greater diversity of ways of being male, then we need to address the constraints affecting boys' subject choices.

BOYS' SCHOOL CULTURES

The most important contributions to understanding masculinity in schools have come from a series of ethnographic and interview studies into boys' school cultures.[39]

One common strategy of these studies is to identify typologies of cultural groups among boys in schools. While authors generally acknowledge the diversity, overlap and shifting nature of these typologies, there is a considerable degree of similarity in the groups described. The most studied group in this context are those boys who represent the stereotype of hegemonic masculinity, the toughs who reject school values in favour of an aggressively rebellious style of conduct, the boys Mac An Ghaill calls 'Macho Lads'.[40]

Willis's classic study established the prototype of this category, and despite criticisms, it remains one of the most complete pictures of a particular type of masculine youth culture.[41] The counter-school culture of his working-class lads opposed authority in very open and direct ways. They joked in class, flaunted their superior sexual experience over more conventional boys, and smoked, drank and swore as public evidence of their independence and rejection of authority.

Their disdain for anyone who did not share their view of the world, and their need to promote their sense of themselves by putting down others, gave them a malevolent attitude to others, one source of their virulent racism and sexism. The lads rejected school for its focus on mental rather than manual work; they dismissed teachers as 'wankers' because teachers lacked the kind of experience in the world they respected; they ridiculed boys who engaged with learning as being weak and effeminate. Willis explains this in terms of the mutually supportive relation between the mental/manual division of labour and patriarchal forms of sexual division and oppression. While the division of labour works against the lads' interests, they turn this around to what they convince themselves is their advantage by rejecting mental work as effeminate. But for this strategy to work it also requires that femininity itself should be denigrated. 'A member of the counter-school culture can only believe in the effeminacy of white collar and office work so long as wives, girlfriends and mothers are regarded as restricted, inferior and incapable of certain things.'[42]

Twenty years later, Mac An Ghaill's study is evidence of the longevity of this form of masculinity. The 'Macho Lads' of his study saw school as 'a system of hostile authority and meaningless work demands', and represented to teachers and other students an anti-school culture. They explained their behaviour at school in terms of supporting each other through a physical solidarity which countered the teachers' control over the school. Their position with respect to teachers, and their placement in lower stream classes, meant that their experience of schooling was what Mac An Ghaill labelled as one of 'domination, alienation and infantilism'.[43]

The Macho Lads responded to this situation by, as they saw it, defending themselves and other students against the teachers by truanting, being late for lessons, not doing homework, and not answering questions. In return, the school authorities practised a form of bodily surveillance by demanding acquiescence in clothing, footwear, hairstyles and earrings and general comportment (such as sitting up straight). To the Macho Lads themselves, masculinity was about 'looking after your mates', 'acting tough', 'having a laugh', 'looking smart' and 'having a good time'. They rejected the school curriculum and regulations in favour of learning to be tough, which for them involved 'fighting, fucking and football'.[44] To be committed to schoolwork was to be inferior and effeminate.

Walker's Australian study describes a corresponding culture in a Sydney high school:

> a culture of youthful self-congratulatory 'Aussie' masculinity, which highlighted standing up for oneself and one's mates, against authority or anything else; physical, especially sporting, prowess; and daring or exciting escapades.[45]

Walker called these boys the 'competitors' and the 'footballers', as sport played a powerful role in their group identity, based on 'the superiority of heterosexuality, of machismo demonstrated through athletic and sexual prowess, physical strength, drinking, and appropriate verbal display'.[46] The footballers were less hostile to school than the boys Willis described, for 'while they would spar with teachers on teachers' territory . . . they did not, fundamentally, wish to contest that territory'.[47] On the other hand, they did practise the strong sexist and racist form of aggressive masculinity which has been identified in all these studies. Boys who were ethnically different or who engaged in practices which were unacceptable to the macho culture, like drama, were treated with disdain or worse.

This aggressive form of masculinity has been most conspicuous in the ethnographies of boys in schools, and clearly looms large in the minds of parents and teachers, to the point where boys showing even some of these traits can be suspected of an anti-school attitude. Its loud, physical and aggressive nature and its potential for disruption give it a significance in the school beyond what the numbers of boys who practise it would suggest. Its dominance in the playground and often in sport, and the physical intimidation it can present to other students, mean that it is a powerful icon with or against which other students must position themselves. It encapsulates many of the problems of hegemonic masculinity and schooling.

However, we need also to acknowledge the alternatives to this form, for there are other ways in which boys can deal with the demands of schooling and masculinity. The conspicuousness of the macho form, which has been both romanticised and vilified, has led to a neglect of those boys who do not practise this strong form of dominant masculinity, and of the fact that in many cases macho performance is intermittent and limited to particular contexts like the playground or sport. Walker observed that the group he called the 'footballers' overtly rejected the formal school culture and defied teachers' authority only when their 'own personal identities and cultural integrity were explicitly insulted'.[48] For the most part, they did not wish to contest teachers' classroom authority.

Thorne's study of primary schools gives some idea of the varied and shifting nature of boys' relationships.[49] In the class Thorne studied, the dominant group included a clear leader, some eight or ten other boys, and one girl. The group shared food, sat together, called each other 'buddies' and routinely played team sports like soccer and basketball, and talked about their games at various times through the school day. The other boys did not form groups. Some joined in the sports but were not otherwise part of the clique; others were part of temporary and shifting pairs and triads who engaged in a range of fantasy play and friendship patterns often thought typical of girls. Finally, there were the loners or outcasts, including one who was overweight, another who was physically uncoordinated, a low achiever, and two recently immigrated Mexican boys.

In secondary schools, these differences seem to harden into more stable friendship groups and more discrete alternatives to the macho style. Mac An Ghaill identified a group of 'Academic Achievers' a small group of male friends who were positively oriented to the academic curriculum, but not unambiguously committed to school itself. Favoured by teachers (though some saw them as effeminate) and privileged in the distribution of resources by virtue of their academic programs, they developed an 'institutionally confident student masculinity that was highly valued by teachers'.[50] Ridiculed and even bullied as effeminate for participating in activities like drama (including the playing of female roles), these boys reported constant harassment of themselves and other boys by the 'yobs' and their gangs. In later years, they became more confident and were able to parody the dominant gender ideology, and challenge the more macho teachers who had criticised them.

Walker reports a parallel case in his study of boys in an Australian school, where boys ridiculed by others for being effeminate replied with a camp exaggeration which challenged their attackers. However, boys who reject the macho form of masculinity still cannot escape it. 'As an oppressed cultural group, much of their practice was developed in reaction, or was the product of a habituated disposition to reject whatever the dominant culture put forward.'[51]

Walker's discussion of the diversity of boys' cultures is a valuable caution to the emphasis on the dominant form. Nonetheless, the identities of all of the groups are negotiated around common issues of sport, ethnicity and gender, with diverse consequences. For instance, Walker describes the groups' different approaches to schooling in the following way:

> The Greeks' striving and commitment to school and upward mobility were absent from ASC (Anglo-Saxon-Celtic) foot-baller culture . . . The footballers competed academically with each other and with other pupils, but short-term status was already theirs through sport and Aussie macho superiority. For the Greek footballers academic competition took on a clear macho dimension in the *way* success was won: through your own merits and independent efforts, not teacher patronage . . . The handballers . . . accepted the credentialist necessity for school, and all wanted good steady jobs.[52]

127

However, these different positions with respect to schooling do not prevent different groups of boys from sharing many masculine concerns and attitudes. For instance, the Academic Achievers in Mac An Ghaill's study still held to a firm belief in their masculinity, claiming, for instance, that their interest in English was different from girls', as it was focused on an intellectual approach to being an expert as distinct from what they saw to be girls' interests in 'feminine writers and all the emotional stuff'.[53] So while boys may not all share the same hegemonic form of masculinity, different masculinities are not necessarily more resistant to traditional gender divisions and stereotypes.

A third group in Mac An Ghaill's study was the New Enterprisers, boys whose masculinities were developed through their commitment to pragmatic values of rationality, an instrumental approach to knowledge and concern for future careers. Their relation to school was worked out in new vocational and technological subjects, and their involvement in utilitarian projects like mini-enterprises. Seeing the Macho Lads as childish, and a threat to the status of the school and therefore their own qualifications, they felt the teachers were too soft, and generally supported the authority of the school.

Finally, Mac An Ghaill describes a group of boys from a non-commercial middle-class background with professional aspirations who saw themselves as cultural arbiters of taste and style. For these boys, teachers and other students were seen as conventional and boring, and they challenged teachers' authority by showing their cultural knowledge and being smart, presenting different and in some respects more difficult problems for teachers than the Macho Lads. They dismissed the school's work ethic, promoting a belief in natural talent, and preferring 'a highly public display of a contradictory "effortless achievement" to each other and outsiders'.[54] They also regarded the Macho Lads as 'trash' and looked down on the Academic Achievers and New Enterprisers for working too hard.

The style is reminiscent of the group identified as the 'gothic punks' in Abraham's earlier study.[55] This was a mixed-sex group who preferred art, music and conversation to the technology, football and violence of the macho boys. Rejecting the macho image, they formed less sexist relationships with girls, and did not objectify girls as sexual objects in the way characteristic of the 'Lads'. They believed they were more mature and worldly than other students, and that school was a boring intrusion into their real lives of bands and nightlife.

The gothic punks seem to be an exception to a widespread feature of boys' school cultures, in that sexuality was not a central part of the distinctions around which they constructed their sense of themselves. Heterosexuality has been found to be a powerful marker of masculine identity in most studies of boys' school cultures. For instance, a study by Haywood shows how the Academic Achievers were seen by others as childlike because of their apparent lack of heterosexual experience, and were called 'wankers', 'gays' and 'poofs' outside the classroom.[56] On the other hand, the Academic Achievers ridiculed the other boys as inarticulate and stupid, referring to them in class as 'cripple', 'cabbage' and 'spanner'. However, this strategy simply accentuated the Achievers' collusion with the school system, and emphasised their childlike nature because they did not use the sexualised abuse of the other boys. As a result, the strategy could not provide them with power outside the class context.

In recalling his own schooling in a Canberra Anglican boys' school, Denborough describes his desire to be part of the dominant masculinity of the 'cools', as membership of this group meant 'benefits, privileges and prestige' which outweighed any competing allegiances:

> The key attributes that one had to demonstrate in order to achieve such membership consisted primarily of excellence at football, drinking, 'sleazing', and remaining always in control. In order to be 'cool' one had to, in many ways, become cold.[57]

Denborough says that while this ethos was uncontested in the early years of high school, in the senior school the imminent Higher School Certificate exams challenged the authority of the 'cools', opening up more space for those previously labelled 'squares'. Of course, as we saw earlier in the discussion of 'intellectual hardness', this may have changed but not fundamentally replaced the masculinist ethos of dominance and aggression.[58] Notwithstanding this, Denborough claims that it was the 'cool' masculinity of the earlier years which were pivotal in his experience, as they coincided with the most important period of his negotiating a masculine identity.[59]

Cool masculinity is a varied creature, depending on many cultural and historical factors. At times, being cool is to adopt the practice of masculinist sports with their aggression, ferocity, commitment and celebration of the risk of pain which construct an ethos of excessive bodily activity. Being excessive, taking risks and taking things to the limit are characteristic of popular images of masculinity. However, in contrast to this is another image of bodily projection through which boys learn to conduct and express themselves in desirable ways—to be cool.

An interesting contrast to the extroverted excesses of rough and tumble play and the intense commitment so valued in competitive sport, is the more detached notion of 'cool', based on a more passive way of carrying and projecting oneself in the world. This version involves a studied nonchalance and a disdain for anyone who chooses or needs to exert themselves, and in this sense it is a ploy to indicate that all is under control, that every thing is cool. Majors[60] traces the cool pose to the African-American expressive lifestyle and its 'high fives' handshakes, spectacular basketball dunks, various dance forms like breakdancing, and street rap talk. To Majors, it is still an aggressive assertion of masculinity, that the protagonist is in control of his space, and should be treated with care. For black Americans, it is a rejection of the demeaning position which the economy and culture have bequeathed them:

> Cool provides control, inner strength, stability and confidence. Being cool, illustrated in its various poses and postures, becomes a very powerful and necessary tool in the black man's constant fight for his soul. The poses and postures of cool guard, preserve and protect his pride, dignity and respect . . .[61]

There is no doubt that Australian boys have adopted much of this expressive lifestyle. The clothes, the talk, the walk, are practised in shopping malls and street corners around the country, and modelled by the icons of televised basketball. Parents and teachers who are frustrated and even provoked by the smouldering hostility which sometimes accompanies the adolescent cool pose will recognise the style.

Majors points out that the cool pose has a cost for the black man, and again there is an interesting parallel with that of boys in their early adolescent years. Majors argues that the cool pose can prevent men from expressing emotions such as fear or affection, sometimes leading to frustration and aggression; and that it can suppress the motivation to learn and to participate in other forms of cultural expression and pursuits. This constriction on feeling and expressing emotion is a worrying development for boys and those who care about them. Majors' comments also bring to mind the ways boys can reject commitment and effort in school as not being cool. The rejection of a participatory ethos beyond a small clique of peers is not only anti-social but limits the range of social experiences from which boys can learn to relate to and work with others.

What is considered cool varies considerably with class culture. The classic studies of boys' school cultures have concentrated on working-class or deviant boys and their rejection of school culture. At the other end of the class structure, Connell et al. have shown that strong forms of masculinity are just as important in the relationship between elite schools and ruling class families. In discussing the father–son relationship in an elite family, they conclude:

> What is needed for success in Mr Walker's world of high-powered business competition is a particular kind of *masculinity*: motivated to compete, strong in the sense of one's own abilities, able to dominate others and to face down opponents in situations of conflict. The school Mr Walker's son goes to is very effectively organized to produce that kind of character structure, even though it doesn't teach the specific techniques of modern business.[62]

Class, 'race' and ethnicity are constant factors in the interplay of different kinds of masculinity, and we will consider 'race' and ethnicity further in the next chapter. Ironically, however, the emphasis in the earlier research on disruptive working-class boys may have glossed over the relational character of class and other social divisions. As Eckert points out in her US study of working-class 'jocks' and middle-class 'burnouts', the separate cultures are in many ways class cultures, and the opposition and conflict between them reflects class relations and differences. 'However, they do not exist separately as inward-looking categories, but in a state of intense mutual awareness and thus of continual mutual influence: each category defines itself very consciously as what the other is not'.[63]

BOYS' IMPRESSIONS OF SCHOOL

The boys' cultures studies reviewed above provide a substantial base for considering issues of boys and schooling. However, there is still much to learn about the specifics of boys' school-related interpretations and attitudes, especially of younger boys who have been underrepresented in the youth culture studies. To balance this focus, and to test the findings of these studies for their relevance to contemporary Australia, we thought it important to add evidence of younger boys at the present time.

A series of interviews was conducted with groups and individual boys in one primary and one secondary provincial Queensland school on a range of issues derived from the boys' cultures research and other questions raised in earlier chapters. The interviews were first conducted with groups of three to five boys, with the intent of identifying the prevailing view, the dominant perspective to which the boys publicly subscribe. If group interviews tend to generate the stereotypical view, the group ideology, then individual interviews are an opportunity to test the variations and differences among boys, as well as their assessments of the views which seem to dominate the groups. Wight has shown how boys interviewed alone express quite different views from those espoused under the influence of the group, confirming that different interview contexts evoke different perspectives on issues.[64] The following discussion reviews what the boys said about a range of aspects of their school experiences.

Nerds, scruffs and schoolwork

The primary school boys interviewed had a pragmatic view of school. In the group interviews the common story was that school was boring, with teachers being too strict and making them work too hard, the strongest comment being that 'it's a load of rubbish'. The only positive feature was that school enabled you to meet your friends. Generally the boys placed themselves between the extremes of the squares or nerds and the scruffier types who actively rejected school. The nerds were seen as quiet, not very popular, and not involved in sport. They didn't 'get around', but just sat and talked with each other, wore the correct uniform, were always neat, never late for school, and did their homework. They would prefer to go to the library and read a book than play basketball. Eric observes:

> Boys who are good at school like being by themselves and sitting down and reading and stuff. They're normally the ones you see pushed out of groups and stuff and sitting by themselves. They're normally sitting in library and reading. I like reading as well and playing with my friends.

Later, Eric reveals that he has suffered in this way:

> I: Are boys who are good at school popular?
>
> *Eric:* Not really. They're normally pushed out of the groups. I'm fairly lucky. I'm in a group with Don and Warren. Normally when we come in here we just talk and stuff except when I come in and read. I'm not really popular with the rest of the class. Most of the kids—because they like to try for the cool image they don't like anyone else except their group. You just hang around with your mates and friends who you get along with and play with. One thing is we all really like computer games. Most of the others mostly like sport and only sport.

The relationship between success at school and being cool and accepted is an important aspect of boys' disposition to schoolwork. An exchange in one group discussion is an interesting illustration. Chris, a member of the group, is identified as a worker, but he evades any stigma this might bring by claiming a pragmatic purpose and explaining that he just gets it done so he can do other things. Chris's main concern seems to be to avoid any suggestion that he works because he likes to, or that he finds schoolwork intrinsically interesting. Ultimately, he is saved by being acknowledged as a sportsman.

> *I*: Tell me about the boys who are good at schoolwork.
>
> *Boy 1*: They like schoolwork.
>
> *Boy 2*: Chris is good but he doesn't like it—he works hard.
>
> *Boy 3*: Chris studies.
>
> *Chris*: I just get it done so I get good marks and can do something else. That's going to be your future job and it's important to do well at grades 10 and 11.
>
> *I*: Are boys who are good at school popular?
>
> *Boy 2*: Some of them are, like Matthew. But the ones who don't play sport aren't—they sit around and read books and stay in class . . .
>
> *Boy 1*: . . . don't get around, just sit down and talk to each other.
>
> *Boy 2*: Sporting people aren't the smartest. Anyone can be popular even if they're not real bright. It depends on whether they play sport or not.
>
> *Boy 3*: Like Chris plays sport and he's popular.

The idea of cool and being popular is quite threatening to some boys who perform well in their schoolwork. Tom's story illustrates the struggle here:

> *I*: Do you know kids who think it's cool not to like school?
>
> *Tom*: Yeah. There's a kid in my class. He's good at his schoolwork but he just says he doesn't like it to be cool. It's stupid.
>
> *I*: Why does he do this?
>
> *Tom*: To get attention from kids 'cause he's not really that popular.

The secondary boys also noted this problem, telling of the 'nerds' who:

> just sit up the front and do all their work during class and get everyone else in trouble for not doing theirs . . . [some-

times] they get away from their work 'cause everyone else starts teasing 'em . . . You get teased a fair bit I reckon.

I: Are some boys discouraged by this?

Yeah they'll start mucking around in class so everyone thinks they're pretty good.

At the other extreme from the nerds were the boys who actively opposed what the boys believed to be the conventional picture of conformity to school values. Oppositional boys were 'home boys, sporting people, people who think they're cool, and wear daggy clothes'. They're 'scruffy' and don't have their shirts tucked in. These boys reject the time required to complete the work at school and home, and would rather 'wag it and to go to the half court and shoot a couple of baskets'. They spend their time walking around in gangs and groups and get into trouble 'to be cool'. In class, they spend their time 'dreaming and playing with toys'.

They don't like the work, the non-stop work—like if they get something wrong they feel a bit ashamed that they're getting it wrong.

The oppositional boys were described as trying to be cool, particularly in their interest in sport and the associated trappings of magazines and clothes, and this gave them a certain power. However, the boys interviewed reject active opposition to school and disruptiveness. Matthew explains:

I don't think it's cool (not to like school) cause you're going to be a bit dumb and being cool's also about being smart. I don't want to be dumb. I don't think that'd be cool.

The pragmatic accommodation

This stereotyped dichotomy between nerds and scruffs presented problems for the boys interviewed, as most of them were quite accepting of and even committed to the notion that school meant doing work and that that was important. When asked about this they invariably pointed out that you needed

135

to do the work for pragmatic reasons—the need to prepare for high school and careers.

> I want a good job so I like to learn about things so that I know about it so I can get smarter, get experience.

> It helps you get a good job when you're older. So you can buy a house and so you don't have to go on the dole and people think you're a bit of a loser.

What distinguished them from the nerds was, in their view, their social lives and sport, though these were so closely connected that they were pretty much the same thing. It was OK to be good at schoolwork if you were involved in sport.

> *I*: Are the boys who are good at their schoolwork popular?

> *Group 1*: Some of them are, but the ones who don't play sport aren't. They sit around and read books and stay in class. They don't get around, just sit down and talk to each other. Sporting people aren't the smartest. Anyone can be popular even if they're not real bright. It depends on whether they play sport or not.

> *Group 2*: Not normally. When you get a really smart person they're alone by themselves. It's alright if you're smart when you do sport. It's not if you're smart and you come to the library and read books and go back to class and read books and don't get into trouble. If you're fun to be with they don't mind if you're smart or stupid.

The secondary school boys were even more blunt in their views. 'Kids that like school are squares', while the ones who reject school and cause trouble are 'idiots'. The boys interviewed, like their primary school counterparts, felt they were in between these extremes.

In the primary group interviews the boys presented themselves as out to have a good time, but pragmatic in their understanding that school success was important. Being able to balance these two commitments set them apart from both the unpopular nerds and the scruffy home boys, who were able to practise only one of these competing desires. (Girls were something else again—not so much a point of comparison but a qualitatively different form of being.) By positioning themselves in this way, the boys found confidence and security in being with the majority. However, this stereotypical picture constructed in the group interviews was not so clear when the boys were interviewed individually. Here the group construction, no doubt influenced by popular myths of what a normal boy should be like, was overlaid with the diversity of personal experience, which was much more complex.

The individual responses illustrated the diversity of experiences and the range of influences on boys' views about school. While they complained that school was often boring, there were also positive times, and their commitment to school was strongly influenced by parental encouragement.

> *Paul*: I guess my mum tells me I have to go to school and she always asks me what I get so I have to do it. And when I get good marks I like it. And I like it on Fridays when I get to go to sport. So we can get out and do something and on Wednesdays we have PE and that's about it . . . If you don't really like school and you don't learn much you'd be more embarrassed when you go to high school 'cause you won't know it. At least you'd know a bit and you won't get embarrassed . . . I'm good at writing up assignments 'cause last year I got 99 out of 100 and after that I liked writing up assignments. I like language and science 'cause we get to do things and do experiments and write it up and sometimes I like maths 'cause now we're making things and that's not that hard and I guess PE. I like PE 'cause I like doing active things.

Paul outlines his own secret pleasure in gaining his mother's approval and in scoring well on assignments. He is also motivated by a fear of being embarrassed if at high school he didn't know the work. Beyond that, he sees himself as someone who likes active things like physical education and science experiments. In these respects, Paul lives out the complexities of boys' relations to schooling. School success is pleasurable, and one must not stand out as being incompetent, but these motivations are combined with a masculine desire to be seen to be active.

Matthew is also motivated by his parents and the threat of high school, and again this is given direction by a masculine emphasis on activity. Part of this is the fascinating link with sport and the image of the loneliness of the long-distance reader. In this case father and son both see a parallel between effort and success in school and commitment to sport, a fascinating construction of schooling as a masculine practice. The influence of the father's interests is also evident, so that sport and computers become attractions in their own right, whereas reading is something that 'you've got to get used to'.

> *Matthew*: Mum says high school's going to be real hard 'cause I play a lot of sport and I don't like to have to sit down and read a book or something. So mum and dad push me to do both. Dad wants me to read for five minutes before I go to bed. He says it's like running in the mornings. You've got to get used to it and get into it . . . I don't like language. It's one of the hardest subjects and I don't have great handwriting . . . I like working on computers and that sort of stuff, technology sort of stuff, 'cause you want to get into the new stuff not the old stuff. Dad's pretty high into computers and he has a few at home. It's important [to do schoolwork] 'cause it's good self-discipline to do homework. If you've got self-discipline you can do other things like sport a lot harder.

These accommodations to the demands of career are no doubt related to the attitude which Connell described in his study of the school experience of young working-class men. Connell identifies a calculative attitude towards long-term career goals among some young men, where the central themes of masculinity are 'rationality and responsibility rather than pride and aggressiveness'.[65] However, while this leads to a more acquiescent approach to school authority, we have seen that even these boys occupy an ambivalent position with respect to teachers and the curriculum, and are still very concerned to proclaim their affinity with dominant masculine aspects of boys' school cultures.

Central to this identification is its difference from girls. We have seen in chapter 3 the importance of sport to boys' sense of themselves, their relations to each other, and to girls. The relation with girls, against whom they chiefly define their own collective identity, was also apparent in other areas.

Boys vs girls

While the continuum from nerd to scruffy could be complicated, the distinction from girls was clear. Girls like school,
and the primary boys attested to the power of this image.

> Whenever I go into the class when there's a test on the girls
> are there asking questions to each other . . . Girls talk for
> hours and don't kick a ball around. Girls try harder 'cause
> they've got nothing else to do.

> My point of view is that girls like working better. Boys tend
> to muck around more, throw the paper aeroplanes. Girls they
> do play sport but they're always smart . . . Boys have short
> concentration. They like to talk a bit while they're doing their
> work.

> I reckon girls like it a bit better than us because they like
> getting good marks. There's three nice girls when they've got
> exams the next day before the test in the morning they test
> themselves for the whole half hour where all the boys go out
> and play basketball. They care quite a lot—more than us . . .
> They won't get teased if they do a lot of work . . . maybe
> their parents expect them to go good in their work.

For the secondary boys, the question of sexuality loomed
larger, but there was still a fundamental difference in boys'
and girls' relation to schoolwork.

> . . . girls tend to get into school but they can get into school
> and still have lots of friends. 'Cause all the guys are always
> looking for chicks and the chicks always want to make the
> choice . . . All the girls respect each other if they do their
> schoolwork—they don't care. They're still good friends. I
> think they're more capable of making friends and doing
> schoolwork. I don't know why. Whereas for guys it's one or
> the other. Yeah, it has to be one or the other.

Eric, a primary school boy, makes a similar observation
about girls' ability to combine social relationships and school
interests. While Eric is himself quite interested in reading, he
is clear on the fact that girls do it differently.

> The girls more like to sit together and grab a book and talk about it. Where the boys who like it just sit by themselves and just think about it where the girls like to share ideas about it. So when you have to share ideas with a group they're normally better at it.

Boys regard girls' commitment to schoolwork as quite different from their own. In contrast with their own pragmatic approach, girls like their work and care about it. In any case, girls have nothing else to do and won't be teased if they do well. This picture presents a problem for boys, for if to care and do well is characteristic of girls, can boys show the same commitment without leaving themselves open to ridicule for being effeminate? The frequent description of boys who do well at school as 'being by themselves and sitting down and reading and stuff' is very close to the common description of girls being inactive and less sociable in their commitment to their work. This is a major obstacle to boys who might want to combine a strong form of masculinity with school success.

The ignominy of trying hard

If a commitment to schoolwork is characteristic of girls, and if to be masculine requires being different from girls, then boys' commitment to schoolwork becomes a challenge to their masculinity.

In a series of observation studies, Adler, Kless and Adler found that, during the middle primary years, boys changed their collective attitudes to classwork and oriented themselves away from adult school figures and more to the peer group.[66] Part of this was the development of 'the potential stigma associated with doing too well at school'. This served to discourage any conspicuous effort from the more able, but the authors suggest it also established a sense of solidarity among the boys. The more able boys engaged in disruptive behaviour to show they were like the others, and the collective lack of effort tended to disguise the shortcomings of, and save face for, the low achievers.

A key problem for schooling is the difficulty that boys face when they like reading or some other aspect of school, but are unable to talk about it with other boys for fear of ridicule. In our interviews, Shane testifies to this problem and the contradictions it generates at the primary level:

> If you like school people tease you that you're a little goody goody and everything so really you've got to hate school if you want to like people. If you like it people will tease you. Some people like school too but they still think it's cool to hate school but they actually like it.

The secondary boys illustrate similar contradictions. They acknowledge the senselessness of ridiculing those boys who are committed to school, but still find it impossible to reconcile this commitment with the need to be popular:

> *I*: Are boys who are good at their schoolwork popular?
>
> *Secondary group*: No. 'Cause they don't spend time looking for friends. They spend time doing their schoolwork.
> And they're just not respected the guys who get in there and do their work.
> It's pretty stupid though.
> Yes it is yeah.
> It's one thing to be good at your schoolwork and another thing to be a teacher's pet and suck up to everybody.
> It'd be good to be social and play basketball at lunchtime and have lots of friends and also do your schoolwork, but rarely do you find that happening. People who don't make friends, don't play basketball, don't do anything, they just stick to one little group if they even have a group and just do schoolwork and . . .
> Talk about computers.
> Yeah, they're not respected. I have no respect for them.

In promoting boys' classroom learning, this must surely be one of the most troubling aspects of the dominant form of masculinity to be found in schools. For some boys, it is sufficient to discourage them from any commitment to learning. For others, a pragmatic compromise may lead them to work to the extent necessary to fulfil their instrumental aims, though this will be done at the risk of being slighted as effeminate. In the cases cited here, those boys who do openly commit to school learning will be ostracised or worse.

CONCLUSION

This review of masculinities in schools shows how varied are the styles and practices of boys' developing sense of themselves, and how each form of masculinity establishes a different relationship with school. It is important to note the tensions among the different groups of boys and the hostility that their differences so often generate. It is as if their struggle to achieve a satisfactory form of masculinity involves competing with and putting down alternatives. The macho form must assert itself by rejecting the softness of the others, but the others also typically define themselves, at least in part, by their difference from the dominant form. Also, while the physical dominance of the macho boys may place them in a powerful position in the peer culture, all the groups present themselves as powerful and superior in terms of some criterion, be it intellectual hardness, coolness and style, or pragmatic careerism. All these qualities can be a source of strength and toughness.

It is hard to see this competitiveness as being anything other than encouraged by schooling, where individualism and competitive definitions of success are rife. On the other hand, despite the school's best attempts, most boys do not commonly apply this individual competitiveness to schoolwork. Here the group solidarity, in which so many boys find security, serves to outlaw a too conspicuous or enthusiastic adoption of school values. To accept the school's invitation to academic learning is seen by many boys, especially the more oppositional ones, to be accepting a position of subservience and immaturity.

Toughness seems to characterise much of the boys' approach to the world and to relations with others. They see success as a struggle with other boys or with teachers, though seldom with girls. Toughness is both a means to the end, in its contribution to school success and group popularity, but also an end in itself, as part of their developing masculinity. It combines with pragmatism and competitiveness as a motivation to schoolwork and sport, but while these values are quite compatible with the dominant values of sport, they tend to limit boys' commitment to learning to those areas of the curriculum which are seen to be useful in getting on. To be seen to commit to schoolwork for its own sake would be seen by a number of these groups as acquiescing to school authority, as taking on the values of the school, as going over to the other side. For most of them it would also risk being seen as effeminate.

The consequence of these cultural practices is to create a series of oppositions which boys must negotiate if they are to be both scholarly and masculine. While the experiences of gender of particular boys is complex, and changes with context, their performance of masculinity is always constructed in relation to a dominant image of gender difference. In schools, the oppositions line up to create two competing discourses within which boys are positioned, and can be represented in the usual way:

active	passive
popular	isolated
sporting	bookish
playing	reading
masculine	feminine

The challenge for schools is to confront this opposition by using it against itself. By breaking down this pattern, the oppositions can be deconstructed, and a more open set of possibilities created. The question of how this might be done will be taken up in the final chapter.

However, while the deconstruction of these heterosexual distinctions is important for all boys, there are also other cultural patterns built around questions of 'race', ethnicity and sexuality which affect some boys more directly than others. For this reason, we need to look more closely at the experiences of boys who are different from the majority in terms of their 'race', ethnicity or sexuality. This is the subject of the next chapter.

Masculinity at the margins

We noted in chapter 2 the need to see masculinity as diverse, dynamic and changing, and to acknowledge plural masculinities rather than to assume a singular discourse. Masculine identity is not constructed as some abstract idea which is then applied to experience; nor is it developed as a dimension of people's lives hermetically sealed from its other aspects. Masculinity is always constructed in relationships and situations which are necessarily impregnated with all those other dimensions of human experience by which we recognise ourselves and others as human. For most people most of the time, particular ways of being male may seem obvious, universal and natural, but this is more a reflection of the pervasiveness of masculine discourses than of some necessary core of masculine identity.

We have seen in the previous chapter, for instance, how class relationships affect the way that male dominance and success are construed. Different positions in the hierarchical relations of class give different perspectives on the meaning of competition, success and status. Since these are important criteria in the dominant image of being masculine, masculinity will, in some respects at least, be experienced differently for different class locations. At the same time, the experience of masculinity in any particular class position will be constructed with the awareness that there are competing forms practised by others, and that these may in fact be a threat to one's own masculine project. Working-class males may be dismissive of the airs and graces of the 'silvertails', who in turn may regard them as unintelligent louts. Both are promoting their own form of masculinity and defending it from attack from the other. So different class masculinities are not simply choices from a range of independent options; they are ways of being male that are constructed in competitive relation to each other. Of course, both forms, along with all masculinities, will be constructed in contrast to being feminine, and will therefore have much in common.

Many boys are not well placed in this aggressive and defensive mix which is the competitive process of constructing masculinity. For various reasons, they are not accorded equal status in the struggle for acceptance within dominant forms of masculinity. Boys with disabilities, for instance, are marginalised if they are unable to conform to the demands for competence in aggressive and competitive performance of play, or do not match the image of the masculine body, or if they are not accepted as potential participants in the increasingly important arena of sexual relations. Gerschick and Miller relate the experience of Jerry, a sixteen-year-old disabled boy who commented on how important it is to be accepted by others as masculine. Jerry explained the difficulty of thinking of himself as masculine if others didn't regard him as a man, 'because if they don't think of you as one, it is hard to think of yourself as one or it doesn't really matter if you think of yourself as one if no one else does'. Jerry also tells of his non-status with girls, who regard him 'as a "really nice person", but not like a guy per se . . . I think to some extent that you're sort of genderless to them'.[1]

Disabled boys are subject to the same cultural images of masculinity as others; that it involves a denial of weakness, emotions and frailty.[2] They will often value sport as much as those who are not disabled, and seek the same success and rewards.[3] Yet disabled boys are often stigmatised as weak, pitiful, passive and dependent. They are often perceived as either asexual innocents or animals with little control over their sexual desires.[4] They may also be subject to further marginalisation if they differ from the dominant group in terms of 'race', class or sexuality. Again we see how masculinity is constructed simultaneously in relation to other boys and girls and the assumptions of heterosexuality, but always in association with other dimensions of being human.

This relational aspect of masculinity is important to bear in mind in this chapter, as we consider how diverse masculinities are constructed in relation to other forms of difference. For just as class location creates different and competing forms of masculinity, and as disability marginalises boys and girls in heterosexual relations, so 'race', ethnicity and sexuality also produce different sets of relations with gender. All boys grow up as members of what are defined by themselves and/or others as particular 'race' or ethnic groups. For some boys in particular minority groups, this definition becomes a conspicuous part of their identity. For those in the majority culture, it may, like dominant masculinity, appear to be the normal way to be, and its cultural practices taken for granted. In this way, dominant ways of being masculine in any society will be a function of the majority culture. Those who are not part of this majority work out a gender identity by negotiating the meanings and practices of their own original culture and that of the dominant majority.

Equally, all boys negotiate masculinity by addressing dominant assumptions of heterosexuality, the view that to be masculine is to be heterosexual. For those boys who identify as homosexual or bisexual, or who are uncertain of their sexuality, this is a challenge made more difficult by the fact that this dominant heterosexuality defines itself as superior and hostile to the homosexual alternative. In this respect, boys who are gay, whether from the cultural majority or from a minority group, are uniquely placed within the multiple forms of masculinity, for they are openly subverting one of its central tenets, the assumption of heterosexuality.

MASCULINITY, 'RACE' AND ETHNICITY

A key aim of this book has been to recognise the diversity of forms which masculinity can take as it is constructed from the discourses available in boys' everyday lives. This aim coincides with developments in research in 'race' and ethnicity, which have increasingly emphasised the diversity of minority experiences and identities. We cannot 'read off the educational, cultural, or political behavior of minority or majority groups from assumptions about "race" pure and simple. Different gender and class interests within minority and majority groups often cut at right angles to racial politics'.[5] Just as minority cultures produce different masculinities, so the construction of gender introduces differences into minority experience.

British commentators have noted the lack of detailed analyses of the lives of black men and black masculinity as 'one of the most striking absences in the masculinity literature'.[6] This applies even more strongly in the Australian context, where, for instance, discussions of Aboriginal men and masculinity are almost completely absent. To the extent that gender relations are seen to be relevant to the experiences of Aboriginal people, and to their educational experiences in particular, researchers have focused on the position of women and girls, but not their male counterparts. Men and boys from immigrant minority ethnic groups are equally overlooked. This is not to say that Aboriginal boys and men have not been researched, discussed, analysed, problematised, etc., but rather that, when they have been the subject of the (usually white) researchers' gaze, they have been ungendered, included in a neutered category of Aboriginal person. In reality, much of this analysis has implicitly been about men, as the dominant image of Aborigines is, like that of white Australians, male. For instance, it is common for commentators to talk about the problem of crime committed by Aboriginal youth, yet over 80 per cent of juvenile offenders are male.[7] Despite this, the issue of gender is simply not considered.

Aboriginal boys and girls experience a range of forms of disadvantage to a greater extent than the population as a whole. They live with poverty, poor health and unemployment to a much greater extent than any other group in the community. Their health problems, especially hearing loss due to otitis media, are particularly significant contributors to educational disadvantage. Also, on a range of educational indicators, Aboriginal children fare less well than other Australians.[8] Absenteeism is a major problem, with Aboriginal students likely to lose the equivalent of between two and four years of schooling over their school lives.[9] Retention rates to year 12 are about half that of the population as a whole, and achievement levels are significantly lower.

These important problems have, however, led research and policy to emphasise deficit theories of indigenous peoples, focusing on what they lack in terms of the dominant culture. They have also highlighted negative images of deviance through drug taking, criminality and violence.[10] In discussing these important issues among indigenous people, and the disturbing incidence of them in some contexts, we must never forget that, while 'the pressures of living in a hostile broader society . . . have led many young Aboriginal men, especially, to lead self-destructive lives and to perpetuate acts of violence against those close to them, the fact remains that that is not the picture for the majority of Aboriginal people'.[11]

In contrast to these negative images, we need to recognise that Aboriginal and Islander[12] children experience many positives in their close-knit community lives, and they share with other young people many of the experiences of growing up in the broader society. Groome and Hamilton studied the educational needs of Aboriginal adolescents in schools in Western Australia, and could not generally distinguish their lifestyles, world views and interests from those of their non-Aboriginal peers in the same socio-economic group. However, they did observe that these young Aboriginal people do have a distinctive sense of identity as being Aboriginal, which for some can be a cause of confusion and embarrassment, but which for most is 'a growth area of their lives which they foster and nurture, valued as a source of personal strength and self esteem'.[13] Groome and Hamilton further comment that we should not ignore the 'strength, courage, resilience and success that exemplifies the struggles and survival of Nyungar families and life'.[14]

So Aboriginal and Islander boys face many of the same challenges of developing masculinity as boys from the rest of the community. However, they face a number of additional tests which mark them off from their white peers: they are all members of a cultural minority in white institutions, with all the misunderstanding, conflicting goals, poor communication and lack of cultural capital that involves; they are all subject to strong forms of racism; and many of them live in conditions of frightening poverty and violence resulting from the destruction of traditional society by colonisation. Seen in this way, the chief issue for Aboriginal and Islander boys is how to deal with the competitive pressures of masculinities in their own cultural traditions and those of the dominant European culture, and how, at the same time, to confront the experience of racism which exacerbates this dilemma. Part of this problem is how Aboriginal and Islander boys are constructed by the white culture which dominates the institutions of contemporary society, especially the school.

In the English-speaking world, white majorities have stereo-typed black masculinity around a number of themes: 'Men of color are constructed as criminal, violent, lascivious, irresponsible, and not particularly smart'.[15] The black stud image, where black men are feared by white majorities for their reputed hypersexuality, is derived from early racist beliefs that black men are subhuman and animalistic.[16] Another theme is the demeaning image of black men as childlike, as in the white American reference to them as 'boys',[17] or the 'slow-witted, lazy, happy-go-lucky creatures fawning on the goodwill of their masters', the Sambos of American popular culture.[18] Yet another image is of a crisis in black masculinity, where slavery and colonialism are thought to have symbolically castrated and emasculated black men, producing a matriarchal culture in which young men bond together in unruly and violent ways in the absence of a fatherly authority.[19]

Australian racism is fed by all of these images. Our racist past has grown from the same Eurocentric origins as Britain and the US, and contemporary Australian culture is still powerfully infused by these media messages. Equally, however, the particular historical and cultural context in Australia has created its own brand of racist treatment of Aboriginal and Islander people (and, of course, other ethnic groups, especially Asian). To understand black masculinity in Australia, we need to combine this analysis of the global and local contexts with a recognition of the great range of ways in which black men have responded to this treatment; no singular stereotype will suffice. This is particularly so for Aboriginal boys who are growing up in a world where many of the old stabilities are in flux, offering new experiences and opportunities and creating new barriers and problems. In this respect, they share many of the uncertainties and challenges facing all boys, but they address these from a position grounded in the unique situation of their 'race' in Australian society.

In their discussion of Aboriginal boys, Groome and Hamilton comment on the boys' preference for sport over academic achievement and their lower academic aspirations relative to girls. They are also seen as being more aggressive and more easily provoked, and feeling a conflict between the more adult treatment and responsibilities they may be given at home, and being treated as children at school.[20] Some Aboriginal families have traditionally encouraged assertive and independent behaviour, admiring cheekiness as one sign of this.[21] As a result, many Aboriginal boys are particularly susceptible to shaming, perhaps because, in their own communities, they are often given more independence and acceded adult status earlier than white communities tend to do.[22] One consequence is that, when in school, they are returned to the lower status of child, and are therefore at risk of and sensitive to being demeaned. In this way, the discourses of masculinity and 'race' heighten the tensions of schooling, creating a fragile set of relations which are easily disturbed. The difficulty here is that this conflict may make an early departure from school an attractive alternative for some Aboriginal boys, where 'the lure of an independent life, with excitement and risk, may be preferable to school if it is a place of stress and pressure, failure, alienation and boredom'.[23]

The most significant distinction between Aboriginal or Islander experience and that of the white majority is the constant racism of everyday life, ranging from verbal to physical harassment and the myriad forms of put-downs, snubs and embarrassments in even the most trivial of everyday situations. Groome and Hamilton point out that children are taught at home how to respond to these negative messages, either by 'giving as good as they get' and challenging any threat, or ignoring or avoiding threatening situations. The experience of racism begins in the earliest years of primary school, but it is especially sorely felt during adolescence, where friendship and dating are increasingly divided by racial boundaries, with sometimes negative and violent results.[24] On the other hand, Groome and Hamilton observed generally 'relaxed and cordial relationships' in most of the schools they visited.[25]

The cultural situation of Aboriginal and Islander students is nonetheless constantly fraught with tension. Their families need to make them independent and self-reliant, and yet at the same time encourage a strong sense of affiliation with and loyalty to the group.[26] While wanting their children to succeed at school, parents must also be wary of the risk of shame, disappointment and failure that their children run in a white institution. Some boys and girls create pressures against commitment by others to academic success, seeing as a 'shame job' any notable school achievement, and questioning whether students who stay on at school are, for example, 'real Aborigines'. On the other hand, students with academic aspirations see their peers as troublemakers. As in any community, tensions exist among Aboriginal and Islander people, but they also sense the imperative to support each other when any of their number is threatened by racism.[27]

The responses to these situations are diverse, but in the process Aboriginal students construct their sense of identity. For some this is a difficult experience in which their Aboriginality is never fully addressed; others achieve it by struggling through a series of 'misgivings and fears'; for others it is a positive journey into a supportive community.[28] Whatever the route, those students who achieve a strong sense of identity are more likely to succeed at school, perhaps because they have the confidence to accept those white values necessary for success without fear of losing their own cultural connection. However, for many Aboriginal students, there is little opportunity to find this security in knowing and identifying with their culture. Beresford and Omaji, in their Western Australian survey of Aboriginal young people, found that over 70 per cent said they knew 'little' or 'very little' about their Aboriginal culture, but, when asked how important knowledge about their culture was to them, a similar proportion said it was 'important' or 'very important'.[29]

Even in remote communities, this need for a positive identity is not always easily met, for drug abuse and violence have in many places become endemic as traditional relationships have been destroyed by years of white rule.[30] The close-knit family relationships which are so important in this process have in many communities broken down as a result of drunkenness and other substance abuse and violence. In these contexts, the traditional cultural transition from juvenile to adult man has in some cases been replaced by an initiation into a culture of alcohol misuse and violence. Domestic violence in particular has been explained as 'one way in which males reassert their lost authority which has accompanied cultural destruction'.[31] The outcome of all this has been referred to as a 'crisis of identity' which has produced a 'new form of male identity' based on regular and heavy drinking, and the new initiation ritual of prison.[32]

In other contexts, forming and maintaining a secure sense of Aboriginal and Islander identity is no doubt becoming increasingly difficult in the face of rapid social and cultural change, especially in urban settings where their communities are less discrete and self-contained than many rural ones. One example of this is the adoption by many Aboriginal boys of black American cultural patterns in dress, rap music, basketball and language, in what Groome and Hamilton describe as 'a strong manifestation of a resistance-type culture'.[33]

While this may well be a form of resistance, to other observers this cultural style is a less demanding assertion of cultural difference than a distinctively Aboriginal expression would require. For the adoption of this style asserts a black identity while avoiding a public association with controversial issues such as land rights, welfare issues and other matters, where an explicit Aboriginal perspective might provoke hostility from whites. In other words, adopting the popular culture of another country, one promoted in media advertising and made attractive to white and black Australians, may be a substitute for and an evasion of the need to confront one's distinctive Aboriginal identity. Dawes' study of Aboriginal and Torres Strait Islander subcultures illustrates this point: one boy explains his preference for American rap over Aboriginal protest music, saying he is 'not into that political stuff'.[34]

Another problem here is whether this adoption of black American culture carries with it that brand of compulsive masculinity, typified by gangster rap, which emphasises sexual aggression, misogyny and toughness.[35] The self-identification of Aboriginal and Islander groups through graffiti tags, borrowed from black American youth culture, suggests that there is a growing connection here.[36] While these groups are not necessarily criminal other than in the act of graffiti itself, the practice does bring them into confrontation with the police, and can be a step into a wider world of crime. In Beresford and Omaji's description of Aboriginal youth groups known to police in Western Australia, there are various elements in the popular notion of gang behaviour. These groups, predominantly boys between the ages of ten and eighteen, are formed around and sustained by the leadership of a 'main man', who is usually over fifteen and a chronic offender. Incarceration increases a boy's status in the group, and crimes increase the group's cohesiveness.[37]

Car stealing in particular is an avenue to fame and notoriety, and is seen as a game and part of the private war with police. Beresford and Omaji see car theft and high-speed chases as a 'function of identity formation' as they 'provide the means to the rite of passage from childhood to manhood central to traditional Aboriginal custom'.[38] A parliamentary inquiry observed that a '15 year old boy in a 208 Commodore' being chased by 'a full grown white police officer in a special pursuit car' is 'the ultimate proof of manhood to some of these boys'.[39] This cultural practice is a fascinating example of the interplay between 'race' and masculinity. A poor and marginalised group of boys uses a powerful status symbol of a dominant culture to challenge male police authority and boost their own masculine and cultural image.

But what can we say in all this about the interplay of Aboriginal and Islander boys and their negotiation of the discourses of masculinity in school? In his analysis of how American black men have responded to the racist impediments to success in a competitive society, Franklin describes five forms of black masculinity, which have parallels among Australian black men.[40] While constructed as ideal types of how black men have addressed the demands of careers and the economy, they also provide a hypothesis about the range of responses which black students might make to the demands of success in school.

The first type of response is the 'conformist', who goes along with the dominant ideology of success as promoted by white middle-class society. The 'conformist' may or may not succeed, but to choose this route will place great strain on their relations with their own community, as they can be seen as going over to the other side.[41] Second, the 'ritualist' accepts this ideology and follows its rules, but without really believing that it will bring him success, going through the motions with neither real purpose nor commitment. Third, the 'innovator' finds ways of beating a discriminatory system, achieving some success in niches like music, or in deviant ways through crime. The parallel in schools might be the achievement of status by succeeding in sporting or cultural arenas, by creating a popular image of cool style, or by bullying other students. Outside school, the graffiti gangs and car thieves just described seem to fit this image, as the boys clearly see these practices as daring and creative ways of confronting the system.

A fourth type is the 'retreatist', who simply withdraws from the attempt to succeed, dropping out, falling into unemployment and welfare or drug dependency, a frighteningly common fate for many Aboriginal and Islander boys, most powerfully depicted in Folds' study of glue sniffers among the Pitjantjatjara people of South Australia.[42] Finally, Franklin describes the 'rebel', who rejects the ideology of success and its false premise of equal opportunity, but who might also in the process find a new understanding of his position and how to make a positive response to it. This might include the many Aboriginal and Islander people who reject school but later return to education through various forms of adult provision, or who achieve success in political, community or artistic arenas.

Of course, this typology of responses might also apply to the reactions of young people whose relations to school are not primarily defined by 'race', reminding us that not all aspects of the black experience are uniquely the result of racism alone. Nor should we see this experience as uniform, for the range of situations of Aboriginal and Islander young people in Australia is considerable, especially in the differences among metropolitan, provincial and remote communities.[43] On the other hand, the particular detail of students' responses will be created by the relations between the discourses of schooling and the class and cultural origins of the students. From this perspective, the diverse responses are, in the case of black boys, joined by a common thread, the experience of racial division and cultural difference.[44]

One boy's experience of school is valuably depicted by Glenn Dawes in his case study of an Aboriginal and Torres Strait Islander boy named Scott, whose account of school life illustrates many of the points raised here.[45] Scott's attitude to school was almost entirely determined by his assessment of whether teachers and principals treated him fairly, and with what he felt was due care and respect. Positive relations in a small primary school, where the principal knew and showed a personal interest in Scott and his family, gave way to a strained atmosphere in secondary school, where the impersonal administration was seen by Scott to indicate that teachers didn't care about him. In this environment, he became antagonistic to teachers who dobbed him in or ignored his complaints or requests. This antagonism seemed to be fuelled by a macho bravado: he dismissed caning as of no concern, saw new teachers as a test to be stood up to, and became angry, resentful and aggressive if he was directly challenged by those he thought were not entitled to do so, or who did so unfairly.

Scott also had a very specific concept of authority, and he was quite ready to accept strict teachers if they were fair. Only the principal was entitled to dob him in to his parents, a view perhaps related to the cultural values of Aboriginal societies where 'only some people, generally the *boss* of a child, have a right to punish a child'.[46] For Scott, punishment was acceptable if it was fair and if warning was given, but a private word on the quiet was much preferred to a public bawling out which he felt was degrading. Again there is the hint here of the importance of public honour and respect, and a heightened sensitivity to shaming, especially if it was seen to be unfair. Many boys feel this masculine sense of honour and public face, and resentment at unfair treatment, and the sensitivities these feelings generate are no doubt at the root of many confrontations between boys and school authority. For Aboriginal boys like Scott, this fraught situation is likely to be exacerbated by a number of aspects of his cultural relations to the school and how they interact with these masculine sensitivities.

First, Scott, like many Aboriginal boys mentioned earlier, seemed to see himself as more mature and independent than the school was likely to accept, so any demeaning of him would be taken as an insult to an extent that teachers may not have understood. Researchers have commented on how the authority structure of mainstream schooling is at odds with the assumptions of Aboriginal students. For instance, leaving class without permission is a common reason for suspension of Aboriginal students which they may see as simply 'exercising their accustomed independence or freedom'.[47] Certainly, there was a mature confidence, courage and independence in Scott's willingness to confront the principal and teachers when he thought his needs were not being met. He also regarded himself as something of a leader among his classmates.

Second, Scott was not academically successful, so his status and public and self-image were, from one perspective at least, at risk just by being at school. Any further threat may have been simply more than he could bear. Finally, Scott was aware that he was a member of a cultural minority, so that, for instance, the Aboriginal counsellor was the only person he felt able to confide in. This membership must have hung like a cloud over whatever expectations and aspirations he held for school success, for he would have been aware of the experiences of most of his Aboriginal peers. The thought must also have weighed on him that any perceived slight or unfair treatment may have been because he was Aboriginal, making him more likely to respond with resentment and righteous indignation.

Of course, while in any particular case the accusation of racism may or may not be warranted, there is no doubt that it is a common part of the black experience. Connolly has provided valuable insights into the connection between racism and masculinity in his analysis of racist incidents in schools. The chief situations in which racist incidents arose were competitive, 'essentially masculine' ones, where student frustration and anger led to aggressive confrontations and then racist abuse. A second type of situation occurred in public spaces where 'there is more at stake for children who are continually in the process of constructing and maintaining their identities and status'.[48] Sport, especially football, was a common context for racist abuse, being a highly public arena where performance was an important test of masculine status. This public and competitive element of racism among children connects in interesting ways with the concern for public respect and the threat of shaming among minority cultures.[49]

For people to be accorded public respect by their peers, they must be accepted as members of a group with common rights and some set of shared experiences on which empathy can be based. Immigrant minority cultures may be placed in a particularly difficult position here. In Australia, a common xenophobic view is that, as immigrants have chosen to migrate, any attempt to retain connections with their origins is inexplicable and largely illegitimate. And yet, such immigrants have no option but to identify with each other and their original culture for at least some time, and are likely to retain indefinitely sympathies, loyalties and affinities with their origins at the same time as developing new ones in their adopted country. In such a situation, defensive and ultimately aggressive feelings of opposition from and to the majority may result. For instance, Moore's study of skinheads and other English adolescent subcultural groups in Perth shows how this violent culture was an aggressive reaction to the disparaging image of 'Poms' promoted by some traditional Australian prejudices. Fighting was physical proof that they were willing to stand with their English mates against the Australian cultural majority, and that they were tougher than their Australian peers.[50]

In other contexts, boys from cultural minorities will react in much less conspicuous ways. Jetnikoff recounts how boys from immigrant minority cultures constructed their relations with other boys through a carefully controlled process of concealment and presentation of self. In order to reduce their difference from their peers, they downplayed their intelligence and the distinctive cultural identity, while working to fit in by joking around and wasting time in class. This public presentation of the image of a less-than-committed student was made possible by long hours of school work at home.[51]

Rizvi identified among primary school children an opposition to immigrant groups which arose from some sense that these groups had fewer rights than long-term residents. Some of the children felt that, while Aborigines had a right to be respected because they had always been here, Asians had no such right. To these children, Asians were aliens who could reasonably be shunned without incurring accusations of racism.[52] This sentiment was also strong among the Anglo-Saxon-Celtic (ASC) boys in Walker's study discussed in the previous chapter. Walker depicts a dominant Australian culture in the school with which other students, including immigrant cultural groups (like Moore's skinheads), had to contend in constructing their identity and status, including that of gender.

In the largely working-class school in Walker's study, the cultural hierarchy was very much connected with that common measure of masculinity—sport. More specifically, the only acceptable form of sport was one of the rugby codes; soccer was seen as 'wog ball'. The footballers set the terms of the cultural agenda, and while this was at its core an ASC group, some boys of European immigrant families, and one Aboriginal boy, were part of it. Asian boys, who did not play football, were at the bottom of the cultural hierarchy, along with three ASC boys who rejected the macho football culture. As Walker observes, 'Male homosexuals were regarded with contempt or loathing', and 'anything "Asian" attracted as intense vituperation as "poofs"'.[53]

Luke has discussed the struggle that Asian men face in constructing a masculine identity 'without any of the defining characteristics of dominant masculinity—white skin, hairy chests, beards and facial hair, big arms and big muscles'.[54] Cheng's American research shows how white males connect this different form of masculinity with a 'nerd' image.[55] The result of all of this for the Asian boys in Walker's study was that they

> retired to outer space (it might as well have been in both senses of the words) on the furthest perimeter of the grounds, often sitting in a small circle, hopefully inconspicuously, but in fact with their strangeness and cultural distance open for all to see and mostly to misinterpret.[56]

The Greek boys in Walker's study felt the tension between identifying as Greek and participating in the footballer culture, dominated as it was by an ASC ethos. Some of them succeeded in this culture; others did not. However, the Greeks were as one with the ASCs in their heterosexuality and disgust at perceived homosexuality.[57] Walker claims that, for the boys he studied, the problems of becoming a man cut deeper on the personal level than ethnic problems, and 'penetrated the centre of the personal identity of each individual'.[58] Yet despite this, the extent of the dominance of hegemonic masculinity meant that boys could not even discuss alternatives. While arguments about ethnicity were well developed among the boys, and often enthusiastically debated, those boys who found dominant masculinity unworkable were unable to articulate their concerns.

In many respects, negotiating masculinity is a universal challenge for boys which is cast in the terms of the dominant heterosexual culture. However, cultural difference produces unique perspectives and experiences of these challenges. In some cases, as Walker claimed of the Greek boys in his study, gender is the more central issue for boys. In other cases, observers claim that 'race' is such a dominant concern for boys that issues of gender tend to be taken for granted.[59] But this will vary from case to case, and the unique interactions among 'race', ethnicity and gender need constantly to be borne in mind. At the same time, we need to be aware that most of the discussion of these issues has been in a context dominated by the assumptions, expectations and prejudices of heterosexuality. While this is problematic enough in itself, for boys who are gay or who are uncertain about their sexuality, the presumptions and prejudices of heterosexuality are a major difficulty.

GAY STUDENTS AND SCHOOL CULTURES

Gay boys occupy a significant position in the performance of masculinity in schools in two respects. Homosexuality is, despite attempts to repress it, a form of masculinity available to students, and the experience of gay students is another instance of boys' school culture. But gays also represent a form of being male against which dominant masculinities identify and define themselves, and so the styles and practices of homosexuality are involved in the construction of masculinity for all boys.

Research has tended to overlook the first of these aspects of being gay at school, focusing much more on how dominant masculinity constructs itself in opposition to homosexuality. In fact, past research has tended to pathologise behaviour which does not conform to heterosexual expectations. For instance, boys who prefer playing with girls have been pathologised as 'sissies', and it has been accepted as natural that other boys would not want to play with them. Also, within this perspective, the assumptions of masculine superiority have seen effeminate boys as a greater problem than tomboy girls.[60] Such views testify to and sustain the privileged nature of masculinity.

Only recently has there been a concerted attempt to study the position of gay boys and their experiences in schools. In the course of this work, the most outstanding point has been the difficulties gay boys face in coming to terms with their sexuality in a context which is negative and often openly hostile to homosexuality. For instance, in Mac An Ghaill's study, teachers represented gays in very negative terms, regarding them as effeminate and mother-dominated, and as suffering from 'arrested sexual development, predatory sexual practices, psychological sickness and disease-related behaviour'.[61] Homosexuality was seldom mentioned in class and when it was it was usually in connection with AIDS. As a result, gay students were isolated, confused and alienated.

Becoming gay is not a simple choice which can be discouraged by not mentioning it, though many parents and teachers seem to wish it were. This has meant that the negative attitudes and treatment surrounding gays have not been adequately confronted. In New South Wales, the Department of School Education was reluctant to move towards an anti-homophobia policy, since many parents and others in the community did not openly support such a policy.[62] A 1989 Australia-wide survey found that many Australians did not believe that lesbians and gay men have a right to equality with other members of our society. Forty-seven per cent of respondents thought it should not be illegal to discriminate against a person because they were homosexual.[63] Being attracted to one's own sex has carried such a strong cultural taboo that school communities and systems will need to work hard to overcome these prejudices. Yet they must do so if the rights of gays are to be protected.

There is a danger that, by focusing on the vilification of gay students, we will portray them only as victims, overlooking their 'courage, fortitude, agency and sheer will to survive',[64] and the intimacy, pleasure and sense of identity which their sexuality, like heterosexuality, can provide.[65] One fourteen-year-old gay boy, who is taking the New South Wales Education Department to court for failing to protect him from vilification, asserts: 'I like the way I am and I can't change the way I walk, the way I act, the way I talk because I've tried it before and I don't feel me'.[66] In Mac An Ghaill's research, gay boys were very politically aware, and were able to analyse and discuss how the hegemony of heterosexuality constrained and threatened them. They felt superior in their ability to talk about feelings in a positive way compared with the hatred, anger and dominance they saw among their straight persecutors. This gave them a confidence which was a valuable resource for dealing with homophobic hostility. One of the boys commented that '. . . I think that one of the main reasons that male straights hate us is because they really know that emotionally we are more worked out than them'.[67] On the other hand, there are cultural differences in boys' attitudes to gays, as when Dawes observed an unusual degree of tolerance of homosexuals among the Aboriginal and Torres Strait Islander boys he studied.[68]

There is also a variety of styles through which gay boys can present themselves. Some fulfil a camp stereotype, some exaggerate a highly macho form of masculinity, while others are quite conventional in style and appearance. As Redman and Mac An Ghaill remind us, 'the existence of gay machismo and heterosexual camp should alert us to the fact that the subject positions made available by discourses of masculinity do not determine subjectivity'.[69]

However, it is still the case that boys known or thought to be gay suffer most from bullying and vilification (defined as incitement to hatred, serious contempt or severe ridicule). In addition, gay students often hide their gayness, even from parents, increasing their isolation and their lack of support in working out their sexuality and dealing with the harassment which it might bring upon them. It should be no surprise that students in this predicament are at risk of dropping out of school or attempting suicide. One study showed that 25 per cent of lesbian and gay students leave school because of harassment,[70] and there is evidence that gays and lesbians are among the high risk groups for suicide.[71]

Homophobia seems a constant feature of dominant masculinity's attempts to distance itself from the threat that homosexuality poses. It is as if the achievement of heterosexuality is thought by many boys to require that they stigmatise and oppress homosexuality.[72] Gays are likely to be seen as a threat by young people who are uncertain about their own

161

emerging sexuality. Students also pick up prejudices from parents and other adults, no doubt strengthened in recent years by the emergence of AIDS and its demonisation in the media. However, students don't have to be gay to be affected by homophobia. 'Any lad who is quiet, or sensitive, or just thoughtful of others' is subject to attack.[73]

This fact gives an insight into the reasons for homophobia. In most cases, perpetrators of vilification, harassment, bullying and gay bashing do not know if their victims are gay; they only presume that they are, or associate them with some stereotype of what typical gay behaviour is thought to be. Terms like 'poof' and 'queer' are routinely used against any boy who does not conform, and yet gays can be captain of the football team and in outward appearance quite conformist to masculine image. On the other hand, studies of this issue show that boys who 'saw themselves as academic in orientation and had good relations with teachers, were often positioned by their classmates as gay, regardless of their heterosexual relationships'.[74]

In his study of homophobic harassment and violence in Queensland schools, Ward interviewed gay men on their experiences of homophobia in school. The ironies of the indiscriminate nature of homophobia are nicely illustrated by two of Ward's informants:

> *Peter*: I don't understand why I deserved to be bashed for who I was. The ironic thing about this is that the offenders were only working on the presumption that I was gay. They didn't know for a fact that I was as I didn't either at that stage of my life.
>
> *Marcus*: Even though I eventually realised I was gay, a few of the outcasts I became friends with did not and were heterosexual. They suffered the same degradation because they were different in various shapes and forms.[75]

Given the range of personal styles which gays and straights take on, and the weak connection between effeminate behaviour and gay sexuality, it seems that, to the perpetrators of anti-gay behaviour, it does not matter greatly whether they are correct in their accusations or not. This is exactly what Epstein believes to be the case. In her view, one that is now widely accepted, homophobia is not motivated simply by a contempt for homosexuality; rather, it plays a key role in policing and constructing heterosexual masculinities in schools.[76] The harassment of those perceived to be gay or effeminate is one way of rendering heterosexuality compulsory, through the punishment of deviance from heterosexual norms of masculinity. 'In this sense, the heterosexist harassment of gay men can be understood as a pedagogy of heterosexuality.'[77]

The pedagogy of heterosexuality is also learned by gays themselves, and studies of gay students cite examples of gay boys who achieve acceptance and status through their success in sport or some other pursuit admired in the dominant masculine ethos, and then protect themselves by using homophobic abuse. In Epstein's study, Simon, a big boy and a successful football player who came out when he was fourteen, explained that 'you would attack, perhaps rather than being attacked yourself'.[78]

Homophobia is not always vicious. Epstein and Johnson describe the 'mixture of embarrassment, fear and homoerotic desire characteristic of contexts like sporting changing rooms, pub sociality and boys' boarding schools', in which the mixed feelings and uncertainties of negotiating sexuality can be expressed through a 'humorous' or 'playful' acting out.[79] However, homophobia is also the pretext for some of the most vicious forms of violence in male culture, generated by dominant masculinity's repression and rejection of what it sees as the threat of homosexuality. Heterosexuality projects its 'anxieties, contradictions and irrationalities onto the subordinate term, filling it with the antithesis of its own identity'. In the process, the 'violence, antagonisms and aversions that are at the core of the dominant discourses and identities become manifest'.[80]

Gay bashing is a serious problem in Australia, and one striking feature of it is the fact that it is done by young people. Various studies have found that the overwhelming majority of perpetrators are 25 or younger. One Queensland study found that 57 per cent of attackers were estimated to be under twenty years old, with only 11 per cent over 25.[81] In New South Wales, there were 24 gay hate murders between 1990 and 1994, and nineteen people had been convicted by 1993. Of these convictions, eleven offenders were of school age, and overall fifteen school children have been involved in these cases.[82] These statistics give rise to concerns that gay bashing is not perceived by young people to be unacceptable. Homophobic community attitudes could easily be read by young people as condoning the practice.[83]

Homophobia and the vilification and violence it generates need to be seen as part of the construction of dominant masculinity. Name calling and physical and psychological abuse are not merely a series of incidental events arising from backward attitudes. They are part of a larger set of practices which assist in the construction of a daily gender and sexual reality.[84] This larger set of practices includes the range of distinctions and exclusions by which hegemonic masculinity is constructed. One of these is the rejection of homosexuality, another is the disparaging of femininity, and both are connected in the equation of homosexuality with effeminacy. Misogyny and homophobia are therefore closely linked in their relation to dominant masculinity.[85] In fact, it is the uncertainty and fear surrounding the construction of masculinity that creates both these forms of hatred.

If boys are to feel secure in their dominant masculinity, they must convince themselves and others that they will have no part of the feminine or the homosexual. Any doubts they might have will only produce a stronger rejection of these feelings, as they will threaten a boy's acceptance into the masculine community. This threat is a serious one, for the masculine community is active in its aggressive rejection of these threats and any who succumb to them. Only by seeing the construction of masculinity in this way can we understand the prevalence of homophobic abuse, the viciousness of homophobic violence, and the indiscriminate way in which boys label others as gay. Fear among adults and authorities of naming homosexuality has meant that much of this has been consciously ignored, leaving the students who have suffered from isolation and homophobia with inadequate support. Students in schools have a moral and legal right to expect freedom from this sort of offence, and school systems, teachers and parents have a moral and legal obligation to ensure such freedom. To fulfil these obligations, we need to put the needs of gay boys firmly on the agenda.

CONCLUSION

Being different from the majority in terms of 'race', ethnicity, disability or sexuality is in many respects an unenviable position for boys. While difference can be the basis of strong group solidarity and support, we have seen in the previous chapter the powerful pressures to conformity which characterise much of boys' school cultures. For boys who are different this presents problems at the individual level as they work out a sense of who they are, but it is most manifest in their relations with their peers. Of course, these two aspects of experience are inseparable, so the prevalence of racism and homophobia is a constant problem for how these boys see themselves and their place in society.[86]

It is important to see how these forms of discrimination work at both the interpersonal and the group level, so that we do not underestimate the importance of racist or homophobic harassment, explaining it away as some understandable comment from young people who 'don't know any better', or who are 'just repeating things they've heard without really meaning it'. To call someone a 'fag' or a 'coon' is not just a harmful personal insult. It calls up and threatens a widespread public communal condemnation. It invokes a powerful discourse and immediately places the victim, not just as someone at odds with the perpetrator, but as the sufferer of abuse by an entire community. It derogates not only themselves, but all those like them whom they know and love. In encouraging the acceptance of difference, we must not close our eyes to the viciousness with which it is sometimes attacked.

From their positions of difference, marginalised boys must come to terms with the dominant practices of heterosexual masculinity. In this respect they share the experiences of all boys, with all that that implies about their relations with girls. Marginalised boys are no less likely to be sexist than those of the majority group. Their cultural traditions, including some strains of gay culture, harbour their own kinds of misogyny. Their relations with girls and women may provide them with a rare opportunity to exert power over others, leading them to exploit the sexist practices that sustain this power. In compensating for their own sense of powerlessness, they may use this position of power with even greater force. On the other hand, their own experience of oppression may be a source of empathy for the powerlessness of girls and women.

Marginality provides an opportunity to see things from a different perspective. To this extent, boys who are different may have privileged insights into the constraints of dominant masculinity. This explains why the gay boys Mac An Ghaill interviewed were able to articulate with considerable insight their relations with heterosexuality. It may also contribute to the apparently greater tolerance for homosexuality which Dawes identified in his study of Aboriginal and Torres Strait Islander boys. On the other hand, their relatively powerless positions with respect to the dominant culture can make the challenges of constructing masculinity even greater.

In these ways, the outcomes for marginalised boys' negotiation of masculinity are as diverse as those of the society at large. At the same time, the problems of boys from marginal groups are more complex than those comfortably placed in a majority culture. Understanding the complexity of these relationships is a first step in helping these boys grow into adulthood.

Bad boys

Some would see anti-social behaviour as a euphemism for the disruption and hurt perpetrated by boys in schools and elsewhere. Perhaps it is, but it is a useful catch-all for the disruptive behaviour, harassment, bullying and violence which so many see as a major issue in today's schools. Two features of these behaviours warrant their consideration as a group here: they are overwhelmingly done by boys, and all are connected with masculine practices and values. This chapter reviews evidence about these anti-social practices and how they relate to the development of masculinity.

The discussion is organised in what might be seen as a continuum from less serious matters like misbehaving in class, to minor or moderate forms of verbal or physical harassment and bullying, to more serious violent acts like assault. However, we are not implying any simple sequence here. There is no reason to believe that the same boys are involved in all these acts, or that one such kind of behaviour leads on to more serious ones.

Rather, these behaviours represent a range of responses to different problems which boys face in their relations with other people. They do not have a common cause, and certainly are not all the result of a commitment to dominant masculinities. However, masculinity is connected with them all, and a key argument in this discussion is that understanding their connections with masculinity is a necessary though not sufficient condition for dealing with them.

One problem with these connections is that some people see all these forms of behaviour as springing from a common cause, with the result that attitudes to the behaviours are determined by whatever this common cause is thought to be. Most problematic are those views which hold that these behaviours are caused by male biology or some essentialist masculine personality. This leads to the belief that the more dangerous kinds of behaviour are simply a natural tendency gone wrong. It sees the lesser forms of anti-social behaviour, like aggressiveness, the small-scale skirmishing of pushing, shoving and punching, and occasional fighting, as just boys being boys. When this escalates to the level of injury, victimisation or public brawls, the reaction is that the natural tendency has simply gone too far, that it has merely overstepped the boundary between acceptable and unacceptable aggression, that it is out of control. The reaction is to constrain but not try to change it, to put the lid back on but to leave the pot bubbling.

This view is quite unsatisfactory. The boys who indulge in the more serious forms of this kind of behaviour are a minority, though all boys may feel they have to prepare for, condone and even silently suffer from it in order to avoid any suspicion that they are less masculine if they don't. The pervasiveness of this myth of natural aggression is one of the greatest constraints on the problem of making our schools safe places to be. Our discussion here considers these issues in the context of a range of behaviours in which the myth of natural aggression is involved.

Contrary to the myth of natural aggression, the tradition of studying boys' school cultures has tended to see all forms of boys' oppositional practice as stemming from a different cause: the rejection by many boys of the school's intellectual and social values and their accompanying regulatory impositions. This has meant that classroom misbehaviour, sexual harassment and bullying have been seen as different symptoms of the same underlying problem. For instance, Willis saw truancy, joking, violence, sexism and racism as different ways in which a class-based boys' school culture expressed opposition to authority and its own claims to independence.[1]

This view needs to be strongly questioned, for, as we will see, it does not accord with the evidence, and it can confound any attempts to deal with these problems. To neglect the specific nature and origins of these different forms of behaviour is to oversimplify, and to see them as just different ways of opposing authority is to ignore altogether the gender system of social relations in which they are implicated. To understand why boys are the overwhelming perpetrators of these kinds of behaviour we need to acknowledge the complex motivations and situational factors which generate them, and, of course, their relations with the construction of masculinity.

MISBEHAVING AND DISRUPTING CLASS

The evidence is overwhelming that boys are the chief culprits of disruptive behaviour in class. In an Australian Council for Educational Research (ACER) survey of gender issues in schools, 57 per cent of primary school respondents, both boys and girls, reported that boys often disrupted classes.[2] This rose to 61 per cent for secondary school respondents. Boys were reported two to three times as often as girls as the perpetrators of this behaviour. How do boys explain this?

The boys interviewed for this study held an interesting but complicated set of understandings which combine common knowledge and popular myth with personal confusion and contradiction. The result is an interesting insight into the difficult negotiations boys have to undertake to deal with this predominantly male behaviour.

When asked why boys misbehave, the common set of responses was that boys who misbehave are the ones 'who don't do their schoolwork', 'aren't as good at their schoolwork', 'try to show off in front of the girls', 'try to be popular', 'try to make people laugh', 'think they're cool', 'are bored'. The boys interviewed generally didn't include themselves in this category, though almost all said they had misbehaved at some time. It seemed natural for them that they would fall foul of school authority at some point. However, in the group discussions, the boys generally criticised as annoying or stupid those of their peers who misbehaved repeatedly.

They want to be cool.

They like to run each other down a lot and end up in fights and stuff.

And show off.

'Cause people laugh at people who make funny comments and stuff and they think they like them but usually they're laughing at them not with them.

They're people who play sport.

People that read don't do it.

People that don't like school. They're not really good at everything so they show off. Try to prove themselves to other people.

Some individual comments were very dismissive:

People think they're the big cool people and the big bosses but they're not really. 'Cause the boy who misbehaves in our class doesn't like school and isn't very bright and even says he likes getting into trouble. I don't think he likes the extra work. I don't think he gets much attention 'cause he doesn't play sport. Some of the sporty people they think it's a bit cool to misbehave. Some other boys think that's the only way they can get attention.

The really dorky people like the kid who sits in front of me he's a real nerd and he likes getting in trouble so he can get the attention or something. He thinks he's good for it.

He doesn't mean to put anybody down. He just tries to be funny and says 'hey everybody I'm here listen to me' and stuff. I didn't get a laugh out of that one . . . like I don't laugh with him I laugh at him. He's being stupid . . . He's tall and he's shaved his head. He tries to buy the gear but his parents aren't so rich so he'll come out with not the best stuff but not the worst stuff. Mrs C put him down the back of the class 'cause no one wanted to sit next to him.

However, the situation is more complicated. The boys distinguished between the disrupters who were rejected as trying too hard and those who were funny and popular, showing that it is possible to create a popular image by being 'funny' (and presumably therefore, in many cases, disruptive) in class. The statements give some insight into the fine distinctions and subtle rules which govern the acceptance of this behaviour.

> Their misbehaviour makes them popular a little bit but it depends who they are. Like Larry if he got into trouble they wouldn't worry about him 'cause they don't like him anyway.

> Boys who misbehave are alright because when you talk to them after they're not so bad. They just do it for a laugh. Sometimes it's funny but sometimes it's really dumb. People who do it in our class are not that popular.

> People laugh at them. But if it's someone else they don't like they think it's stupid. If it's someone they like they think it's funny. So when you see them again you say 'nice joke' and stuff. So you think it's not so bad if you get detention.

> Ian tends to get too stupid. He does make you laugh but he sometimes goes over the top. He puts people down and he makes other people laugh. But he makes [the one put down] feel bad. They're trying to get friends. It gets boring after a while.

> *Do guys gain popularity through mucking up?*
> Some people do, depends what they're saying to teachers. It makes the lesson a bit interesting. If a square starts giving the teacher crap everyone just tells them to 'shut up you're not funny'.

> It depends. If the guys who are misbehaving are quite popular no one cares. You have a laugh and it breezes over them.
> It's cool if he just does it a few times but if he's sitting there always trying to make jokes it's not funny.
> If it's not funny it's like shut up.

One boy was quite puzzled by the fact that disruption could make boys popular.

> For some strange reason they are [popular] 'cause most of the boys like them. I don't really know why they're so popular. I suppose it's because most kids are trying to be like them and stuff. They normally get a laugh from most kids for making stupid comments which they see as their great thing to do.

When disruption was seen as attention seeking, it was generally as an attempt to gain approval from other boys, but one boy saw it in more overtly heterosexual terms, a way of showing off to girls, behaviour for which he had little sympathy:

> Girls are quieter and boys try to show off more than the girls. They try to show off more than the girls 'cause they want the girl to like them. Teasing, putting other people down, shouting out. It makes me cross 'cause people show off and I can't cope with people showing off. They just do it to show off to girls. They're people who don't work and don't pay interest in homework and work. I'm fed up with them. I just think it's a waste of time. I don't like dobbing on people so I keep it quiet so when they get in trouble I think finally they've got in trouble.

Distinctions were also made among subjects as contexts for disruption. If subjects were interesting and engaging, then disruption was a nuisance; if not, disruption relieved the boredom. The following cases illustrate how boys can both practise and disapprove of disruptive behaviour depending on their interest in the subject. This again shows that we are not talking here of disruptive behaviour as some personality trait or socially deviant behaviour type, but as a contextualised response which has clear social rewards.

> I muck around a bit in science, not in stuff I enjoy like Shop A and Shop B. I get annoyed when people muck around 'cause I'm trying to do something good like make a dart board cabinet. They just keep on mucking around or something so you can't do it. *Do many guys muck up in Shop A and B?* A few blokes that are not really good at it. They just go to muck around for a bludge subject. I like going in there and doing it straight away. If a boy's getting bored with their classwork they start giving teachers flak and muck around a bit. *Why would you muck up in science?* I just don't like it, never liked it.

> *Do you muck up?* Not really. I usually just sit there. I do occasionally. It's not like an everyday thing.
> *What do you think of guys who give the teacher a hard time?* It depends on the class. If you're in a class that's really

important say like a maths class or a science class or something I don't think the people tend to muck up as much, but if you're in something like PE or music or something people might tend to mess around a bit 'cause they think it's a bludge class.

Related to this is the way in which the teacher is seen to be a part of the context for disruptive behaviour, sometimes to the point of provoking it. A typical comment was that teachers impose more punitive penalties on boys than girls for exhibiting similar behaviour. In other claims, teachers' discriminatory or unacceptable actions were described as unfair and as justification for retaliation. In the last example, even ·the hard core disrupter can raise a laugh at the teacher's expense.

Like people with earrings in our class Mr J gets up them more than other people . . .
There's this kid Alan who's got an earring.
Yeah he gets in trouble so much. And he talks only a little bit and he's the one who gets in trouble 'cause he's got an earring.
Every time he turns round to borrow an eraser or a sharpener or something.

Sometimes I misbehave and I don't mean to do it and I get in trouble and I'm just sick of them so I keep on doing it to get 'em annoyed . . . Sometimes he thinks I'm doing it and he blames it on me and I haven't done anything bad. And if someone does it he says one more warning and if I do it he doesn't give me a warning . . . That's when I got really annoyed.
In grade 4 the teacher used to throw blackboard dusters.
Cool! (Exclamation from other group members)
And you'd be dodging all these blackboard dusters and one day he threw one at Jimmy and it hit him on the back of the head and Jimmy turned around and went whack and hit him in the face. And he didn't get in trouble for it.

And Lou in Japanese in grade 5 . . . didn't say 'konnichiwa' or something and he ran out the door and ran out of school and someone told me that he was crying. He got kicked out of every school in the Northern Territory and he was proud of it too.

He was giving all the teachers brown-eyes and Mr Y said I'll break your leg or something and he said 'I'll shoot ya' and just walked off. He'd just walk off. (laughter)

We can see in all of this the distinctions boys make between acceptable and unacceptable behaviour, and the grey area in between where there is a grudging admiration for the excitement of behaviour which openly confronts authority, all tied up with more general social relations of popularity and heterosexual image, and contextual elements of curriculum and teacher relations. As part of boys' school cultures, misbehaviour is a source of a laugh, a game in which boys, either as performers or spectators, cement a certain camaraderie, where outstanding events become legend, and where even mediocre performances can be celebrated by backslapping and congratulations in the playground after class.

We can see also the excitement of pushing the boundaries, of showing one's independence and strength by challenging authority, sometimes with good cause, often not. Classroom misbehaviour is for many boys another opportunity for risk taking and experiencing the thrill of transgression. For others, it is an opportunity 'to acquire or defend privilege, to mark difference, and to gain pleasure . . . rule-breaking becomes central to the making of masculinity when boys lack other resources for gaining these ends'.[3]

And yet it is easy to fail in this public arena where reputations are made and broken. Trying too hard attracts ridicule, and constant disruption can class a boy as stupid. The competitive ethos of masculine popularity no doubt contributes to this situation, but if there were any further need to establish the links between this behaviour and the construction of masculinity, it can be seen in the way boys distinguish their disruptive behaviour from girls' transgressive practices. The boys interviewed were clear that, while girls did misbehave, it was a completely different practice from their own.

When girls are bored by schoolwork, their reaction is not the boys' confrontational and public display, but a private withdrawal.

When girls are frustrated they fiddle and when boys are frustrated they get angry.

I don't know many girls who misbehave and usually when they misbehave it's not for back-answering or not doing their work. One girl always gets in trouble for reading when she's not supposed to. But boys, it's a hard thing to see a boy reading when he's not supposed to.

In the boys' eyes, disruptive behaviour among girls was often caused by their bringing into the class difficulties in friendship relations.

There's this girl in our class who was crying because a girl liked another girl better than her. And another girl was crying because she was upset. She nearly had a heart attack. She went downstairs and you could hear her from miles away.
Was that Barbara? (laughter)
She was saying 'You stole my friend away from me. You stole my friend from me'. (mimicking whining voice) If a boy has a fight they have a bit of a hustle and then they come into class and everything's alright. If girls have a hustle with one of their friends they put their head in their arms. If we get angry at someone in class we take it. We get it at lunch time. We never do it in class.

When groups were asked to compare the behaviour of boys and girls, their answers were characteristically accompanied by laughter. It was a matter of amusement that boys were more disruptive than girls. Even to ask such a question was funny, as it was taken to be obvious. The following group exchange was in answer to the question 'why do boys misbehave more than girls?' Some of it was said tongue-in-cheek, but the tone was one of pride spoken from an assumed superiority.

They're just made to be. The king of the Indian tribes was a man. It's just the way they're made.
It's probably just because we think we're better. We are though.
It's the way we're built 'cause we're stronger and I think we use that strength but girls don't. They use their verbal strength.
Girls just sit there and polish their nails.

Boys' disruptive practices are a complex of public claims to notoriety, a yearning for recognition, a rejection of imposition, a playful testing of regulatory limits, a vengeful reaction to failure, and a refusal to be treated as non-adult people. They can be seen as resistance to school values or the performance of masculinity or the expression of some other interpretation of self and one's relation to the world. Connell et al. make the interesting observation that when the interaction between school authority and class and gender dynamics becomes overly strained, resistance becomes a struggle which is expressed in different ways.

> Among ruling-class kids resistance appears as taking on working-class styles, among girls it means acting like a boy, among boys it is liable to mean hypermasculinity: in each case there is an appeal to something felt to be potent and objectionable.[4]

Thus, the project of constructing masculinity does not account for all of this complex set of motivations, interpretations and behaviours. However, it is equally true that we cannot understand why boys misbehave unless we also realise the significance of such behaviour for their public persona, their social relations and their sense of self. A central part of these elements of identity is the need to establish an acceptable position in the arena of masculine gender relations.

BODILY AGGRESSION

In the previous chapter, the discussion of the Macho Lads highlighted the embodied reality of masculine practice in the combination of sexual discourse and physical aggression. Masculine characteristics like competition, domination and control are not inherited or socialised psychological values applied to behaviour. They are better seen as ways of conducting oneself in the world which we confront and take up in various ways in the discourses and social practices of everyday life. How, then, do boys learn these characteristically masculine ways of relating to the social world?

It is clearly part of the public image of the desirable male, as our discussion of sport and the media pointed out, but it enters also into the very personal realm of the body in demeanour, dress and the presentation of self. Revealing expressions of this are the T-shirt slogans whose messages are paraded in those temples of masculinity—the nation's sports stores.

Guts is good. Balls is better.

A true test of one's courage lies not only in the heart but directly between one's legs.

Balls a.k.a. cojones. You should have several. Preferably brass or steel. Extra large.

Life is a contact sport.

No scars. No proof.

No such thing as unnecessary roughness.

Here boys and men are enjoined to proclaim an 'in your face' kind of masculinity where designers are obviously convinced that to be outrageous and shocking is to be marketable. It should not surprise that the key sites of this outrageous masculinity are the body and its male organs and the practices of aggressive sport. However, the ideology derived from these symbols is held up as an approach to life as a whole, and, presumably, is thought to be appealing even to women.

These slogans can be seen as a culmination of the bodily aggression which is a key part of masculinity, and boys begin to learn it at a very early age. One aspect of boys' early experience which has attracted researchers' interest is rough-and-tumble play, that playful mix of reciprocal chasing, teasing, pushing and hitting evident in any schoolyard. The general view of this behaviour is that it is a benign way of developing social skills, as long as the roles of victim and victimiser are alternated so that domination is avoided, and as long as it remains playful, usually taken to be indicated by a play face or wide smile.[5] This is surely a naive way of classifying behaviour as benign. It leaves open a whole range of questions about the consequences of such behaviour, and places its faith in a very simplistic notion of motivation and intent.

For rough-and-tumble play is a complex range of behaviours where boys are playing out (in the senses of play discussed in chapter 3) various ways of relating to others. Some of these behaviours can quite easily be seen as experiments in domination, testing one's power and ability to catch, push, hit and ultimately hurt. In such an activity aggression is rewarded, and while reciprocity might be the researcher's wish, the children are also establishing a pecking order of physical power. The fact that boys' smiles show that they enjoy all of this is not very reassuring.

Rough-and-tumble play can be seen from a different perspective. Thorne describes the conspicuous physicality which was both a feature of the activity and a topic of the conversation of the children she studied. Their rough-and-tumble play was a constant feature of playground life, and in their desire to present themselves as tough, they threatened, insulted and competed with each other. This hostile behaviour is, ironically, also a way of developing friendships. From a range of elementary school studies, Thorne concludes that

> boys more often publicly violated rules, for example, against saying 'dirty words' on the playground. Their larger numbers give a degree of anonymity and support for transgression that is lacking in girls' friendship pairs. Boys bond through the risk of rule-breaking and through aggressing against other boys (called 'girls', 'fags', or 'sissies') who are perceived to be weaker. Boys also bond by aggressing against girls . . .[6]

Pellegrini discusses the developmentalists' argument that boys prefer rough-and-tumble play and that it is an arena for establishing friendships and positive social relations with other boys.[7] However, Pellegrini's research showed that engaging in rough-and-tumble play did not make boys more popular, and that for twelve- to thirteen-year-old boys it was more a function of aggression than prosocial play. There are also grounds for seeing mixed-sex rough-and-tumble play as a context in which young boys learn to see girls as legitimate targets for physical assaults of a sexual nature.[8]

Rough-and-tumble play is only one aspect of bodily physicality. To this we might add boys' fascination with farting and other bodily functions not least because it provides them with the opportunity to revel in a facet of life which adults have ruled out of polite conversation and proper behaviour. One illustration from our interviews shows how this is seen to be an acceptable and amusing but nonetheless transgressive act.

> Sometimes I get in trouble—once at parade I did this fart and I had to write out the code of behaviour. Martin said do it, do it, do it, so I did. One boy thinks he's funny when he does it. He does really smelly farts all the time.

In the realm of farts, burps, and smells, every boy has the power to transgress adult rules, and to challenge the hypocrisy of adult conventions, all with the knowledge that these are natural functions which can hardly be seriously punished. Chapter 4 has shown how this interest in anal and genital masculinity is constructed as a part of boys' game culture through the language of advertising. It seems that boys and advertising writers are both aware of the playful transgressions which boys can achieve this way.

The physicality of boys at play is an important exploration of the potential of one's body, a form of personal expression and a means for participating in social activity. None of this should be confused with aggression, and there is no reason why physical play should be predominantly male. The fact that it is both aggressive and male highlights its gendered character, and when applied to relations between boys and girls, it becomes a means for sexual oppression.

SEX-BASED HARASSMENT

Aggressive sexuality is commonly introduced in gender relations through language, where sexist put-downs give boys premature access to an aspect of adult male sexual discourse and the power that goes with it. Wood suggests that using sexual slang is a way for boys to expel sexual anxieties, confusions and self-doubts,[9] and it is an important means for the regulation and normalisation of masculine identities among boys and their peers.[10]

Mac An Ghaill's study supports this view, showing boys 'compulsively and competitively' discussing and playing out sexuality in a discourse where penis size, penetrative sex, and sexual potency were the main preoccupations.

> Their sexual narratives carried the predictable misogynous boasting and exaggeration of past heterosexual conquests and male heroic fantasies, in which women were represented as passive objects of male sexual urges, needs and desires.[11]

Mac An Ghaill sees this compulsory heterosexuality, along with misogyny and homophobia, as the constitutive elements of the process of learning to be men. For the boys in his study, this involved a difficult sacrifice, as they were forced to avoid close relationships with other boys for fear of being accused a 'poof', and were left with no one to talk to about feelings, affection or intimacy. The interviews in Mac An Ghaill's study provide clear evidence of the tensions between the public performance of confident, independent masculinity on the one hand, and their private insecurities and desire for intimacy on the other. An inability to reconcile these contradictions is likely to lead at least some boys to reject what they see as the vulnerability and potential weakness of the latter dimension, and to promote an unfeeling, obsessional version of the former.

In the studies reviewed here, peer relations among boys seem to be routinely characterised by potential and actual hostility, as boys struggle to establish for themselves a secure place in the network of relations, and a respectable and respected sense of themselves as male. As this struggle is most obviously among boys themselves, it is easy to overlook the fact that underlying the competing forms of masculinity is the presumption of difference and superiority over girls. The boys' culture studies have been criticised for overlooking this fact, but any understanding of boys in school which takes a relational perspective on gender must place this point at its centre.[12] The relation between boys and girls in the context of sexuality is a key part of the process of the construction of masculinity in schools.

Part of the neglect of sexuality arises from the sanitised

view of childhood innocence which does not consider the harmful effects of what is often seen as playful behaviour.[13] Yet the physical aspects of the sexed body are never far from view in the play, expressions and interactions of children and adolescent boys. Walkerdine's startling depiction of two nursery school boys, who intimidate their teacher by calling on her to strip and show her 'tits and bum', is a grim reminder of how accessible is the harassing power of males over females, as is Connolly's observation of the sexualised behaviour of five-year-old boys imitating sex on a restrained girl in a playground game.[14]

Dixon depicts one boy's sexual display in a design and technology classroom as he uses a wooden mallet, 'Pete's tool', as a symbolic penis, masturbating it and making it erect, and flaunting it to the girls.[15] As this is a common occurrence, the girls appear untroubled by it, seeing it as just another example of male immaturity. Yet in failing to object, they are reproducing the indulgence of society at large of the dominating behaviour of boys and men, and sustaining the myth that this is natural male behaviour which must be tolerated. This lends support to Kenway and Fitzclarence's point that certain femininities 'unwittingly underwrite hegemonic masculinity' through compliance, subservience and self-sacrifice and constant accommodation to the needs and desires of males.[16]

From the earliest years, children in schools police the boundaries of gender difference, and reproduce the power relations of adults, becoming, in Thorne's words, 'familiar strangers'.[17] From the girls' perspective, this 'shifting presence' of gender evoked by their relations with boys in school is highly problematic, and we need constantly to consider the effects of masculinity on those who, apart from the boys themselves, are most affected by it. Thorne's study paints a disturbing picture of gender relations among younger children, where boys routinely stigmatised and teased girls, invaded and disrupted their activities, and controlled their access to space.

Of course, the verbal harassment and put-downs of girls is only part of a more general ethos of the domination of women. Studies of English teaching have shown that in writing classes boys' stories construct aggressive tales in which women and non-macho boys are often outcasts and victims.[18] The following report from our interviews illustrates a similar episode.

> And we were talking about how men should be polite to women and they said how men, if there's a muddy ground, they put a coat on the ground so women can walk on it. And Mark said they should chuck the woman on the ground and walk over her hair so they didn't get dirty. A couple of people laughed but Mrs R. got really upset at him, and he's always making comments like that, every chance he gets.

The oppression of women is part of our culture, and boys are aware of this. For the most part it remains part of that dark area which is not talked about, other than in fiction, jokes and whispered asides. At other times, it becomes a weapon in a gendered contest with the teacher. For girls, however, it can become open hostility, when sex-based harassment leaves them vulnerable to what can only be described as insult and assault. Wight's study of Scottish working-class boys shows that this situation is problematic for boys, as there is a growing discrepancy between the norm of masculinity among boys' peers, with its disdainful attitude and obscene objectifying references to girls, and their personal relationships with and emotions towards girls, which may be a source of affection and comfort.[19]

While it might be problematic for boys, for girls it is simply offensive. In an earlier study by the present authors of secondary school girls' experiences of schooling, girls spoke about their relationships with boys.[20] Most of the girls clearly felt discriminated against in the ways boys were treated differently in families, in the classroom, in sport, in relationships, and in general social life. They often compared themselves less favourably to boys, describing how boys seemed to have an easier time than they did and how people treated them differently.

> They treat you different. Just because you're a girl you're weak you know. But a boy: they're real macho and proud to be a man or whatever they think they are.

> . . . they think they're much better off for being a boy and that girls, you know, just can't do anything because we're

girls and we're hopeless. Yeah, because we're girls and boys think that they're just it because they're a boy.

Sport—the provision of better facilities for boys and the greater recognition boys' performances received—was a key area of inequality, but life in classrooms and the playground could also be very difficult. For these girls, male harassment, violence and indignities were a significant aspect of life at school. Boys seemed to be a constant threat to girls' physical, emotional and linguistic space. Many of the girls talked about how groups of boys were almost out of control in classroom contexts. The teachers couldn't establish a classroom order in which quieter boys, and most of the girls, could get on with the set curriculum.

Well, the boys when they're mucking around like, the teacher would tell them stop sort of. Do their work and something. But they won't listen. Because they just like to impress each other and not do their work. And while they're mucking around no one else can get the chance to do their work because if they're making noises or anything, no one else can hear what the teacher's saying. So the boys should be put in place and told who's boss. Because most of the teachers here are too soft on them.

We just sit there and we wait for the boys to shut up, 'cause the teacher says 'I've had enough of this, we're just going to wait now until they're all quiet'. And we wait there, wait there, wait there. And they never shut up, and we're waiting there fifteen minutes and the next thing you know the bell's gone and we're out. So we've done nothing.

Like in Life Ed the boys don't take it seriously. Us girls take it seriously and we'd have an open group discussion and all they'd do is laugh about it and make jokes and all that . . . I think we should have a teacher more in control of the situation and not let the boys take control of the class and make jokes . . . [when] we're trying to be serious.

Time and again the girls offered examples of how much harder it was to 'get on' with schoolwork, because of the domination in classrooms by groups of boys, and because of the teachers' inability to control boys' behaviour.

The boys' domination of classroom time and space was also documented by teachers we spoke to in this project, and is clearly a well-recognised issue in gender equity debates. But there were additional implications of this domination that were noticed by both teachers and girls in the study. The boys openly harassed the girls—verbally and physically—in the classroom and the playground. The girls were continually positioned in the school as sexual objects and read in terms of their sexuality.

> They've got sex on their mind all the time and they take it out on you and say all these things . . .

> Stupid bitches, losers, bangers. You know they make up really stupid things that don't mean anything, but to them it's just a big laugh if they see you getting upset. They just laugh over it. You know they say to all their mates, 'Look I made her really upset' and all this.

> Like you feel like what they call you. They call you a whore and you feel like it. Because they actually come up behind you and you know touch you on the bum, or 'how much do you charge for an hour baby'. They have a credit card thing and they come up with a ruler or something and they hit you on the arse with it and say '$20' or something like that and they reckon it's credit card. It's like so pathetic, you just sit there and think 'Yes, sure, whatever you reckon'.

> I'm pretty heavy up top and I went home one day and I was crying and that. All these boys were picking on me, you know, saying turn your headlights off and all these stupid comments and I went home and I was crying . . .

> . . . the guys are always putting shit on girls about, you know, stupid things like their periods. It makes the girls really embarrassed. Embarrasses them. It happened to me a couple of times . . . You know, you'd have [tampons] in your bag or something and they'd pull them out and chuck them around the classroom and they'd just, really make you feel like . . .

. . . a few guys that are a bit older and they used to feel you up and everything and you just really shake and you just get up and don't know what to do. You don't know whether to just sit there and put up with it, or get up and walk out. And I ended up just getting up and walking out . . .

This constant harassment affected girls' confidence at school, and their willingness to choose subjects that they knew would put them in with a lot of boys. They expected, with good cause, that they'd get teased and humiliated. The girls reported that, if they dressed in the appropriate mechanics' clothes for Metal Module subjects, for instance, the boys would laugh at them and make disparaging remarks about their femininity. If they dressed in swimming togs when they were in a Marine Studies class, the boys would embarrass them by making offensive remarks about the sexuality of their bodies. In both cases, the girls were made to feel excluded from subject choices in the curriculum because of the way they were read as sexual subjects.

This perspective on boy–girl relations in school is an important antidote to the tendency in much of the discussion of boys' schooling to overlook their position of power over girls. The need to promote the educational welfare of boys can be justly served only if we acknowledge that the culture of masculinity, which creates problems for many boys, most powerfully impacts on the school experience of girls. The 'poor boys' syndrome must never lead us to overlook this.

While girls may see boys as dominant, powerful, and privileged, the boys, of course, do not necessarily see themselves this way. From the boys' perspective, school experience presents a number of challenges to which they must measure up if they are to see themselves as successful and secure. One important threat is that of bullying.

BULLYING

Bullying has been the subject of considerable research and development in recent years, and while much of value has been written about it, most of this writing has been curiously devoid of any clear focus on masculinity.

One of the most well-known international studies of bullying is based on the decades of work in schools in Scandinavia conducted by Dan Olweus. Olweus defines bullying or victimisation as occurring when a student is 'exposed, repeatedly and over time, to negative actions on the part of one or more other students'.[21] Clearly, to identify a negative action we need to posit an idea of a student's welfare, including an appropriate set of gender relations and rights. The bullying literature generally leaves this ideal unelaborated, assuming that it is self-explanatory, that negative actions are a general class and that nothing is to be gained by analysing them further.

However, we have seen in this study that some actions which might be deemed negative can also be taken for granted as normal behaviour. When some children are excluded from activities because of their sex or because they are seen as 'wimps', or when students are embarrassed by the flaunting of sexist or homophobic comments in classroom jokes, or when conscientious students are ridiculed as weak conformists, are these actions to be seen as bullying? To judge whether such behaviours constitute bullying we need some interpretation of gender relations and rights, and to understand them we need to realise that they all share a connection with the project of constructing masculinity.

The ACER survey paints a worrying picture of bullying and harassment. Verbal sex-based harassment, in which a student's sex is the ground for insults, is the most common form of harassment, reported by more than 90 per cent of students surveyed. A striking feature of the findings is that overall the victims of sex-based verbal harassment are as likely to be boys as girls; at secondary school it is worse for boys. Homophobic verbal harassment is a common form, with 44 per cent of boys reporting that it happened often to males, while the corresponding figure for girls was only 19 per cent. About 30 per cent of students reported that verbal harassment by groups of the same sex happened often, and this was reported by both girls and boys.[22]

However, bullying and sexual harassment were more predominantly, though not exclusively, male activities, victimising both girls and other boys. While the survey confirmed that concerns over the harassment of girls were well founded, the authors concluded:

the rights of boys not to be constructed and intimidated through sex-based harassment must also be addressed. It confirms that harassers, as the literature has suggested, tend to be boys. They use sex-based harassment as a dominance 'game' in a regime in which gender stereotypes are used as weapons. It also suggests that some, though fewer, girls play an active part inside this regime, accepting it as a framework and joining in the power game with the same sex-based harassment weapons.[23]

These findings support the view that the construction of masculinity is a powerful component of harassment and bullying in schools, one that does not receive the attention it deserves. A reason for this is that commonsense explanations of bullying have generated a series of myths which might deflect attention away from the construction of masculinity as a factor in bullying.

One such myth is that it is a reaction to the frustrations of failing at schoolwork. Olweus found no evidence of this. The bullies of his study had 'unusually little anxiety and insecurity', did not suffer from poor self-esteem, and were not disproportionately from low socio-economic groups.[24] Rigby reports similar findings in Australia, though he finds no Australian evidence on the socio-economic factor.[25] A related point comes from an American study which found that men with better heterosocial skills used more sexual coercion than those who were less skilled.[26] Given such evidence, there can be no easy explanation that bullying and harassment are a compensation for social failure. Most perpetrators are socially competent and secure.

Another myth is that big strong boys somehow naturally become bullies. Olweus says that bullying is characterised by an '*imbalance of strength* (an asymmetric power relationship)' which renders the victim somewhat helpless.[27] However, there is in fact only a weak relationship between strength and bullying, since most strong boys are not aggressive. Rather, Olweus suggests that bullies have a more positive attitude to violence, tend to be impulsive, and have a strong need for power and dominance over others. Their behaviour is often aimed at coercing others to give them money or other goods, and is often rewarded by the prestige they achieve. Group

187

mechanisms are important, as bullying behaviour can generate power for some members of a group, while other group members learn that such behaviour can be rewarding.

In the Australian context, the most well known and extensive work on bullying has been done by Rigby, whose recent text is a valuable review of research and suggestions for practice. However, the book is strangely silent on the relation between bullying and masculinity. Early in the book, Rigby defines sexual harassment as 'only one aspect of the bullying problem, and a very serious problem in its own right', but because sexual harassment has been dealt with by others, Rigby explains that he does not intend to examine it further.[28] The consequence of this decision is that gender is not mentioned at all as a part of the system of bullying, other than to point out gender differences in the incidence of things like absenteeism, attitudes to bullying, incidence of victimisation and group and individual bullying.

In other words, it is recognised that bullying for various reasons affects and involves girls and boys differently, but these differences and other aspects of bullying are almost never related to a system of gendered power relations. And yet the discussion of bullying is replete with findings and explanations which are clearly gendered. This is not just because boys bully more and more physically than girls (in Rigby's study, 69 per cent of boys and 24 per cent of girls who were bullied said that they were always bullied by boys, while the corresponding figures for bullying by girls were 4 per cent and 25 per cent), but also because the findings are presented in a way which glosses over their gender significance.[29] For instance, in Rigby's most extensive survey of 6000 boys and 2500 girls in sixteen schools, by far the most frequent kinds of bullying reported were being called hurtful names and being teased in an unpleasant way. But the ACER survey shows the prevalence in this kind of bullying of sex-based and, in the case of secondary boys in particular, homophobic put-downs. To neglect the importance of this powerful form of bullying is not very instructive.

Rigby asks why there should be a continual sense of enjoyment on the part of the bully in repeated victories over the weak. Students of masculinity would answer that at least some of it can be explained as a confirmation of one's masculinity, based as it is on the sense of power that comes from dominating others. For instance, Rigby cites the case of Big Bully Billy, an inveterate bully whose school performance is poor compared with that of his more academically successful brother and sister. Rigby explains Billy's behavior in terms of the reputation and admiration it gained for him, but there is no reference to the masculinist ideology on which this admiration is based, even though Billy himself hints at it by calling himself 'cock of the school'.

Even more puzzling is the one reference Rigby makes to a form of masculinity. Listing the values and attitudes which are centrally associated with bullying, Rigby includes such ideas as 'might is right', valuing the ability to dominate others, lack of sympathy with weaker people, and the belief that it is weak to be gentle and compassionate. Rigby observes:

> Now although these values are more likely to be embraced by male students, there are schools in which they are strongly held by girls also. Macho is gender-neutral.[30]

This comment seems spurious, since the dominance of boys as perpetrators of bullying is clearly evident, and dominance, physical power and lack of compassion are much more central features of masculinist ideology than a feminine one. Rigby repeats here the misconception that only boys can enact masculinity, and that if girls do it, it can't be masculine, simply ignoring the sex-gender distinction.

The parliamentary report into youth violence in New South Wales reviews a range of submissions on masculinity and bullying. For instance, the Men Against Sexual Assault organisation identifies key dominant messages traditionally given to boys about masculinity which must be eliminated if the connection with violence is to be broken, including

- the importance of dominance and control in being a successful man;
- the justification of violence to achieve such control;
- the attribution of responsibility for violence to other sources, such as alcohol or women;
- the rejection and disparaging of the feminine both in terms of women and any feminine qualities within men; and

189

- the rejection and suppression of any homosexual expression.[31]

Rigby's idea of a gender-neutral macho is but another indication of the apparently strong desire to deny that the construction of masculinity is relevant to an analysis of bullying. It is no surprise then, that in discussing cultural influences on bullying, Rigby mentions only social class and ethnic identity, omitting the powerful presence in our culture of gender and the power relations that flow from it.

A particular cause for concern among educators is the connection between bullying and/or harassment and student commitment to the ethos of schoolwork. A major feature of Australian classrooms is the tendency for boys to ridicule those boys and girls who might be seen to be committed to their schoolwork. The ACER survey found that 26 per cent of primary students said that boys made fun of others' answers often in their class while only 9 per cent said that girls did this. At secondary school level these figures were 37 per cent and 10 per cent.[32] Here we have a crucial disincentive for boys to commit to school, but the lack of a gender awareness on the part of those researching bullying has led them to ignore it.

On the other hand, as we saw in the last chapter, while boys carefully avoid any suggestion that they are conscientious nerds, they are also quick to criticise what they see as stupidity. Achieving at school may leave boys open to ridicule, but boys have their own criteria of what it means to be smart, and this is also an opportunity to distinguish the strong from the weak. Willis's early study nicely captures what is involved here.

> In certain respects obvious stupidity is penalised more heavily amongst 'the lads' than by staff, who 'expected nothing better'. Very often the topic for the 'pisstake' is sexual, though it can be anything—the more personal, sharper and apposite the better. The soul of wit for them is disparaging relevance: the persistent searching out of weakness.[33]

Our interviews with boys provided a classic example of a bullying victim, Richard, whom Olweus might classify as a provocative victim, in that some of the bullying seems to be aroused by annoyance at his strange ways. Of course, Richard's behaviour could equally be an ineffectual attempt to establish some self-respect by irritating the others. We see here the association with being cool, and some signs of the threatening atmosphere which forces boys to conform. In trying to explain what was involved in not being cool, the boy interviewed said:

> The not-so-cool go with the not-cool-at-all. It's hard to explain, and they get picked on a lot. Richard is the most hated person in the class and he's always getting something thrown at him and he cries a lot so people know that if they're going to make a crack at him they're going to make him hurt so they're always throwing things at him. But now if anybody does that their parents get called up. It's only for Richard. If you pick Richard your parent gets called up because it happens so much. The things he does are really stupid. We'll be sitting in class reading a book and he'll go nanananana, you know, make silly noises like from nowhere and he'll just sing or just make funny noises out of nothing and make weird noises.
>
> It's better to be the same as everybody else so you're not really going to make so much of yourself so people know you're there but they don't always *know* you're there, like mix in.

This image of being there but not being there is an interesting illustration of the fine distinctions boys make in deciding how to negotiate an acceptable balance of independence and conformity, of individualism and group identity.

VIOLENCE

Boys' bullying and sex-based harassment are forms of violence defined by victimisation. Bullying is the repeated singling out of particular victims, while sex-based harassment targets girls and boys who are classed as targets of a hegemonic gender regime. Beyond this is the more diffuse and pervasive arena of violent acts, where victims and perpetrators are more interchangeable and violent acts more random. Putting these forms together, we can say that violence is therefore both discriminating and indiscriminate.

As the evidence in chapter 1 demonstrated, more general acts of violence are just as dominated by males as are bullying and harassment, and are related to masculinity in similar ways. In the words of Kenway and Fitzclarence, a focus on violence 'points to the vulnerable underbelly of all masculinities, to the driving force of such emotions as confusion, uncertainty, fear, impotence, shame and rage'.[34]

Kenway and Fitzclarence argue that violent males draw from the repertoire of masculine values, attributes and practices and 'exaggerate, distort and glorify' them, so that, for instance, a masculine belief in the superiority of men becomes a hostile contempt for women. Similarly,

> assertiveness may be exaggerated to become aggression, physical strength to toughness associated with physically beating others, bravery to bravado and cruelty . . . emotional neutrality to emotional repression on the one hand and to extremes of rage and shame on the other, competitiveness to hostility, rationality to the rationalisation of violence, sexual potency to control over and contempt for women's bodies and so on.[35]

An interesting insight into the nature of violence amongst boys is its ritual character. For the most part, violence amongst boys is not an individual pathology caused by an inherently violent nature. The great majority of violent acts do not involve psychological illness or disorder. Nor do they result from a sudden outburst of an uncontrollable urge. Most violence is an extension of normal masculine behaviour exacerbated by unforeseen events in contexts where incentives, controls and inhibitions are out of the normal balance.

Willis noted this point when he described the violent events among his working-class lads, who recognised violence as a 'dangerous and unpredictable final adjudication which must not be allowed to get out of hand between peers'.[36] The lads preferred verbal or symbolic violence, and if a real fight occurred 'the normal social controls and settled system of status and reputation is to be restored as soon as possible'. This fine line between acceptable and unacceptable violence requires careful negotiation, but boys learn the distinction through long and constant training.

In a more general way the ambience of violence with its connotations of masculinity spread through the whole culture. The physicality of all interactions, the mock pushing and fighting, the showing off in front of girls, the demonstrations of superiority and put-downs of the conformists, all borrow from the grammar of the real fight situation.[37]

This controlled ritualistic violence was well illustrated in our interviews when one boy, David, recounted an incident in which the normal level of 'little push-ups' escalated into a 'big punch-up'. Note that David draws on the common notion of losing control as a rationalisation, while at the same time providing evidence that such explanations are inadequate, as there is a clear distinction between the classroom and the playground as contexts of opportunity for the different kinds of violence. Interesting also is the observation that this is an occasional but regular event. It seems that the 'big punch-up' is a necessary part of the ritual, since it sustains the connection between the relatively harmless and normal pushing and shoving, and the real thing for which this minor aggression substitutes and yet symbolically stands.

> Boys get in fights—about one a month—a big punch-up. That's why Mum has to sew on different buttons. I got in one a couple of days ago . . . He said something and I told him to mind his own business and he grabbed my throat and he swung about ten punches before—'cause I don't like to get into a fight—and he kept swinging at me so I just lost it. We are usually having little push-ups but we'll have a push-up and then five minutes later we're friends again. That's how we are usually. That's usually how all the boys are. Like we have two groups, the cool group and the not-so-cool group and usually if someone from the cool group gets in a fight from the not-so-cool group—they always fight in class but when they get into the school ground they really go for it.

This ritualised distinction between normal acceptable violence and 'really going for it', its escalation in particular contexts, and its connection with the opportunities and rules applying to different social spaces, is chillingly reminiscent of Polk's analysis of case studies of homicides committed by

193

youth in Australia. The common pattern in these killings was a meeting between groups of boys in some public place, the exchange of insults and challenges which provoked violence, usually between individuals from each group, which became lethal when weapons were introduced. Polk distinguishes these incidents from gang conflict found in the United States, because in these Australian cases:

> the conflict seems to be moulded to the contours of Australian life. Virtually all of the youthful homicide was contained within what has been termed elsewhere the 'confrontation' scenario . . . The violence is definitively masculine, and involves threats and challenges to masculine honour or reputation.[38]

The control of space and the symbolism of territoriality play important roles in the securing of and threat to masculine potency. This is an important aspect of violent behaviour which again is active in the school context.[39]

Male violence in Aboriginal communities is a major issue that cannot be put aside, and like violence in the community as whole, is closely related to masculinity. The picture of Aboriginal violence on many remote communities is a horrifying one, and some Aboriginal men and boys in these places seem to have come to see violence, especially domestic violence, as a normal part of life. The chief victims of this violence are women and girls in their own communities. While popular prejudice may see this as evidence of the inferiority of Aboriginal culture, it is important to realise its origins in the effects on men of the destruction of traditional Aboriginal communities.[40]

The emasculation theory mentioned in chapter 6 is only part of the story, for it can sometimes imply that black men simply choose violence and other forms of anti-social behaviour as a reaction to a relatively benign process of being replaced as authority figures by white settlement. This ignores the powerfully violent and destructive effects of the colonisers themselves, including the rape, prostitution, child sexual assault and other forms of masculinist violence which were common-place and even condoned on the frontier. These crimes were rare in traditional Aboriginal society, and when they did occur were dealt with harshly by traditional law. As Atkinson explains:

Instead of traditional methods of control, the patterns of violence learned from those who now held the law—the invaders—grew to become a way of life and a way, like alcohol abuse, of dealing with frustration and feelings of powerlessness and anger. Combine this with an official status as inferior, unable to survive without protection, a loss of personal freedom, a destruction of the recognised relationships between men and women and others in the community, and the violence within much of Aboriginal Australia today is understandable.[41]

Racist attitudes, bolstered by sexist assumptions of both white and black men, may tolerate such violence as a normal part of Aboriginal culture, and are no doubt part of the explanation of why this situation has been allowed to continue. The chief significance here is how this violence in the community relates to the negotiation of masculinity by Aboriginal boys. In a recent Western Australian survey, 98 per cent of young Aboriginal people had had an older brother, father or uncle in jail.[42] Ninety per cent of trust area families experienced domestic violence, which is clearly a part of the experience of most boys in these situations. Atkinson refers to a 'cycle of abuse' where boys may learn that this is acceptable male behaviour, and argues that 'Some men have a macho image to maintain and have the impression that women are quite happy to accept the violence . . .'[43] Of course, both black and white men and boys share an attraction to this macho image, which can heighten tensions between them. For instance, it has been known to contribute to the tensions between young black men and police.[44]

CONCLUSION

We need to reject explanations of violence which do not adequately recognise the role of masculinity. Biological and general psychological theories simply cannot account for the pervasiveness, diversity and institutionalised nature of violence, and its deeply gendered form. On the other hand, we need to avoid seeing all kinds of violence as originating in some general masculine anxiety, where 'The masculine subject becomes a catch-all category in which the psychological and social-historical dimensions of violence find their locus'.[45]

Moon argues that not only is this theoretically misplaced, in that there is no general form of masculine consciousness, but that it makes any progress in dealing with male violence dependent on a revolutionary end to patriarchy. He sees violence as related to goals of power rather than a form of masculine subjectivity. It is functional to the operation of a system of power controlled by men.

> This is why the notion of patriarchal power, patriarchal violence, is potentially more useful than the notion of 'masculine' violence. The former designates a structure in which gender and power are systematically linked, and which gives rise to forms of consciousness, and to ideologies; whereas the latter implies power's obedience to consciousness.[46]

While dominant masculinity is not a simple and certainly not the only cause of violence, the connections between the two are incontrovertible.[47] No serious attempt to understand and deal with violence can overlook this. In discussing the normality of violence within dominant masculinities, Braithwaite and Daly give some indication of the magnitude of the problem here, and the huge task ahead of those who would try to change it.

> For men, status competition through physical force, domination-humiliation of the less powerful, and knowing no shame have substantial cultural support. Few societies today contain majoritarian masculinity that sets its face against violence. In general, women's and men's social movements have failed to nurture credible competing non-violent identities for heterosexual men.[48]

If schools are to address the bullying, harassment and violence which is of such concern, this cultural context is a major challenge. But schools have little choice but to take up this challenge, for if they are to promote the educational and general welfare of all their clients, the harm and injustice which violence causes must be remedied.

Boys and books

BOYS AND LITERACY: THE ISSUES

Boys' poor performance, achievement and participation in literacy is seen by many teachers and parents as a major educational problem. And, certainly, when taken as a single group, Australian boys do less well than girls in early literacy tests and in high school English results, and are less likely to participate in literacy-based school subjects. Literacy tests in the primary years invariably show boys behind girls, and in secondary school, boys not only perform less well in English and literature subjects, but they avoid curriculum areas like the humanities and the arts that make literacy demands. Boys typically complain that English is a 'girls' subject' and, when given a choice, opt for a stereotypically gendered mathematics, science and technologically focused curriculum selection. There seems to be an abrasive rub between boys, literacy and schooling.[1]

As we discussed in chapter 1, boys' poor performance in literacy tests was one of the main arguments used for mounting the New South Wales Inquiry into Boys' Education in 1994, and the subsequent O'Doherty Report from that inquiry provided telling data about boys and literacy. It described, for instance, various ways in which boys were significantly over-represented in special language and reading classes. Of 317 children identified with serious language disorders in the New

South Wales Department of School Education, for example, 256 were boys, and three times more boys than girls in New South Wales schools were receiving special assistance for reading.[2] The issue was also clearly not just one associated with the early years of schooling. Boys' poor performance and participation in secondary school English and literature subjects—and their absence from the humanities and the arts areas—had also been documented in the national report, *Who Wins at School?*.[3] More recently, the release of 1995 data from national literacy testing of year 9 students in Australia has been used to argue that 34 per cent of boys of this age, compared with 26 per cent of girls, are now without 'basic literacy skills'. This figure is compared with national figures from 1975 which show that there has been a widening of the gap in the past twenty years between boys and girls. 'In 1975 the gap was three percentage points; in 1995 it was eight percentage points.'[4]

Of course literacy test results are only a small part of any picture of literacy competence and success. Literacy tests and literacy testing notoriously reflect class and cultural bias, privileging some groups of students and marginalising others.[5] Some students are socially and culturally positioned in ways that help them to understand the particular 'text-talk' that goes with testing, to make meaning from the text types selected, to use intertextual links to unlock testers' purposes. Literacy tests can be used—and have been used—to confirm a 'natural' social order of privilege, whereby children from middle-class Anglo cultures outperform other groups, thereby confirming an apparent superiority of white middle-class family culture. Before we could be confident that poor performance on literacy tests was a significant indicator of students' abilities with language, we would want to know what types of literacy a test was attempting to monitor, and to examine test construction carefully. In the case of working-class boys, Aboriginal boys, and boys from non-English speaking backgrounds, this will be particularly significant.

Literacy tests are also limited by their own technologies: only some forms of literate knowledge are assessed in such tests. Many forms of literacy cannot be easily assessed by standardised, computerised, national tests. It is difficult for a test to measure how capably, for example, students can use language in its many media forms, and in a range of sites other than the school literacy test site. And again, for boys, this may be significant. There may be other 'literacy' sites that boys excel in that are not easily tested or monitored. We might want to ask whether the forms of literacy commonly assessed on standardised tests represent functional social literacy in its popular and contemporary genres.

However, leaving aside these obvious problems associated with literacy testing—which can apply to groups of girls as well as to groups of boys—there are still complex issues to unravel in connection with boys' school literacy performance and participation, and it seems clear that the issues need to be addressed at the beginning of the compulsory school years. Early childhood teachers, for example, frequently comment on boys' reluctance to write and to read, and the trend continues through middle primary and secondary school. However statistics on the disproportionate numbers of male students in reading remediation groups (as well as in behaviour modification and discipline groups) have seldom been kept by schools. This may partly be because schools have tended to expect boys to perform less well than girls at school tasks like reading and writing, and to assume that the causes are preordained. By predominantly drawing upon biological models of male genetic predisposition to mathematics and science, and to physiological differences in female and male brains, research on sex differences in reading and early literacy acquisition has predominantly read female–male difference with reading as 'natural'.[6]

This is not to say that the situation was left unchecked and that boys' needs were not addressed through early literacy intervention strategies. Considerable school resources have been allocated across this country (and internationally) to programs that both directly—and indirectly—provide back-up strategies for boys who do not want to participate, or cannot participate effectively, in literacy classrooms.[7] Many early literacy programs, for example, reflect how text selections for such programs often focused on boys as chief story protagonists and on narrative content seen to be of interest to boys.[8] This was also particularly noticeable in secondary school English programs, where teachers were worried to select texts that might be described as 'girls' books' for fear that boys would not participate in English classes.[9] It was assumed that books for boys would need to have boys or men as chief protagonists, and that they could not focus on romance, relationships or issues of female sexuality.[10]

Hence, it would be incorrect to say that schools have not tried to address the needs of boys within the literacy and literature classroom. However, it might be correct to argue that the ways in which these needs have been addressed have often been ineffectual because they have not taken sufficient account of the gendered construction of the boys they work with. While schools have developed a range of practices that offer help for the 'reluctant' reader, or the 'remedial' reader—both of whom are often male—these strategies have not often attempted to engage with the experiences of masculinity such readers bring with them, or critically to reflect on the ways in which various technologies of literacy learning might conflict with social constructions of masculinity.

The result is often that, by the end of their compulsory schooling years, many boys have not only moved away from literacy and English as domains of significance or of pleasure, but they have also identified literacy and English as feminised subject domains.[11] Surveys of teenagers' reading habits and preferences show not only that boys read less than girls, but that they also read and engage with different material: material that is less likely to be used for textual study in the school.[12] Ways to 'do' masculinity are much more likely to be found in sport, electronic and gaming magazines than in novels—and in multimedia net-surfing rather than the literacy classroom. English, as it is taught and constructed at school, is not positively linked with masculinity in the ways that science, technology and trade work are, and boys seem not easily able to insert themselves into the practices and technologies associated with literacy learning and teaching. On the contrary: literacy and English can be too closely linked with the feminine and with non-masculine practices.

So literacy *is* an issue for boys, although we do need to unpack its complexity carefully. While there is clearly some difference between the performance of boys (as a group) and girls, as a group, on measures of literacy, it is important to keep this in perspective. As we have argued, all boys do not do poorly on literacy tests—nor do all boys score poorly in secondary school English and literature. And not all girls perform well. Rural Aboriginal girls, and working-class girls from non-English speaking backgrounds, for instance, do less well than some groups of boys. While gender is certainly a factor affecting literacy results, so too is ethnicity, the socio-economic status of a student's family, Aboriginality and rurality.

Also, we need critically to evaluate what is being tested in any literacy test or high school English examination to determine what 'doing well' on that test or exam might signify. What is it that boys do not do as well as girls? How socially important and culturally valued are the knowledge and skills being tested? For instance, are boys disadvantaged in terms of post-school options if they do not do as well as girls do in the forms of literacy valued and tested at school?[13] Are there other forms of literacy, for example, in which boys do perform well, and which may be more valuable in terms of future work and leisure? It has often been argued that performance in mathematics and science, for instance, is more valuable than performance in English for students seeking tertiary entrance to the more elite professional areas. It has also been argued that, given the technologies of the future, print-based literacy skills will be less valuable than multimedia literacy skills. (Is there more long-term and vocational advantage for a boy to spend two hours surfing the net than two hours reading his school English novel?) If there is a disadvantage for boys associated with poor performance in school literacy tests or English exams, where does it lie?

In addition, we need to ask if boys' lack of interest in literacy and in English education is connected with the way literacy and English have been pedagogically and ideologically constructed. If boys, as a group, are reluctant participants in these domains, and if boys, as a group, do less well in these educational areas, is there some incompatibility between masculinity and the curriculum areas? Do we need a critical assessment of dominant assumptions underpinning these areas to see how they may sit beside hegemonic discourses on masculinity?

DEFINING THE PROBLEM

In this chapter we argue that there are important issues to focus on with boys and literacy—but that there are also important issues to address here for girls, and that the two need to be read in tandem. In this regard much can be learnt from the work that has already been undertaken on girls and literacy, in terms of how gender impacts upon literacy learning and literacy practice. In this book we have argued that gender plays an important role in the way in which boys and girls position themselves within the curriculum. As we discussed in chapter 5, masculinity and femininity are played out in school arenas in sexual and social ways, and school practices support, reinforce, and even rely upon, stereotypical discourses of male and female sexuality. Of these, the imperative to be demonstrably and unequivocally heterosexual is powerful in its impact upon young men. The importance of embodying and playing out a hegemonic form of masculinity within the school becomes a critical and crucial challenge.

As we argued earlier, a masculinist position can be achieved in a number of ways: through participation in sport, through attention to the physical and cultural embodiment of masculinity, through participation in male culture, and through resistance to the position of 'child' or 'little boy' offered by teachers. It can also be achieved by subject selection. Boys lined up within a mathematics and science stream are demonstrating their preference for masculinist subjects. Boys lined up within an arts or humanities strand are more ambiguously positioned. They will need to demonstrate in other ways— through sport, through talk, through their bodies, through their behaviour—that they are still heterosexual; that they are 'megaracers' and not 'girlie-men'.[14]

The construction of literacy and of English as feminised areas has an impact on girls as well as on boys, because it lessens the significance and cultural value of literate competence and literary sensitivity. It has also meant that the positive and important role that literacy and literature study might have for boys is lessened. We would argue that there is much on offer through contemporary approaches to critical social literacy that is of value for boys in reading and rewriting their social construction. Of all the subject domains at school, English has most opportunity to engage students with issues of masculinity and power, and to provide them with opportunities to critique, to interrogate and to subvert texts.

We would argue that boys need more than the limited

repertoire of texts made available through male youth culture, more than the restricted range of reading positions such texts offer, and more than the stories made popular through electronic game culture, violent film genres, and sport journalism. We would argue that the issues for boys in relation to literacy are important ones to consider—not because boys might perform better on literacy tests, but because, like girls, they need opportunities to explore the possibilities of language in making and re-making their lives as masculine subjects.

In this chapter we look at what can go wrong for boys in literacy and English classrooms: at how their histories in families, in peer groups, and in male youth cultures position them in relation to the reading/writing classroom, and at how practices commonly in use in such classrooms might be incompatible with boys' developing understanding of masculinity. We then consider positive agendas for change, so that literacy, and the literacy classroom, might become more desirable spaces for boys—and yet still be attractive and desirable learning domains for girls.

BECOMING A SCHOOLBOY

As we described in chapter 4, it is not unusual for boys to have different sets of experiences in families from girls, as mothers and fathers struggle with what is seen to be appropriate ways to talk to their sons, play with their sons, and love their sons. In that chapter, we described research which demonstrates the different ways in which male and female children are spoken to and handled in families; the different speech practices of fathers and mothers; the different interactive patterns children engage in with gender-marked toys.[15] Of particular significance, however, is the implicit—and explicit—value given to literacy by mothers and by fathers, as work by Sue Nichols demonstrates.[16]

Nichols' Australian work indicated that literacy was clearly linked with mothers and with women, that fathers often identified themselves as non-readers, and that a 'negative identification with reading was associated with a positive identification with perceived masculine activities and qualities'.[17] Nichols argues that most parental involvement programs at school rely upon women workers, and as we described in chapter 4, Lareau[18] demonstrates how in both working-class and middle-class British families, the 'work' of school falls predominantly upon women, particularly in terms of homework completion and parental classroom support.[19] Boys' earliest experiences of reading, of literacy and of the home–school nexus are likely to be associated with their mothers, rather than with their fathers: with femininity and the female, rather than with masculinity and the male.

Consequently when boys arrive at the literacy classroom they are already inscribed by expectations and understandings of literacy, schooling and masculinity. We should hardly be surprised, therefore, if many of them have difficulty finding a desirable subject position to occupy within the dominant discourses of 'literacy' and 'schooling' on offer in the early years of compulsory schooling. There may well be little here that links easily with other important learnings in their lives. Rather, the regulated 'nursery-style' environment of the early literacy classroom, with its preponderance of women teachers, women aides and mother assistants, could seem to represent an extension of the maternal domain of the home—the domain that so many of the popular parent guides insist boys must break with if they are to become 'men'.[20]

Because so much time in the early years of school is devoted to learning to read and to write, and to learning the discourse patterns of school talk and discipline, it must be easy for boys to see 'reading' and 'school' as almost synonymous, and for literacy and schooling discourses to become closely intertwined. Learning how to 'do' school becomes very much about learning the appropriate patterns of talk, of listening, of writing, and of reading for the school context.

The schoolchild subject constructed within these discourses is assumed to be a regulated, disciplined body who will accept the surveillance and control naturalised as part of schooling practice. The schoolchild is assumed to occupy a position of submission: to accept the authority of teacher, textbook, classroom practice and work; to accept the regulation of body, of voice, of space, of time. Learning to *do* school in the early years is often about learning to perform school and about inserting the body into the gendered, social landscape of the school. The tendency to timetable eating, drinking, toileting, playing and working, and to urge uniformity in clothing, body adornment and behaviour is part of the landscape schools construct. Much of what children learn in their first years of school is learned through the body: how is the body to be performed in the classroom? in the playground? in the home? on the sporting field?

The schoolchild has to learn how to construct a school 'self'—how to perform as a schoolchild—and this learning is not disassociated with gender.[21] Whereas much of a girl's social learning has introduced her to performances of submission, passivity and courtesy, much of a boy's learning has been different. His learning is more likely to have introduced him to performances of activity and maverick individualism. As we have argued in chapter 4, boys and men in families, and boys and men in relationships, can often expect to do less of the 'work' of the family or the work of the 'relationship'. They can expect girls and women to do the 'social' work necessary to maintain human social interaction. And as we have also argued in chapter 3, boys' experiences through sport and leisure reinforce an association between masculinity and active individualism. Masculinity, as we have argued, is a performance—but it is a performance reliant on physical control, autonomy and independence.

The physical performative masculinity many boys come to see as acceptable and desirable ways of being male could be seen to be potentially at odds with the performances expected, and required, in the early literacy classroom. As Luke argues,[22] much of learning to do literacy is about learning to regulate the body in particular ways. Learning how to hold writing implements correctly (to be tidy and neat), learning how to hold and manage books (to be careful and custodial with texts), learning how to perform literacy practices like morning talk presentations, whole class discussions, teacher–child interactions (to be socially competent) are important aspects of early literacy learning and become markers of children's success with literacy. Questions to ask here are whether these practices may be seen as particularly undesirable to some boys because they are potentially in opposition to masculinity. Angela Phillips, for instance, suggests that: 'At primary school good work is encouraged but it does not enhance a child's

sense of masculinity. It is just like being good for Mummy
. . .'[23]

The position of schoolchild on offer within the discourses
of schooling, and particularly the position of literate child
constructed within discourses of literacy in the early years of
schooling, is potentially at odds with discourses of masculinity
boys have practised in their families and their leisure groups.
Sets of binary oppositions emerge very obviously here. To
perform literacy effectively, students have to accept conditions
of inactivity; tidiness and neatness; surveillance and regulation;
and discipline by an infant teacher who is likely to be female.
And this is potentially a conflict for boys. Primary school age
boys we interviewed[24] recognised the connections between
literacy, reading, and acceptance of school. For them the
'schoolboy' and the 'literate subject' produced through early
schooling discourses had begun to coalesce. They claimed that
the sort of boys who liked school were:

> . . . the ones who like books . . .

> . . . They're into work. Wear proper uniform. Always neat.
> Never late for school. Boys who are good at school like being
> by themselves and sitting down and reading and stuff.

Reading and books were frequently associated with girls, with
'work', with boredom, with anti-masculine practice.

> . . . I don't like to have to sit down and read a book or
> something, so mum and dad push me to do both.

> . . . I hate reading. I like PC magazines and sport magazines.
> It tells you more stuff. It's got pictures. Books you just have
> to read over and over. Reading magazines is interesting. Books
> are boring.

> . . . I don't know many girls who misbehave and usually
> when they misbehave it's not for back-answering or not doing
> their homework. One girl always gets in trouble for reading
> when she's not supposed to. But boys. It's a hard thing to
> see a boy reading when he's not supposed to.

> . . . Girls only play sport when they get sick of reading.

The link between being positioned as a 'nerd' at school, and being associated with books was often made.

> . . . when the girls are good at school nobody really notices it if they study and everything. But if a guy were to go out and like study and not go out with his friends, and just go home and study, they'd think he was kind of mad.

> . . . For girls it's pretty good for them to do a lot of work. They won't get teased if they do a lot of work—but boys if they do a lot of work . . .

> . . . it's pretty much a matter of getting grades, going out with your friends and not always just sitting in front of a book.

As we have argued in chapters 5 and 6, there is obviously a clear tension here for boys, and discourses of race, ethnicity and sexuality compound this tension. Taking up an acceptable schoolboy position requires a balancing act of considerable skill, for the world of the classroom is not the world of the playground and of boys' cultures. 'Teachers don't know what goes on in the playground', said one of the boys in our study. In the gendered landscape beyond the classroom it is critical for boys to find an acceptable masculine position to occupy, and yet, ironically, it is still critical to find a masculinist position within the classroom: one that will be approved not only by teachers but also by other students—both male and female students. This classroom terrain is obviously far harder to negotiate and to read.

Yet there are rewards for boys who succeed in this classroom arena. Valerie Walkerdine's work indicates the association teachers make between the inquisitive, intelligent learner and masculinity—and of the difficulty teachers have in expecting intellectual curiosity or cleverness with girls. Other work by Stanworth, Clarricoates, Evans and Currie[25] supports these findings, indicating how teachers often prefer to teach boys, how they find boys more interesting, how they expect boys to be more intelligent. The boy who learns how to perform a successful version of masculinity within the classroom is likely to be rewarded by teachers and respected by his peers. He learns how to position himself within a masculinist discourse that has been adapted for the classroom.

FALLING OUT OF READING

However, for young boys beginning school, this is not easily achieved. The young literacy learner is still clearly a child, although most boys, as we have argued, perceive some tension between being treated as a child and as a boy, and also some tension between becoming a literate child and a boy. Given the early lining up of oppositional constructs for childhood, masculinity and literacy, it hardly should be surprising that more boys than girls end up in teacher-identified remedial reading groups or support programs. Flynn, for instance, observed that the ratio of boys to girls in North American programs at first and third grades was 2:1.[26] Other major studies have indicated that a majority of students identified as having 'learning difficulties' are male. Gottlieb and colleagues, for instance, found 70 per cent of such groups in large urban American school systems were male[27] although as Nichols[28] argues, these figures need careful scrutiny. How is 'learning difficulty', for example, defined?

Flynn suggests that the reason that more boys than girls are identified as having 'learning difficulties' may be because of boys' aggressive and disruptive classroom behaviours: because, we might argue, they are trying to perform an unacceptable form of masculinity within the school context. She suggests that, by comparison, 'girls may only be noticed when their intellectual abilities are significantly lower than boys and their academic difficulties more pronounced'.[29] This is the argument also made by Currie in a study of the imbalance of boys to girls receiving special help in a British school region. Currie concludes that teachers have different perceptions about girls and boys which influence decisions about who needs special help. Her argument is that while teachers believe that girls generally work to capacity and will cope in whatever group they are put, teachers have different perceptions of boys as learners and tend more frequently to provide them with special help groups. Generally teachers in her study believed that boys had more natural talent than girls, but that they needed encouragement to use it; that boys' lack of success was due to 'problems' they had; and that boys needed help to concentrate.[30]

The negative effect of these perceptions on girls is clear: girls who do need help may well be passed over because they are not undisciplined and troublesome in class; because they perform femininity successfully. However, there is also a negative effect upon boys. As Nichols argues, 'placement in remedial classes, if not an indicator of a pre-existing learning disability can certainly be the cause of low achievement'.[31] She notes that placement in such classes not only labels boys and leads them to have a low opinion of their own ability, but it also limits their access to the mainstream curriculum. She also notes however that a disproportionate number of the boys who are identified for special help are boys who come from low socio-economic status backgrounds. Not all boys are likely to fill remedial classes. In a discussion of American data on learning difficulties Nichols suggests that 'the problems of black and working class boys are being used as evidence that boys as a whole suffer from learning difficulties which are not being sufficiently well addressed by the current school system'.[32]

The 'problems' that black and working-class boys have with literacy at school, however, may well be linked with teachers' preconceptions of intersections between ethnicity, poverty and schooling. In a major Australian study of literacy practices in low socio-economic urban communities, Freebody, Ludwig and Gunn observed that teachers often expected 'disadvantaged' students to have low interest in schooling, to lack home support and resources, and to be potentially disruptive at school. They argued that teachers then constructed literacy practices for such students that reflected this bias. The Freebody et al. study noted that in 'disadvantaged' classrooms '[t]he focus on and interpretation of student talk and action as oriented to disruption of classroom order often interrupted and sometimes completely obscured the curriculum topics of lessons', and that '[b]ehavioural and procedural directives were longer and more complex than literacy task directives, which were often cursory and non-explicit'.[33]

Masculinity may well be an additional complication to this uneasy mix. The 'doing of masculinity' ('bad behaviour'?)

within the controlled environment of the literacy classroom could easily lead to increased teacher surveillance and discipline, and ultimately to the withdrawal of particular 'disruptive' students from the mainstream classroom. Those groups of boys who are not regarded as 'advantaged' may well be perceived by literacy teachers as potentially at risk of failure, and be positioned by teachers as oppositional to 'the literate self' assumed to lie at the heart of literacy discourses.

BECOMING CIVILISED: THE TECHNOLOGIES OF ENGLISH LITERATURE

Clashes between literacy and masculinity do not just occur in the early years of literacy instruction. They are equally as likely to occur in later years of compulsory schooling, as the discourses about literacy become more closely connected with those of literature. English as a high school subject bears traces of English literature as a university discipline, and as such, carries a similar history. English could be called, for example, a discipline with a mission. Originally seen to provide a common culture offering access to spirituality in an increasingly secular nineteenth century,[34] it became, in the twentieth century, the repository of moral values—offering opportunities for students to improve themselves through close reading of great texts.

No other key subject in the school curriculum proposes itself in this way. While other curriculum areas are likely to be promoted for their functional, vocational or contemporary relevance, English literature is most likely to be promoted as good for the soul and the mind. Unlike 'serious' professional subject areas like law, medicine or engineering, English literature could easily be regarded as something to study if you didn't have vocational or professional ambition. Not surprisingly, at university level this discipline with a 'mission' is predominantly taught by men and studied by women, and despite various philosophical shifts in literary theory, has maintained its position as a key liberal discipline.[35]

The translation of university English literature into school practice carries strong traces of the humanist and personalist discourses that characterise its university designation,[36] and are imbued, as Hunter and Patterson[37] would argue, with aspects of moral training and self-regulation. Patterson, for instance, suggests that all models of English education have a pedagogy through which students might 'freely' assume the task of self-regulation: 'that combines spontaneity and restraint, autonomy and supervision, the free response of the student with the correcting limits set by the teacher'.[38] This is not to say that the approach to working with literacy and literature in this country is monolithic. Australian schools operate with a wide range of language and literacy strategies. Personal growth models of literacy learning, skills-based models, literature-based language programs, cultural studies programs, critical literacy programs, and feminist post-structuralist practices have all found space within Australian classrooms.

However, certain sets of strategies or technologies can be identified which characterise much classroom 'work' on language and literacy.[39] They are technologies designed to produce the literate self within the institutional context of compulsory schooling. For example, many of the most familiar school literacy practices require that students accomplish the processes of self-disclosure, introspection, empathetic response, and personalised and creative expression.[40] The truly literate subject, for example, is able to lay bare the soul: to engage in literacy practices that describe feelings and emotions, and which locate the writer/reader as a sensitive and aesthetic subject who derives pleasure from print and the literary experience. Even in the early years of schooling, the focus in the literacy classroom is often on personalised expression and response to teacher-sanctioned texts.

Such typical technologies of the literature classroom as these—personal response to literary and cultural texts, creative writing programs, empathetic readings of character and character relations in textual fictions—are indicative of how self-regulation and moral training might occur in the classroom. Because the dominant missionary purpose and ideological goal of literary discourse is to be a liberal and humanising discipline, *some* responses, *some* creative writing, and *some* character readings will be deemed preferable to others. While traditionally it has been male reading responses and reading positions that have been privileged through the study of literature,[41] these have not always been easy for all boys (and certainly not for all girls) to imitate and reproduce, relying, as they have very often, on specific cultural capital.[42]

But even when alternative responses and positions are sought which challenge traditional literary readings, the moralising, regulatory possibilities of literature are often still in evidence. For many students, literary or text study has come to be associated with toeing an acceptable ideological line—whatever the ideology of the classroom might happen to be: liberal humanist, feminist, postmodernist, Marxist . . . Evidence of this coercion can be seen through the production of the mass of 'appropriate' stories and descriptions, or response journals and literary essays that school students produce for English classrooms.[43] Evidence can also, of course, be seen in the 'inappropriate' stories, descriptions, responses and essays that boys, in particular, produce in resistance to this coercion.[44]

Boys' stories, for example, are notoriously different from girls' in their use of violence, and draw far more extensively on non-literary sources for characters, narratives, settings, themes.[45] It is far more likely for boys to use characters and plot sequences based on action toys, films or TV programs—and to focus on an external public world of battle, aggression, retribution. For some boys this is the only discursive world that is familiar and known. For others, it is a world that can be deliberately brought into the classroom *because* it is known to be unacceptable to the mission of the English classroom.

And boys' reading responses can be similarly ignorant of, and/or resistant to the moral imperative lurking behind literary study. Colin Kenworthy, for example, provides an intriguing example of his efforts as a teacher to promote students' understandings of how 'some texts and reading practices work together to condition readers to perceive and evaluate the world from a masculine point of view'.[46] The point of Kenworthy's lessons for teenage boys was ideologically commendable: he was trying to help them to understand and 'resist' the seduction of masculinist literary readings. For this to occur, he needed to move the boys towards alternative readings and preferred reading positions: to encourage them to shift ideologically in their thinking about masculinity; to read differently, acknowledging the naturalisation in literary readings of misogynistic and patriarchal positions.

However, boys who worked together on a poem in a single-sex class group—unlike boys who worked in mixed-sex groups, or girls who worked in single-sex groups—resisted this attempt at moral training. Instead of reading against the masculinist stand the poem offered, they introduced contemporary masculinist discourse into the lesson which allowed them to resist the 'missionary' discourse of the lesson. The result was an entrenchment of masculinist positions rather than a liberal and humanistic broadening of positions, and, as Kenworthy observes:

> [The boys] were not unintelligent in doing this. Their response to the task I set them showed them as fearful of the feminine. [The poem] was difficult for them because it challenged their view of how they would like the world to be. The lesson was difficult for them because while pretending to offer a set of neutral . . . reading practices, it offered what they saw as a set of feminist (or even feminine) reading practices. I was difficult for them because while bearing the outward signs of maleness and masculinity—a beard and a tie—I asked them to reject the view of the 'real men' in the poem and the masculine point of view which their own talk had constituted as the objective truth about what it was to be a man.[47]

For many boys, the texts marketed at children's culture and the compulsory years of English study, and the teaching practices or technologies associated with those texts, tacitly endorse dominant standards of morality, and could be interpreted as feminised. While hegemonic masculinity is lined up oppositionally to sensitivity, emotion, disclosure, regulation and surveillance, literary study is potentially unmasculine. It is also, as we have argued in chapter 3, in marked contrast to the discourses supported by and endorsed through male youth culture and boys' sport and leisure practices. And it is also in contrast, as we argued in chapter 5, to much of boys' experiences of life at school.

While the literacy classroom encourages boys to express their inner selves, to appreciate the canons of literature, and to observe community standards of morality, the wider school context subordinates them within the student–teacher authority structure. Although boys may maintain a privileged position in relation to girls in the school context, the schoolboy nevertheless 'is required to accept inferior status to the teacher, to experience powerlessness in the face of adult rule, to be regulated by the demands of the institution, and to be controlled by the state authority'.[48]

Yet outside the context of the school, boys are encouraged to understand themselves very differently and to position themselves within sets of masculinised practice. But they also quickly learn that masculinist discourse as it is practised in the playground and peer group is not acceptable within the classroom. As Alloway and Gilbert argue, '[h]egemonic masculinity is not done in terms of self-disclosure, introspection, personalised and creative expression, but rather in terms of an outside-of-self, objectified expression . . . Outward-looking, hegemonic masculinity prefers to concentrate on things outside of self, rather than on the self.'[49] Masculinist discourse therefore becomes a discourse of opposition, signalling resistance to the discursive constitution of 'schoolboy' or 'literate subject'. It is a discourse of power that not only has the potential to sexualise female teachers and female students, thereby diminishing their status and authority, but also has the potential to enforce and legitimate heterosexual masculinity as the only possible form of maleness.

Constructions of the literate subject, the schoolboy and masculinity therefore open out a field of play where abrasive interactions are inevitable. Some groups of boys, as we have seen, may find the press to become insiders to the literacy and literary experience particularly threatening to their masculinity, and issues of class, ethnicity, race and sexuality may be crucial in determining how boys resolve these tensions.[50] Martino's interviews with Australian secondary school boys, for example, show how homophobia may feature in regulating boys' engagement with English.

> English is more suited to girls because it's not the way guys think . . . this subject is the biggest load of bullshit I have ever done. Therefore, I don't particularly like this subject. I hope you aren't offended by this, but most guys who like English are faggots.[51]

Some boys may reject the requirement to engage in the 'feminised practices' of the literacy classroom as the friction with their masculinity is too keenly experienced.

CONSTRUCTING AN AGENDA FOR CHANGE

The challenge to develop a constructive and positive agenda for boys and literacy is clearly very difficult and is not without serious internal contradictions and complexities. One of the most pressing is, as Martino's student explains above, the association of English literacy with feminised practice and the pride and confidence which boys can voice in their opposition to English and reading. It seems entirely appropriate to many boys to reject literacy. If the masculine self is oppositional to the literate self, then it must seem to many boys that literacy is relatively unimportant and irrelevant. Given that hegemonic masculinity is such a powerful and enabling discourse, it is difficult to see why boys would willingly give up its strengths for the less attractive and less powerful discourses of literature and literacy. Successful acquisition of masculinity seems almost to demand separation from literacy and the technologies associated with it.

In a study of fathers and literacy, Sue Nichols found that many fathers identified themselves as non-readers at some stage of their schooling years, and that this 'negative identification with reading was associated with a positive identification with perceived masculine activities and qualities'. Nichols found that rejection of reading seemed to be associated with four main stances.

1 Reading and physical activity defined as mutually exclusive
 . . .
2 Rejection of fictional narrative . . .
3 Reading along with 'schoolwork' and 'homework', being associated with the subject position of conforming to authority . . .
4 Interest in maths and reading seen as mutually exclusive . . .[52]

Significantly the women in Nichols' sample shared these views about the inappropriateness of reading for men, leading Nichols to suggest that the women made a 'positive association between their partner's valued masculine qualities and his perceived rejection of literacy'.[53] Reading was linked with passivity, with fiction, with regulation—whereas real men were

215

active, interested in facts and information, and slightly maverick and beyond the control of the school ma'am. Nichols concludes that 'associations with literacy and schooling are evidently an important building block in the construction of the masculine/feminine dualism'.[54]

This potential opposition between masculinity and literacy can also be seen in some of the strategies often proposed for addressing issues to do with boys and literacy. For instance, while there is considerable interest in involving boys more in reading programs, so as to make them competent readers in the school culture, there seems to be little interest in extending the range of reading positions for young men, or in making a variety of reading practices accessible.[55] Similarly, despite clear evidence of the violent, aggressive and combative content of boys' written school texts, there is no reference to boys' writing in the O'Doherty Report, and almost none in the recent Browne and Fletcher[56] edition on boys and schooling. And yet as we have argued earlier, boys' written texts are often restricted in their generic range, subject matter and linguistic structure.

It would almost seem as if literacy is constructed in terms of functional and vocational technologies when boys are its subjects, so as to make it implicitly less oppositional to masculinity. And this is in marked contrast to the strategies adopted for issues to do with girls and literacy in the 1970s and 1980s. While many groups of girls tended to perform well at literacy, there was concern that school-based literacy practices were not necessarily advantageous for girls. The compatibility of the 'literate' self with a 'feminine' self has not necessarily served girls well in terms of introducing them to a range of other ways of taking up social positions as girls and women. In addition, as we have argued earlier, there is little social valuation of school literacy competence. Being good at reading and writing has not necessarily led to careers in language-based professions—or even to well-paid jobs.[57] It is still predominantly girls who become secretaries and typists for male managers and bosses; it is still predominantly women who do the word-processing while men write software programs.

Although initially concerned with issues of access and equity as they pertained to girls' participation and involvement in classroom talk, to female representation in textbooks and literature, and to sexist language practices, the girls and literacy agenda soon moved to a focus on the symbolic language order and the literate self constructed through such an order. Feminist critiques of patriarchal literary traditions, of masculinist reading frames, and of unequal and discriminatory gendered language practices,[58] provided eloquent testimony to the masculinist, patriarchal self assumed to be at the heart of the literary experience.

Such critiques asserted the need for a female literate self and posited various ways in which such a self might be experienced and constructed. The impossibility of a singular female self—and the possibility of variously reconstructing and redefining what such a self might look like—became increasingly the focus of feminist education reform in the 1990s.[59] Yet while feminist educators developed a range of new technologies that would enable girls to reject the literate (masculinist) 'self' offered through traditional literacy discourses, there has so far not been a corresponding interest from those working with boys. This may again indicate the implicit desire for a male literate 'self' resistant to the compliant and morally regulated subject of English education discourses: a reconstruction of literacy that can be embraced within hegemonic discourses of masculinity.

The boys and literacy arguments grew initially out of what might be labelled equity and essentialist arguments: boys were not achieving as well as girls in literacy tests, and maleness and masculinity were being derided and attacked through what might be regarded as an increasingly strong focus from feminist educators on sexual harassment and male violence to women. There has been comparatively little emphasis in boys' literacy education on moving beyond gender dualisms, towards theories of multiple subjectivities and the complexities of the multi-located social subject.

This suggests that it is this level which will become increasingly critical to the boys and literacy agenda, because it is only at this level that the oppositional constructs of literacy and masculinity can be unravelled and reconstituted. While issues of access and equity are obviously important to highlight and emphasise, and while a recognition of desirable aspects of maleness and masculinity needs to be sustained, a crucial aspect of reform for boys will need to involve a reassessment

of constructions of the male 'self' and of how such constructions sit beside the discourses and technologies of the school.
In terms of literacy, this means that constructions of the literate
'self' through school discourses on literature and literacy need
to be seen beside constructions of the male 'self' that educators
posit for boys through reformist agendas.

This conflict is likely to become even more problematic
when the issue of male youth culture—and its place within
the school—is addressed more widely. Feminist educators have
seen the potential of working constructively with the texts of
popular culture, and of building connections from these lived
texts of community to the more literate texts of the school.[60]
Girls' popular culture provides an ideal site for exploring
constructions of femininity, of reading practices and positions,
and of the gendered construction of narrative. However, boys'
popular cultural texts, and the performative, embodied nature
of such texts, might require other approaches. As we have
argued in chapter 3, the male culture of Nintendo and Sega
electronic games, game playing, and game magazine reading
provides a different set of options for the classroom. Similarly
TV shows and films that are more popular with boys do not
offer the same stepping stones to print and literate culture
that many of the programs aimed at girls do.

In addition, it would also be a mistake to appropriate male
youth culture narratives into children's picture books or junior
and teenage fiction, without problematising the competitiveness
and violence of such narratives and the masculine subjectivities
they legitimate. And yet there will be a temptation to use such
high interest source material because of its attractiveness to
the reluctant reader, and to avoid considering how gender
relations are implicitly involved in the technologies employed.
In constructing text material for boys—or textual activities for
boys—we need to avoid a construction of literacy which merely
embraces and appropriates masculinist discourse and fails to
tackle the opposition between literacy and masculinity.

CRITICAL LITERACY AND THE BOYS' AGENDA

The technologies developed within discourses on 'critical literacy'[61] may be more appropriate for this task. While such

discourses are not hegemonic or monolithic, and while they can encompass a wide range of positions and viewpoints, they do have common elements. On the whole, critical literacy discourses acknowledge the crucial link between language and social practice, and they support a critical investigation into the way language practices can transform social practice. They make it possible to advocate a more critical approach to literacy and to textual practices both in and beyond the school, as a strategy for enabling boys to read both their own practices, and the practices that inscribe and construct them as masculine, literate and institutionalised subjects.[62]

We would argue that such an approach makes it possible for both students and teachers to see how they have been textually inscribed and constructed in various ways, through the access they have had to various discourses and social experiences. Discourses and social experiences of masculinity and femininity will be critical here, as will discourses and social experiences of sexuality, ethnicity, class and privilege. Unlike femininity, masculinity—as a dominant and powerful discourse—has seldom been held up for scrutiny and reconstruction in classrooms.

We would also argue that there are many forms of literacy, and that schools tend to work with particular print-based versions of literacy. It is important that this base be broadened: that texts from a much wider range of cultural experience be enfranchised within the classroom and serve as legitimate texts for inquiry and interrogation; and that a much more extensive range of pedagogical practices be embraced in this inquiry and interrogation. In particular, the practices associated with the teaching of literature need very close scrutiny. It is doubtful whether the literate self lying at the heart of literary discourse is a subject position of value to girls or boys, and given the cultural loading it carries, it has potential to seriously marginalise and silence many students.

If classrooms are to foster critical deconstruction of 'the self', and to support critical inquiry and interrogation, then they need to establish teacher–student relationships and classroom environments that are supportive of student-focused learning. This may be particularly problematic if other aspects of masculinity and schooling are not understood and acknowledged. Successful literacy classrooms are those in which teacher–student power is distributed more evenly, so that students are recognised and valued, and their knowledges and skills enfranchised and respected. This is important for all students, but given the connection between power and dominant forms of masculinity, it may be critical for boys. Boys are more likely to participate and achieve in school literacy work if they don't see participation and achievement in such work as being in conflict with desirable constructions of masculinity: if they can see, instead, how such work is relevant and useful in understanding their lives, in making their lives richer and fuller, and in offering them new and different ways of re-making their lives.

Critical literacy can certainly not be read as a panacea for boys' underachievement and underperformance in school literacy. However, when adopted with other understandings of the social constructions of masculinity, literacy and schooling, it can provide strategies that not only strive to meet the challenge of developing a defensible and positive agenda for boys' education, but that also sit compatibly within the education of girls' reform agenda of the past twenty years.

CONCLUSION

As we have argued throughout this chapter, literacy learning has become closely intertwined with schooling. Learning to 'do' literacy is very much about learning to 'do' school: learning what counts as an appropriate response; learning how to write within school-sanctioned discourse modes; learning when and how to speak and perform. Reading and writing become associated with conforming to school demands. To understand more about student failure at literacy—and student resistance to literacy—we need to look carefully at these schooling and literacy connections.

For some groups of boys the rub between masculinity and literacy may be much more abrasive than many teachers have assumed, and it may well be linked with implicit parental, social and cultural assumptions about a mismatch and disjunction between masculinity and literacy. As long as literacy is associated with feminised activity, and as long as literacy is also associated with conforming to the regulation of the school, boys may well choose to reject a position as literate subject. And yet, as we have also argued in this chapter, attempts to 'masculinise' literacy and to legitimate masculinist discourse in literacy classrooms will not only serve boys poorly, but will also disadvantage girls.

Yet boys need language skills and language experiences. They need opportunities to engage with the discursive construction of themselves as masculine subjects, and with the discursive construction of textual practice. They need experiences of how language works in a range of media sites and a range of social contexts. They need understandings of language practices that will allow them to use language in ways that will enrich and broaden their experiences of social life. Discourses about literacy and about 'English' have to engage much more deliberately with the ways in which boys · are positioned in literacy/English classrooms, and have to place links between masculinity and language practice firmly on the schooling agenda.

Strategies for change

In our discussion of boys' construction of masculinity and its relationship with schooling, we have focused on the images which represent to boys what it is to be masculine, and the practices they must engage in to be accepted and to recognise themselves as masculine in culturally acceptable definitions of the term. Many of these images and practices of masculinity pose threats to the welfare and security of boys and girls, as well as boys' engagement with schooling, and their relations with adults and peers of both sexes. Society as a whole is the loser, and many boys suffer from the restrictions imposed on them and the uncertainties they face.

If boys are to be shown how dominant masculinity constrains as much as it advantages them, they need to see how these images and practices are sustained, and at what cost to their opportunities to live lives which are open to diverse experiences and positive relationships with others.

Seeing masculinity as a performance suggests that we need to focus on how boys interact with others in various contexts if we are to offer them different ways of being male. We have also argued that masculinity is relational, that it is constructed within a system of gender which places dominant masculinity in hostile opposition to alternatives. Boys will need to see the folly of believing that there is only one form of masculinity which is narrow, rigid and inflexible, and whose integrity and viability depends on its opposition to femininity and more diverse concepts of masculinity. Acknowledging the range of alternatives, and understanding their combination with other kinds of difference, make this a complex task.

Performing masculinity is never complete, but is always struggled over, a constant part of everyday life which pervades all its aspects, including the experience of schooling. We have seen how schools as institutions can be masculinised in their administrative and pedagogical ideologies and practices, and how these influence teachers' relations with students and with each other. We have also seen how masculinity is infused in the practices of sport, leisure, and learning in a range of curriculum contexts. If we are to consider reforming the anti-social and anti-educational aspects of dominant masculinity, action will need to be taken on all these fronts.

IDENTIFYING THE PROBLEMS

The school response to the call for a focus on boys' education has been diverse, uneven and tentative in its development of goals and appropriate strategies, but there is a growing body of work which needs to be considered by those concerned to address the issue. For instance, the recent Australian collection, entitled *Boys in Schools*, illustrates the issues and strategies developed by practitioners in the field as they have addressed those aspects of schooling thought to be relevant to the education of boys.[1]

The problems identified in the book and the strategies applied to them illustrate the range of ways in which the boys' education agenda has been taken up. The collection identifies a long list of concerns among the contributors, which can be categorised in terms of what is seen to be the origin of the concern.[2] The contributors address four main kinds of problem: the attributes of boys, where they are seen to be fragile, maladjusted, and anxious; how they relate to other people, where they are seen as intolerant, harassing, aggressive, and anti-social; their lifestyle, which is largely destructive to themselves and others; and the problems of their relationship to schooling. The most frequent problems identified are those in the first two categories—boys' attributes and personal relationships. These two categories play a more fundamental role in the explanation of the problems, since they are often seen to underlie the other two areas of concern. The key point, however, is that there is no consensus over just what the problems are, nor how the various dimensions are related.

The focus on boys' attributes implies a form of essentialism, as if boys have a set of characteristics which are uniform and distinctive to them as a group. This approach focuses on these aspects of boys' experience primarily as features of boys' personalities or character, rather than as a cultural repertoire of masculine behaviours, relationships and practices which construct their responses to situations. Locating these elements of masculinity in boys in this way also overlooks differences among boys, the similarities between boys and girls, and how the same boys can act differently in different situations. Similarly, the focus on interpersonal relationships, important as it is, nonetheless fails to locate these in wider structural relations, such as sexuality, race and class, and to acknowledge the tensions and differences which result. This is evident in the almost universal tendency to speak of 'boys' as a homogeneous, undifferentiated mass.

In these respects, the analyses of the issues for boys' education in *Boys in Schools* lack important aspects of the perspectives we have outlined in earlier chapters. However, the Browne and Fletcher collection was primarily intended to review the strategies available for working with boys in schools, and it is better judged in these terms. The collection reports on a range of strategies developed by educators to deal generally with behaviour problems, social welfare issues and various target groups in schools, and applied to the education of boys.

For instance, a common strategy is to discuss boys' relationships in group sessions where rules of interaction are developed to prevent put-downs, conflict and aggression.[3] Another approach uses encouragement, affirmation, role play and close physical contact to develop feelings of safety and self-esteem.[4] Others use conflict resolution,[5] the Glasser method of behaviour management,[6] or role play and improvisation[7] to deal with bullying and harassment. Strategies like self-esteem exercises, role play and values analysis and clarification predominate in this collection, and while these strategies are problematic,[8] each of them has its uses.

However, the relation between particular aspects of boys' education and the strategies included in *Boys in Schools* is not clear. Any particular concern is addressed using a number of strategies, and any particular strategy is justified in terms of a number of concerns.[9] As a result, it is difficult to identify the specific goals of particular strategies, and to gauge their success. It also raises interesting questions about the relationship between diagnoses of need and schools' curricular and pedagogical responses. To do this, we need to analyse the various strategies, clarify their purposes and assess their relevance. The following discussion tries to map the types of strategies available for boys' programs and consider their relative merits.

APPROACHES TO BOYS' EDUCATION

Strategies for addressing the needs of boys in the various programs, projects and prescriptions in the area can be discussed in five major categories. First, there are those disciplinary responses which attempt to control the anti-social fallout of boys' behaviour, like bullying and harassment. Other strategies consider the knowledge content needed if boys are to understand how they are influenced by contemporary masculinity. A third approach develops boys' ability to discuss and reflect on their experience and how it is influenced by their social context. A fourth tries to develop skills such as interpersonal communication which might assist boys in their relations with others. Finally, another approach emphasises the need to deal with boys' attitudes, values, emotions and sensitivities through strategies approximating personal therapy. We will consider each of these broad kinds of strategy and what they have to offer as ways of dealing with the issues of boys' education.

Disciplinary approaches

Some educators have seen the problematic aspects of boys' behaviour as generic problems, and developed disciplinary policies to deal with them. Bullying is a good example.[10] Rather than seeing bullying as a response to some problem in boys' relations with others, the approach is to see bullying itself as the problem, and emphasising strategies which will suppress it. Programs designed to address these generic behavioural problems tend to ignore any connection with the cultural practices of students and their wider society. For instance, bullying policies may treat as identical any harmful acts, irrespective of their different motivations or whether they have racist or sexist or homophobic dimensions. In such cases, the policy will address the symptoms while leaving the cause untouched. It is for these reasons that the O'Doherty Report recommended that programs on sex-based harassment and violence in schools should be brought under the umbrella of the school's gender equity strategy.[11]

It is crucial that policies on bullying, sex-based harassment and the like should exist, and the protection of the targets should be guaranteed as securely as the school can possibly achieve. In a national survey of Australian schools conducted by the Australian Council for Educational Research (ACER), around 91 per cent of teachers claimed that their classrooms were free of sex-based harassment, but student responses gave a different picture, with over a third of boys and girls reporting that verbal sex-based harassment happened often. In addition, 40 per cent of primary and 50 per cent of secondary pupils said that nothing happens when a student makes a complaint about sex-based harassment.[12] Programs to combat bullying and harassment are clearly needed.

However, unless these programs are combined with other approaches, including those addressing gender, race and disability, they will give students no understanding of the practices which the policies are designed to control. Students need this understanding if they are to recognise racism and sexism and how it can give rise to or be incorporated in threatening and harmful behaviour. They need to be able to name these injustices if they are to respond appropriately by demanding their rights to be left unharmed. Boys who may feel that such behaviour is reasonable or required for acceptance by their peers also need to understand how these perceptions are created in their culture and how they impugn the rights of others.

Disciplinary responses such as anti-discrimination policies

that rigorously police expressions of sexism or homophobia, and protect vulnerable groups from harassment, may still be incomplete. Redman points out that they are unlikely to shift boys' fundamental investments in forms of discriminatory behaviour. Boys may learn not to be racist or sexist or to bully in front of teachers, but, when not under surveillance, may revert to the kind of dominant and aggressive behaviour which makes these acts acceptable in certain definitions of masculinity. In fact, these practices then have the added function of being protests against authority, which increases their value as a form of 'protest masculinity'.[13]

The difficulty with many disciplinary approaches is that they can be seen to use the same methods in retribution as the perpetrator used in the initial offence. Domination and intimidation as strategies to achieve an end are just the kinds of strategy which bullies and harassers use. For this reason, we need to avoid shouting, corporal punishment, bullying passing for discipline, and other masculine disciplinary strategies. Also, the disciplinary approach tends to focus on individuals when much of this behaviour is a group response to the culture from which it draws much of its sustenance, kudos and rewards. As Askew and Ross observe, removing one troublemaker often means he will be replaced by another because of group pressure.[14] Dealing with the individual should be part of a broader strategy.

A useful example of the disciplinary approach is the sex-based harassment policy developed at Keira Technology High School, where perpetrators are dealt with according to a carefully worked out program which confronts them and firmly challenges their behaviour. The policy details a staged set of procedures which clearly signal that such behaviour is unacceptable, and which protect the victims, and confront perpetrators with the need to accept and change the wrong in what they did. However, this disciplinary process for dealing with harassment events is preceded by meetings and lessons for all the students where they are informed about sex-based harassment, how to combat it, and the policy for dealing with those who transgress.[15] On the other hand, the program lacks any clear connection with the broader issues of power and gender which would give it a wider effectiveness.

Of course, while there is a mutually supporting affinity between the cultural significance of bullying and aggressive masculinity, bullying cannot be entirely attributed to aggressive masculinity. There are instrumental reasons why some boys and girls will find bullying a profitable way to act. Yet even in these cases, the ideology of dominant masculinity will make such actions seem more acceptable, respectable, even laudable, in the eyes of many boys. Understanding how these cultural meanings are established and fed by a wider culture of masculinity is an important need.

Knowledge-based approaches

This brings us to a second group of strategies, which emphasise knowledge and understanding rather than the punitive control of the disciplinary approach. Of all the strategies available to educators, surely this should be central to any school response. However, in the survey conducted by the ACER, only 35 per cent of teachers said they used 'critical analysis of practices and contexts which limit educational and life possibilities on the basis of gender'. This was the second lowest frequency of use of the thirteen gender related strategies in the survey.[16]

If we are to reform the more damaging aspects of dominant masculinity and its effects on gender relations, students need to understand how gender operates as a system which positions them with respect to each other, encourages and discourages certain ways of being, and offers them models and resources for creating their sense of identity. Kenway and Fitzclarence have noted the tendency for some gender equity programs to become highly rationalistic and even authoritarian in their approach to these issues. As the issues are themselves highly emotive for many students, this can simply be alienating, for 'approaches which preach rather than teach and which are destructive rather than deconstructive and reconstructive do not work'.[17]

However, this difficulty should not prevent us from treating understanding of gender as a central need in school learning for boys and girls. Gender is one of the most powerful social institutions which construct their world; to leave them ignorant of it is simply to fail them educationally. The O'Doherty Report offers a useful starting point in its list of important learnings, which it recommends as necessary core content of the curriculum:

- the construction of gender; what it is to be 'male' or 'female' in our society, including different types of masculinity and femininity,
- living as part of a community; how relationships are affected by gender issues,
- relationships in families and in the community,
- gender stereotypes; their effect on attitudes and behaviour,
- media images of men and women and their impact,
- peer group pressure,
- self-image and the development of self-esteem,
- the nature of power in relationships and in society; the abuse of power through sex-based harassment (same-sex and other-sex harassment), bullying and violence,
- conflict resolution techniques,
- understanding the opposite sex, including the impact our behaviour can have on others,
- the things we value in relating to each other and in living as part of our various communities—family, school, our neighbourhood, the workplace,
- the things we value from individuals around us, male and female, and the ways these may run counter to predominant gender stereotypes.[18]

Part of this understanding must include the question of boys' curriculum choice and the narrow range of subjects to which concepts of masculinity seem to restrict them. In the ACER survey of gender and education in Australian schools, Collins et al. observed that 'In our school visits, we got the sense that this narrowness of what many boys did was not perceived as a problem'. The students surveyed perceived that girls were encouraged to cross gender boundaries in subject choice much more than boys.[19]

Group strategies

A focus on knowledge also underlies the third approach to be reviewed here, but the source of the knowledge is not the concepts of social analysis and the construction of gender, so much as reflection on personal experience. Redman labels as 'participatory rationalism' the approach which uses participatory strategies like small group discussions, case histories and role play to allow pupils to think through beliefs and values and come to more rational and objective conclusions. However, he points out that boys often self-censor the beliefs they express among their peers, so this kind of discussion doesn't necessarily shift boys' feelings or their investments in their peer group's values. It can also be a rather uncritical discussion where boys clarify their values but do not locate them in their culture or ask how they are related to power relations among boys or between boys and girls and men and women. Nonetheless, such an approach is a necessary complement to the study of gender relations as a system, since it allows boys to see how their own experiences are produced by that system and how they might be able to change it through their own actions.

However, the evidence is that boys do not often have the opportunity to discuss these issues. The ACER survey concluded that 'Few schools appear to be doing well at the task of helping students to discuss gender . . . at least in the kind of personal way which might develop the level of understanding of each other, and of the impact on others of their own behaviour, on which real friendship and respect are built'.[20] Reflection on personal experience in small groups will be an important part of any program addressing the needs of boys.

Skills training

The fourth approach through skills training emphasises that gender identities are forms of learned behaviour that can be replaced by alternative skills. Examples in gender education have included assertiveness training for women, or strategies for negotiating sexual activity between men and women. When applied to the problem of dominant masculinity, this approach has been widely criticised as underestimating the power invested in men by existing gender relations, and therefore their interest in retaining a dominant position over women.

We need to acknowledge that currently dominant forms of masculinity may '"feel right" or "make imaginative sense" to the men and boys who inhabit them'.[21] When applied to schools, the evidence is that bullying or sex-based harassment is not caused by a lack of social skills in the perpetrators.

In her work on sex-based harassment in schools, Hinson has been highly critical of this approach. She argues that the first problem is that 'harassment is a social phenomenon, driven by a web of identifiable interrelated cultural practices', and that these practices need to be addressed at the individual but also at the group, school and system levels.[22] Accordingly, any approach which regards the problem as being based in a lack of individual skills must be inadequate. In fact, Hinson cites research which suggests that men who were better able to get on with women, that is, with more heterosexual skills, were more coercive in their relations with women than those who were less skilled. Boys do not harass because they lack skills, but because of the power advantages it offers, and the fact that in certain situations such behaviour is socially sanctioned. Hinson points out that boys who harass do not do so indiscriminately, but in situations where they feel able to do so. She found in her 1994 study of Australian schools that there were seldom any consequences for boys who harassed girls or women at school.

Hinson makes similar comments about the approach through conflict resolution or mediation, which she says assumes that sex-based harassment occurs as a conflict between two equal parties. While such strategies are useful in certain circumstances, they are not adequate for sex-based harassment as they frame 'explanations and responses in ways which tend to obscure those cultural and institutional practices which sustain sex-based harassment'.[23] Addressing sex-based harassment requires that we teach students about gender relations and the power relations that go with them, and that we lead them to challenge and change the practices which sustain harassment.

However, while the approach through skills is not adequate to the task of dealing with issues like harassment, there is a need to show students not only the injustice and constraints placed upon them by unequal gender relations, but the strategies they might use to deal differently with these experiences.

In this sense, the development of social skills is an important part of a comprehensive approach.

For instance, school programs dealing with counterviolence strategies, such as effective intervention tactics in violent confrontations, have been reported as lowering the levels of violence in schools. Ways of handling violence have been enhanced when teachers and students have rehearsed in advance in class the respective roles to be played when anger or violent behaviour erupt in the playground.[24] Katz reports a project in which college sportsmen discussed and rehearsed scenarios for dealing with harassment perpetrated by their peers. Participants considered options for intervention and how they might act against such behaviour.[25]

Such skills and strategies are an important part of a comprehensive approach. The ACER survey on gender programs showed that 69 per cent of primary students but only 62.5 per cent of secondary students agreed that they had been taught 'ways to handle hassles from others about how they want a girl or a boy to look or behave'.[26] Kenway's research on gender equity programs found that students were not given 'much advice about or practical experience in how to become active citizens for gender justice'. She argues that it is important to offer students 'visions of alternative worlds and ways of being', and 'negotiated, practical or hands-on experiences of political organisation and strategy'.[27] While skills-based approaches can disguise the real nature of the problems many boys face and cause, when combined with other approaches recommended here they have an important role to play.

Personal development

The final approach to be discussed focuses on the affective experience of students, how they feel about their relations with others, and their associated self-concept, self-confidence and self-esteem. Redman sees such strategies as motivated by the need to 'find the real man within', with its false distinction between the 'real or true self' and the way boys have been socialised to feel and behave. The fallacy of this distinction has been pointed out in chapter 2. However, Redman accepts that the strategies of American ego therapy, which are associated with this concern for the self, do connect with boys' active investments in heterosexual power relations. Since these are not necessarily open to rational argument nor easily redirected through skills training, the therapeutic approach does offer a way forward. The problem is that this focus can ignore how masculinities interact with and are part of a wider set of social relations, and how this wider context accounts for the investments men and boys make in the forms of masculinity they occupy.

Kenway's research also identified this therapeutic approach to gender programs, with its emphasis that participants enjoy themselves and feel good about their gender. This sometimes dominated to the neglect of a focus on becoming critical, informed and skilled advocates for gender equity.[28] Hinson criticises the focus on self-esteem more fundamentally, partly because of its vagueness and theoretical weakness, but also because there are no established causal links between the everyday practice of sex-based harassment and constructs such as self-concept, self-esteem or self-confidence. She quotes examples in her own research of boys who were popular, confident leaders among peers and in the school, but who nonetheless severely harassed girls.[29] Olweus also found no evidence that bullies lacked self-confidence, though, understandably, many victims of bullying did.[30]

This approach reflects the focus on the inner struggle with masculinity rather than what boys do, which we criticised in chapter 2. The focus on the inner self lays the emphasis on an internal harmony rather than one's relations with the world, and in this sense can promote selfishness over care for others. As care for others is commonly seen as a problem for men and boys, this seems a dangerous strategy. As McLean observes, ' . . . what is most seriously absent in male social development is the capacity for empathy and emotional connectedness *with the experience of other people*—not simply an inability to express one's *own* feelings'.[31]

However, personal work is important if boys are to be enabled to see why certain ways of being masculine seem desirable, why their anxieties might lead them to conform to these models, and how this conformity can prevent them from developing their humanity in all its forms, and from enjoying rewarding relationships with others. Kenway argues the need 'to include in the theoretical apparatus of gender education pedagogies such concepts as pleasure, nurturance, pain, blame, shame, risk, investment and fantasy'.[32] Addressing these emotions will require strategies for dealing with these affective elements of becoming masculine.

Just as masculinity is not singular or uniform, no single approach will address all the problems boys will have in confronting the demands of masculine discourses. Each of the approaches reviewed can make important contributions to boys' needs. The most successful programs then will have the following characteristics:

- they will be part of a wide ranging policy on gender equity in which the education of boys and girls, and school policies on discipline, bullying, harassment, and curriculum choice and content will be integrated, along with strategies which address racism, sexuality, disability and other relevant issues;
- they will ensure that an understanding of the social construction of gender is integrated throughout the curriculum, including its operation as a social institution in the wider society, and its role in constructing opportunities and responses for boys' and girls' sense of themselves and their relations with others;
- the strategies for dealing with these issues will include small group reflective exercises where boys and girls, in both mixed and single-sex groups, will share their experiences and interpretations relevant to the formation of their gender identities and relations, and explore the possibilities for improving these relations;
- strategies will also include the development of skills involved in resolving conflict, resisting sex-based harassment and bullying, and gathering support for the promotion of personal safety and the freedom to be different;
- strategies will address the affective needs of boys and girls, providing experiences where they are able to receive and provide cooperative, nurturing, comforting and empathetic experiences.

In devising these programs, we need to see the construction of masculinity as a process where boys are constantly presenting themselves to the world through whatever repertoire of behaviours, styles and forms of expression are most readily available to them and most appropriate to their context. The challenge for schools is to make available a variety of educationally constructive positions and positive experiences, and to endorse these as acceptable ways of being male. This will not be an easy task, for, as we have seen in this book, powerful forms of masculinity will compete for boys' allegiance in ways which conflict with the educational aspirations of schools, and many of the conventional processes of schools themselves are complicit in this.

SOME CURRENT EXAMPLES

There is an increasing number of valuable models to follow, as workers in the field produce programs, materials and strategies which translate the understandings of the construction of gender into productive learning experiences. Much of this work began in programs for dealing with sex-based harassment and violence, and was motivated largely by the need to combat the worst excesses of masculine behaviour, and to protect girls and other boys from being dominated.

For instance, Herbert's work on sex-based harassment combines a range of approaches outlined above.[33] Through discussions of personal experiences and interpretations, harassment is named and distinguished from other social practices like flirting, and a series of myths about harassment shown to be fallacious. The program then relates harassment to power relations between men and women at individual and institutional levels, and considers how the presumptions on which it rests are related to sexist stereotypes. Harassment is studied in relation to homosexual harassment, bullying, racism and sexism, and domestic violence. The program raises issues of sexism in the curriculum as part of the context which must be changed if harassment is to be seen to be inimical to the school ethos. There is a focus on skills and strategies for confronting and dealing with harassment, as well as strategies by which boys can avoid actions which girls might find threatening.

The *Hands Off!* program is similarly broad-ranging.[34] It begins with a series of group building activities which establish cooperation, negotiation, the tolerance of difference and class cohesion and trust as the bases for the program. This therapeutic approach is followed by an analysis of violence and its relation to power in gender and race relations, and a skills-based approach which addresses ways of dealing with anger, being assertive and resolving conflict. The final section analyses popular culture to raise awareness of how gendered and other messages in sport and the media perpetuate violence in Australia.

The advantage of these and similar approaches to issues like harassment and violence is that they relate specific anti-harassment and anti-violence strategies to broader under-standings of gender relations and the power differences which make such behaviour possible. They do this in a comprehensive fashion which relates these issues to the social construction of gender at a range of levels from the individual to the social, and they combine critical analysis, participatory reflection, affective and skills-based approaches which give students a broad repertoire of resources for understanding, judging, responding to and acting on the issues involved.[35]

Other programs address the wider range of boys' problems by focusing on the construction of gender as a central issue, though they still address violence and harassment as a part of that issue. For instance, the *Boys-Talk* project focuses on masculinity, non-violence and relationships by encouraging young men to resist aspects of gender identity that harm them and the rights of others, and to examine how they are inducted into predominant practices of masculinity. The program includes topics of gender expectations and relations, violence, sexuality and personal relationships, and addresses these across dimensions of understanding, feelings, skills and planning for change. This and similar projects are ideal sources of ideas for developing programs for boys in schools.[36]

Other approaches try to develop alternative ways of becoming masculine in situations where young people are relatively free of the public pressure to compete and perform and match dominant expectations. These might include activities where collaboration is more valued than competitive dominance. Much of popular culture is of this kind. For instance, popular music seems to be one area where creative performance can give form to a wide range of images and relationships, and create the possibility of expressing a counterdominant ideology which is more accepting of difference. This is not to deny the sexism and conventional masculine ideologies which remain a significant part of this culture, manifest in such styles as gangster rap and cock rock. It is simply to recognise that artistic pursuits can generate a sense of release from traditional constraints where alternatives can be more freely voiced. Similar effects seem to result from community projects, especially where young people are given more responsibility than they might be granted in school. This should not simply be an option for those students who volunteer, as this is likely to exclude those very students who most need a cultural experience which is not dominated by aggressive competitiveness. It should be an expectation of all students, a taken-for-granted aspect of schooling.

Other important work is being done in the *Boys and Literacy* project, a professional development program which addresses the problem of boys' poor performance in English.[37] The distinctive aspect of this program is that it deals directly with the relationship between the construction of masculinity and boys' involvement in language practices in the classroom and in their leisure pursuits. For instance, the program notes that literacy strategies which ask students to discuss their personal, emotional responses to stories may disadvantage boys because disclosure, potential vulnerability and surveillance are at odds with dominant ways of being male. The project advocates that in encouraging boys to engage in such work, we must also address the cultural disincentives which may prevent them from doing so.

The project examines why some boys consider literacy to be feminised and/or culturally exclusive, and how literacy activities, resources and pedagogies reflect particular social constructions of what comes to count as literacy in contemporary society. This implies that while addressing the practices of dominant masculinity, the school should also scrutinise conventional literacy strategies and assess their suitability for boys. As part of this, the project considers

237

other forms of literacy, like those popular in boys' culture, and their implications for school literacy which is predominantly print-based.

While all these programs address issues of relevance to all boys, few of them focus specifically on strategies for groups of boys who may differ in terms of disability, ethnicity, race or sexuality. Many of them deal with race, ethnicity or homophobia as issues, but the presumed audience is those boys in the mainstream who need to be more tolerant of such differences, rather than gay or black boys themselves. Anti-racist and anti-homophobic work is important, but needs to be supplemented by work which addresses the needs of minority boys. The *Boys and Literacy* project does consider the special positions of Aboriginal and immigrant minority boys with respect to literacy. For instance, Ann Queitzsch reports work with young Aboriginal and Torres Strait Islander men which developed critical readings of how Aboriginality and masculinity are discursively constituted in popular texts.[38] Coleman and Skeen suggest strategies for teaching nontraditional boys in early childhood settings. Nontraditional boys in their terms are those who, because of their sexuality or gender identity, do not wish to conform to traditional heterosexual self-image, expression or behaviour. Their recommended strategies suggest teaching styles which do not presume or require traditional heterosexual norms of attitudes, interests or behaviour. They also discuss ways of conferring with parents, and evaluating the curriculum for its openness to different ways of being masculine.[39]

This review of approaches to boys' education is evidence of the increasing range of work being done in schools, and while it is still relatively unformed, and not extensively tested, it provides an excellent support for those planning to address the issue in schools. There is evidence of successful work across a wide range of issues and contexts, well illustrated in Salisbury and Jackson's collection.[40] While much of the work has addressed the concerns of adolescent boys, there are also valuable models of practice with children in the earliest years of schooling.[41] However, in implementing these programs and using their materials, there is an important set of issues relevant to them all which need to be considered.

ISSUES OF IMPLEMENTATION

Innovation in any institution is notoriously difficult if it challenges customary practices and ways of organising them. Gender education reform in schools is a classic example, and dealing with boys' issues in the ways advocated here will not be easy for a number of reasons.

Many of the strategies recommended for addressing boys' issues are not widely practised. Schools tend to operate with a standard range of strategies, and dealing with a new issue like the boys' agenda is a matter of activating them to address this new set of concerns. In the course of their application, the strategies bend the nature of the problem to ways that the school can deal with. Aspects of the problem which cannot readily be accommodated by the standard strategies are overlooked. Seeing boys' education strategies in this way explains the neglect of class, 'race', ethnicity and disability; the evasive treatment of sexuality; and the lack of a skills or therapeutic approach to gender. Schools historically have not developed or institutionalised strategies for dealing directly with such issues. This is especially so in secondary schools, and it is not surprising that the ACER survey found that secondary schools were less receptive to gender policy initiatives.[42]

This also accounts for the difficulty of integrating approaches to issues of boys' education. Boys' issues tend to be seen as problems of behaviour management or counselling or pastoral care or pedagogy or (less often) curriculum content, when what is needed is a more integrated and socially contextualised approach. (Similar difficulties plague the implementation of gender equity for girls.) Bringing these approaches together to develop a common understanding and a shared commitment is very difficult given the nature of schools and schooling. Yet there is a clear consensus among those experienced in this kind of work that only an integrated whole school approach is sufficient.

A whole school approach

Given the pervasiveness of masculinity in school practices, action addressing boys' issues needs to be equally pervasive.

This may include changing aspects of school organisation, disciplinary systems, the images and practices of sport, science, art and literature, peer group interactions and relations between teachers and pupils.[43] As Collins et al. observed in the ACER survey, 'taking action consistently is systematic, whole-school work, requiring focussed attention and team work by staff while a system is being set up, and mindful professional judgment thereafter'.[44]

Martinez has set out a useful list of elements of school practice which need to be addressed if schools are to respond to the boys' agenda.[45] Among these are the need for school leadership in publicly affirming gender equity principles, identifying the problems and how they may have been unwittingly endorsed in past practices, and modelling gender equity principles in relationships. This leadership role needs to be combined with partnerships between men and women in running boys' programs. If only women teachers are involved because they are seen to be the initiators of gender work, the programs will be marginalised, and the lack of male teachers' involvement seen as a sign that the program is irrelevant to male concerns. On the other hand, if only men are involved, the program will find it difficult to avoid a 'them and us' opposition, and to demonstrate positive gender relationships.

Partnerships are also needed among teachers, parents, students and the wider community to address masculinity in local cultures, and to enlist support in optimising the range of versions of masculinity available to boys. In addition, Martinez argues, the curriculum needs to address explicitly the critique of social practices which support gender inequality and violence, and develop the knowledge, skills and commitment to allow students to develop more equal and positive gender relations in school and family. It must equalise access to educational resources for boys and girls, and allow them to make choices which are less constrained by gender expectations and discriminatory attitudes. Finally, Martinez calls for the promotion at all levels of the system of gender equity policies, and a priority for the resource needs which they generate.

The whole school approach is necessary because of the wide variety of ways in which gender is practised in schools. Gender relations and practices are involved in all facets of the school's operation, and therefore need to be addressed across this range. This will also mean involving all staff in some way, and developing a broad commitment to the philosophy of gender programs.

Gaining staff commitment

The need for the whole school approach and Martinez's calls for leadership and partnerships raise the vexed question of how a broad staff commitment might be developed, for there is no doubt that dealing effectively with boys' problems in schooling will challenge a range of personal commitments among both male and female staff. Some boys and men see gender-related programs as a feminist plot, a threat to their status, and special steps need to be taken to pre-empt these reactions.[46] Discussing his experience with boys' programs, Dunn notes a backlash perspective among some male teachers who believe that women are taking over in schools, that gender equity is some 'dark feminist plot', and that girls' programs have been promoted at boys' expense. Dunn observes that these views have been the reason that some male teachers have become involved in boys' programs.[47] But developing a critical approach to gender and masculinity creates challenges for some women as well as some men. In discussing anti-violence strategies in schools, Kenway and Fitzclarence point out that:

> Some sorts of femininity unwittingly underwrite hegemonic masculinity . . . this particular version of femininity involves compliance and service, subservience and self-sacrifice and constant accommodation to the needs and desires of males. This indicates that anti-violence education is not a boys' only matter.[48]

Dunn also reports that, despite the years of work on gender equity and the general exhortations in policy documents, there remains a lack of specific understanding of gender among many teachers. Gender equity is often seen as being about non-sexist language and giving equal time to boys and girls, neglecting the need to value male and female contributions to society and to challenging discriminatory social structures. This problem is confirmed in the ACER survey, which found that some principals understood the construction of gender as being indistinguishable from the more general and familiar area of equal opportunity. Another group of principals operated on the premise that education should focus on the individual child, not on boys and girls and the social constructs underlying their behaviour and attitudes.[49]

In addressing boys' issues, schools should not underestimate the need for careful preparation of staff understandings. Allard has argued the need to prepare the ground with staff in a way which allows them to explore and investigate their own understandings and knowledge about gender and inclusive teaching practice, and which recognises their different starting points and understandings of the construction of gender. This will involve the trialling of teaching practices negotiated and developed by teachers, assisting them to monitor and reflect on experience, and ensuring regular reflection on progress and process of change.[50]

Male teachers and segregated classes

The involvement of men in the education of boys has become an important part of recent debates. Despite the continuing dominance of men in authority positions in schools, concerns in much of the boys' debate focuses on the fact that men are a minority in the teaching force, especially in the earlier years of school. It has been argued that the feminisation of the teaching force, especially in the early years, has contributed to the problems boys face by depriving them of adequate role models of masculinity.[51] The recommended solution is that there should be more male teachers in these early years. However, the rationale for this argument has been framed in two ways.

The conservative view is that more male teachers will reinforce traditional sex-role norms, giving boys the security of a clear role model. The reformist position is that having male teachers will show boys that men can be nurturing, loving and understanding, just as women are perceived to be. Clyde is attracted to this latter concept, which she labels androgynous, because it 'seems to offer the young child a balanced program because an androgynous adult has the psychological freedom to engage in whatever behavior seems most effective at the time'.[52]

There are difficulties in both the conservative and the reformist positions. First, there is no guarantee that the kinds of men who enter the teaching force would satisfy the role model desired by either the conservative or the reformist position. The conservative position is weakened by the lack of research evidence that male and female teachers treat young children differently. Clyde cites one study that 'male and female care workers' personality, characteristics and methods of reinforcing children's behaviour are similar'. Second, researchers studying the effects of modelling believe that 'the sex of the model is less important than the sex-appropriateness of the modelled behaviour relative to the observer'. If this were true, the reformist argument is not very compelling either.[53]

Others have argued that lamenting the absent male teacher is dangerous, as 'It places little responsibility on adult men to question their own behaviour', as if 'it is their gender presence that matters, not what they do and how they do it'.[54] It is certainly the case that the dynamics of gender are too complex to support any simple predictions about the effects of having male teachers; neither the presence nor absence of men determines the lessons boys might learn about masculinity. We saw earlier, for instance, that traditional versions of compliant femininity can reinforce the presumption of privilege among men and boys.

In contrast, there is evidence that boys can pressure women to be authoritarian and aggressive, and to prove themselves to be tough. Askew and Ross quote a teacher in a boys' school whose positioning by the boys transforms the gender significance of her teaching:

> I feel in a dilemma as a woman teacher. Whatever I do, I feel I end up reinforcing the norms of how teachers should behave in a boys' school . . . By adopting a more authoritarian style, I feel I'm validating this way of teaching and invalidating alternative methods. Yet if I take a more creative approach, I'm 'acting like a woman'.[55]

If boys can have this effect on women, they are equally likely to expect and try to evoke the same responses from those male teachers who do not conform to dominant ideologies of masculine authority.[56]

Having more male teachers would be a good thing if it signalled a dissolution of the gendered division of labour which is still so strong, and of the dominant masculine view that intellectual work is effeminate. To the extent that this occurs, then any effects on the children, however slight, are likely to be positive. On the other hand, if men (and women), who are encouraged to teach, provide restrictive, stereotyped discipline styles, gender attitudes and subject preferences, they will simply do more harm than good.

The push for separate boys' programs can be viewed in a similar light. The need for such teaching is probably exaggerated, and has been criticised for failing to recognise

> that men in our culture have always been separate from women, and that this separation is fundamental to traditional masculinity. Male bonding has always involved the exclusion of women, and this exclusion has been based on superiority, exploitation and a deep, unspoken fear of women's difference.[57]

If separate programs for boys reproduce these exclusionary understandings of masculinity, they can only aggravate their problems. On the other hand, segregated groups can provide both sexes with the opportunity to consider issues which might be difficult to air, at least initially, in mixed groups. Nonetheless, given that one important goal of boys' education is to promote better relations with girls, it is difficult to see how this can be achieved if boys never consider and act on these issues with girls. The need is for programs which deal with gender issues for both boys and girls, including segments which might best be done in segregated groups, but which are always followed up in mixed groups. An unfortunate consequence of the history of gender education reform is that, while there are excellent programs devised to deal with the gender oppression of girls,[58] and with the problems of boys,[59] they are not equally targeted at both sets of issues. Schools will need to adapt this range of excellent work to construct a program which caters for boys and girls together as well as separately.

The conclusion on the issue of segregated classes must be similar to that on the need for male teachers:

Sex segregated education can be used for emancipation or oppression. As a method it does not guarantee one outcome. The intentions, the understanding of people and their gender, the pedagogical attitudes and practices, are crucial, as in all pedagogical work.[60]

What's in it for boys? Problems of motivation

There are clear challenges for men in taking on the critique of dominant masculinity, so working with the issue of masculinity in schools will be difficult. While men and boys may sense that they have a problem, they may not want to acknowledge where the problem actually lies. Men (and boys) profit from what Connell calls 'the patriarchal dividend',[61] and most men are complicit in the social conditions which produce it. We cannot therefore accept the 'poor boys' stories as if boys are simply socially disempowered. Connell argues that masculinity is not 'an impoverished character structure. It is a richness, a plenitude. The trouble is that the specific richness of hegemonic masculinity is oppressive, being founded on, and enforcing, the subordination of women'.[62] This richness and plenitude are in question in the minds of many men. Some acknowledge the injustices on which it has been based; others resent the challenges to it. Both groups are unsettled in the process, though as we have seen, the power differences between men and women remain significant.

Boys will need to be convinced that to accept a critical view of dominant masculinity, they are not simply being asked to sacrifice a position of privilege in order to conform to someone else's idea of what is good and right. It may not be difficult to convince those boys who suffer bullying, intimidation, teasing and exclusion because they are different in some way. It will be harder to shift the allegiances of those who have found some security in conforming to aspects of the dominant image, or who relish the kind of power it provides.

Dunn's experience is that boys feel under siege with the heightened awareness and publicity of male violence and harassment and domestic violence in particular. They are also sensitised by the media to the backlash perspective, adding to their confusion and encouraging a defensive reaction.[63] Connell also cautions against 'a certain kind of feminist criticism, which emphasises blame and treats men as an undifferentiated category'. He recounts the experience of men in his university courses on gender, who have been discouraged by 'the endless facts of sexism, experiencing feminist ideas mainly through guilt, and turning away because the alternative was to be overwhelmed'.[64] Similar reactions have been reported in boys' programs in schools, but these are not impossible to change if teachers understand how boys see the problem, and are flexible and skilled in their response to it.[65] As Kenway and Fitzclarence point out, peer relations are more important among adolescents than relations with adults, and apparent criticisms of their culture will not be easily accepted. In a context where they face economic and cultural uncertainty and instability, further destabilising of gender identities can be very disruptive.[66]

Denborough's strategy is to refuse to blame particular boys for the problems of masculinity. While he is often approached to help schools deal with a 'problem year group', he believes this is not a useful way to approach the issue.

> In order for our work not to participate in the pathologising and individualising of what is a broad societal issue, we must ensure that our work does not remain at this level. Year 9 boys are *not* the problem—the problem is the ways in which gender, race, class, and sexuality dynamics are organised in our society. If our work is not at this level then we will be participating in the blaming of relatively powerless boys for far broader social systems.[67]

This is a difficult issue, for we want boys to recognise the harm caused by the aggression, violence, sexism and other anti-social consequences of aspects of masculinity, and to accept that they, like all males, need to accept responsibility for abolishing them. To suggest that boys and men are somehow the innocent victims of some anonymous social structure seems less than frank. On the other hand, boys and men are not inherently evil, and most of them will rightly resent any suggestion that they would willingly harm others and perpetrate injustice. The need is to show them that, in trying to accommodate the demands of dominant masculinity, they could contribute, however indirectly, to a set of practices which, taken together, do result in harm and injustice.

There is a range of ways of motivating boys to question masculine practices and to engage in the process of improving gender relations. Boys may simply be curious about gender relations and the intellectual challenge of understanding their own development and culture. They may be experiencing personal crises such as domestic violence against themselves or mothers and sisters. They may sense a lack in their relationships with others and want more sharing and emotional intimacy. They may have their own experiences of oppression under masculine power, such as the threat of violence, or being put down or bullied. They may want to participate in a wider range of activities without being labelled a 'wuss'. They may simply want a more peaceful atmosphere at home or school. Just which of these will be most successful will depend on the context and the boys themselves, but this is a useful set of possibilities.[68]

We still need to be able to present a critique of dominant masculinity in terms which will not only interest boys, but which will also appeal to their social commitments and their sense of personal welfare. We should not underestimate the ability of boys to appreciate the injustice of many gender practices, and this will need to be a constant emphasis. However, this commitment will be most effective if it is incorporated into their sense of who they are, and if they can see how it might be applied in a way that makes their lives more rewarding. It is for this reason that the negative critique of injustice needs to be combined with a positive agenda for change.

In criticising dominant masculinity, we need to be able to replace it with a sense of being male to which boys can aspire. Ridding the dominant image of its worst excesses is important, but it needs to be replaced by some alternative vision and sense of direction. Jordan takes up this issue and argues that we need to define masculinity in such a way that violence and aggression are seen as weak and cowardly, while 'proposing the idea that true masculinity lies in self-control and moral courage, and using as the subordinate term lack of volition in behaviour—being swayed by impulse and rage'. Selfishness and impulsive aggression can be countered by promoting the ideals of fatherhood; the sort of commitment to the community that impels men to fight bushfires, search for lost children, join in rescue operations; the public spirit that leads them to devote themselves to union activity, conservation campaigns, righting what they see as legal injustices. Some of these definitions are built around physical courage and strength, while others that are not nevertheless involve some sense of the battle between good and evil that underlies the 'warrior' definition of masculinity and the little boys' super-hero play. With all of them it is possible to use male greed, selfishness, and lack of public spirit, rather than female passivity, as the subordinate term.[69]

The idea of 'true masculinity' has connotations of a masculine essence to which only boys could aspire, and needs to be rejected. The social actions so much admired are, of course, also done by women, and this needs to be emphasised. However, the central point is a valuable one, that certain values of dominant masculinity, like strength, courage, public leader-ship and independence, can be interpreted in action in different ways. Much of the anti-social behaviour of boys and men is rationalised by a very narrow, self-interested and ultimately oppressive interpretation of these values. Boys and men are often pressured to adopt positions in the name of these values, even though they may be aware that the consequences are anti-social and that the values are corrupted in the process. If, for instance, it is seen as strong to react to insult or offence with impulsive aggression, rather than to take control and deal with the situation in ways which don't simply escalate violence, then the masculine value of strength will be anti-social.

The argument is relatively clear when the concern is with issues like violence and harassment. In other areas of mascu-linity, it is not so obvious. For instance, we have shown in chapter 3 how dominant masculinity is valorised and reinforced in schools by the ideologies and practices of men's sport. But does this mean that participation in sports like football should be banned or discouraged? The best approach here is likely to be a gradual one, acknowledging that politics is the art of the possible. The task is one of identifying the harmful and anti-social elements of any practice and ridding it of them. If the practice remains viable, well and good; if not, the loss is justified.

248

In the case of sport, there can be little argument that sports like boxing, whose chief purposes are to harm others and which endorse personal violence, must be abolished.[70] In football, the strongest action must be taken to rid the sport of its dangerous and harmful elements, including its misogynistic culture, coaches' and parents' use of intimidation, ridicule or metaphors of battle to motivate players, and the incitement to violence as a winning strategy. At the same time, we need to promote alternatives which are known not to be harmful or belligerently competitive, and which are not sexually exclusive.[71] This will require that the valorisation of football and footballers in the masculinist culture of schools, where the team is the flagship of the school, will need to be replaced with a more balanced recognition of students' sporting and other achievements.

This pragmatic and cautious approach will be necessary in other areas as well. For instance, Kruse reports a strategy which recognises that students' awareness and attitudes will differ, and that a staged approach may be necessary.[72] She recommends that, in promoting a critical approach to gender, the first step should be to help students understand the contradictions in dominant gender relations. Segregated classes were useful to help students see their gender group in a new way, and to make power structures and strategies apparent. The process is one where students explore, analyse and express their own feelings about and understanding of these structures.

This would be followed by a process of critical thinking and consciousness raising, where teachers confront, ask provocative questions, and encourage students to explore the effects of gender in their own lives. Teachers challenge stereotyping, sexual harassment and inequality through pupil-centred, cooperative and interactive methods, and then broaden the focus to a study of inequality locally and globally using historical and current evidence. After having named their own experience (step 1), and together having gained new insights and a new awareness about the issues in their own lives and in general (steps 2 and 3), the pupils (still in their respective single-sex settings), with the support of teachers analyse what they have learned and apply their learnings to their own context. They consider what in their daily environment they no longer accept, what is within their reach to change, and how they might work on changing their attitudes and behaviour.

The final step involves the expressing, communicating and acting on these decisions. This might include drama or dance performances, information boards, tape-recordings, video and slide displays, writing songs, poems, essays etc., or taking action in school and neighbourhood to implement change. The expressive component of this is important as it allows students to connect their learning with their own processes of making sense of their world. Redman quotes Cohen's work on anti-racist education as an example of what is needed here. Cohen points out that

> . . . popular racism cannot be tackled by simply giving students access to alternative sources of experience, or new means of intellectual understanding; rather it is a question of articulating their lived cultures to *new practices of representation*, which make it possible to sustain an imaginative sense of social identity and difference without recourse to racist constructions.[73]

The same need applies to students' developing a sense of themselves and the processes of gender construction which are such an important part of it.

CONCLUSION

Changing the practices of dominant masculinity will sometimes not be so difficult. The experience of many programs for boys has been positive, offering encouragement that, properly handled, boys' programs will be responded to positively. Dunn's experience seems likely to be the norm—that boys are 'mostly intelligent and sensitive people', believers in 'the principle of the "fair go"', and with a basic understanding of social justice; that they will often freely acknowledge their prejudices, and the irrationality of such prejudices. 'They claim to like and respect girls and while admitting the existence of sexual harassment, rape, domestic violence, and other gender abuse, they almost invariably claim such behaviour to be unthinkable in their own relationships with girls and women.'[74]

In dealing with boys' relations with others, especially women and girls, there is a fairly clear set of needs and an increasingly well-established set of experiences and resources from which to proceed. Without wishing to underestimate the powerful interests involved, we believe that there is cause for optimism that work on these issues can be successful.

On other problems facing boys, and the role of masculinity in them, the situation is not so clear, as the nature of the problems and their solutions are less obvious. While research on masculinity is increasing our understanding of why many boys may express feelings of insecurity, why they are so conformist and intolerant of difference, and why the dominant image of unfeeling, solitary and competitive masculinity has been so powerful, there is still a lack of clarity on what we want to replace it, and a reluctance to address the question of masculinity in any fundamental way. It may be that this is the wrong question to ask, that we should simply be promoting a set of broad human values in combination with a commitment to diverse gender identities among boys and girls and men and women. By focusing on the needs of boys, and what kind of masculinity we should promote, are we simply reproducing the problem of wanting boys to be special? Is the concern about boys and masculinity so strong because we have put boys on a pedestal? Is our anxiety about boys just another result of the higher expectations and aspirations we have for them? Are the adolescent male angst themes of the coming-of-age movies simply evidence that we invest greater cultural significance in boys than girls?

If this is so, then a key part of the problem boys face is our own expectations of and aspirations for what kinds of men they will be. The answer then may be to stand back a little, to give them a more secure and less demanding context in which they can work together with men, women and girls to construct different ways of being male.

Notes

Chapter 1

1. *Courier-Mail*, Brisbane, 13 January 1996.
2. *Bulletin*, Sydney, 25 April 1995.
3. 'The trouble with men', *Economist*, Vol. 340, No. 7985, 28 September 1996, pp. 17–18; K. Gold, 'Hard time for Britain's lost boys', *New Scientist*, 4 February 1995.
4. 'The war on boys', *Men's Health*, October 1994.
5. See discussion, for example, in Yates, 1997.
6. Australian data on this appears in Australian Council for Educational Research, 1997, p. 9.
7. Teese et al., 1995, p. xiv.
8. Teese et al., 1995, p. 1.
9. Teese et al., 1995, p. 3.
10. Collins et al., 1996.
11. Collins et al., 1996, p. 73.
12. Collins et al., 1996, p. 75.
13. Girls, too, lose from gendered subject selection, and the Teese report documents the number of ways in which girls' lower participation in high level mathematics and physics is particularly damaging.
14. Teese et al., 1995, p. 10.
15. Richard Teese discusses the complexity of these achievement patterns in considerable detail in pages 45–75. This chapter can only sketch general patterns that emerge from his analysis.
16. Teese et al., 1995, p. 82.
17. Teese et al., 1995, p. 79.
18. Alloway and Gilbert, 1997.
19. Alloway and Gilbert, 1997, p. 52.
20. Yunupingu, 1994.
21. Teese et al., 1995, p. 83.

22. Teese et al., 1995.
23. Teese, McLean and Polesel, 1993.
24. Teese et al., 1995, p. 86.
25. Australian Council for Educational Research, 1997, p. 2.
26. Australian Council for Educational Research, 1997, p. 2.
27. Australian Council for Educational Research, 1997, p. 9.
28. Lemaire, 1994.
29. Martinez, 1994, p. 8.
30. Martinez, 1994, p. 8.
31. New South Wales Government Advisory Committee on Education, Training and Tourism (Chair: S. O'Doherty), 1994, p. 16.
32. Fletcher, 1993.
33. Quoted in Maslen, 1997.
34. Commonwealth Department of Human Services and Health, 1995.
35. Maslen, 1997.
36. See Graham, 1994. Also, O'Brien, 1997, p. 5.
37. Commonwealth Department of Human Services and Health, 1995.
38. Gray, 1995.
39. National Committee on Violence (NCV), 1990, p. 33.
40. NCV, 1990, p. 19.
41. NCV, 1990, p. 19.
42. Polk and Ranson, 1989, cited in NCV, 1990, p. 22.
43. NCV, 1990, p. 101.
44. Fletcher, 1994, p. ii.
45. Fletcher, 1994, p. iii.
46. Fletcher, 1994, p. 2.
47. Fletcher, 1994, p. ii.
48. Teese et al., 1995, p. 11.
49. Gilbert and Gilbert, 1995.
50. New South Wales Government Advisory Committee on Education, Training and Tourism, 1994, p. 17.
51. Fletcher, 1994, p. 4.
52. Davies, 1989a, proposes this framework for gender and educational reform.
53. Fletcher, 1994, p. ii.
54. Lemaire, 1994; Martinez, 1994.
55. See Frith, 1981.
56. See Patterson and Lee, 1993.
57. See Swann, 1992, and Gilbert and Gilbert, 1995.
58. See Mac An Ghaill, 1995. This issue is discussed more fully in chapter 6.

Chapter 2

1. Close, 1996, pp. 1, 4.
2. Close, 1996, p. 1.
3. Bly, 1991.
4. Biddulph, 1994.
5. Biddulph, 1994, p. 24.

6. Biddulph, 1994, p. 12.
7. Biddulph, 1994, p. 19.
8. Miles, 1991, Sabo and Panepinto, 1990.
9. Biddulph, 1994, p. 24.
10. Elium and Elium, 1992, p. 17.
11. Biddulph, 1994, p. 187.
12. Biddulph, 1994, p. 31.
13. Formaini, 1990, p. 3.
14. Formaini, 1990, p. 38.
15. Biddulph, 1994, p. 186.
16. Biddulph, 1994, p. 166.
17. Taylor, 1996.
18. Biddulph, 1994, p. 14. Emphasis in original.
19. Formaini, 1990, p. 18.
20. Connell, 1995, p. 233.
21. Moir and Jessel, 1991.
22. Moir and Jessel, 1991, p. 5.
23. Moir and Jessel, 1991, p. 11.
24. Elium and Elium, 1992, p. 19.
25. Shaywitz et al., 1995.
26. Tavris, 1992.
27. Gibbons, 1991; Kimura, 1992.
28. Kohn, 1992; Kimura, 1992.
29. Klama, 1988.
30. Moir and Jessel, 1991, p. 48.
31. Ridley, 1994, p. 249.
32. Vincent, 1996, p. 23.
33. Peters, 1991, p. 519.
34. Hoptman and Davidson, 1994, p. 203.
35. Hoptman and Davidson, 1994, p. 200.
36. Kimura, 1992, p. 86.
37. Rose, 1992, p. 249.
38. Star, 1991.
39. Elium and Elium, 1992, p. 17.
40. Kimura, 1992.
41. Greenstein, 1993, pp. 53–4.
42. Moir and Jessel, 1991, p. 7.
43. Goldstein, 1989.
44. Bettencourt and Miller, 1996.
45. Laursen and Collins, 1994.
46. Turner, 1994.
47. Prentky, 1985, p. 29.
48. Turner, 1994, p. 247.
49. Gilligan, 1996, p. 215.
50. Braithwaite and Daly, 1995, p. 222.
51. Klama, 1988, p. 152.
52. Rose, 1992, p. 89.
53. Segal, 1990, p. 63. See also Kaplan and Rogers, 1990.
54. Collaer and Hines, 1995, p. 61.

55. Jones, 1993, p. 180.
56. Tavris, 1992.
57. Biddulph, 1997, p. 61.
58. Connell, 1995, p. 52.
59. Connell, 1996a, p. 56.
60. Vance, 1995.
61. Connell, 1995, p. 231.
62. Connell, 1996b, p. 211.
63. Brittan, 1989; Connell, 1995.
64. Butler, 1990, p. 140.
65. Butler , 1990, p. 33.
66. McMahon, 1993, p. 691.
67. Smith, 1996.
68. Smith, 1996, p. 30.
69. Connell, 1995.
70. Segal, 1990, p. 289.
71. Dawson, 1991, cited in Edley and Wetherell, 1995, p. 157.
72. Walker, 1988.

Chapter 3

1. Kline, 1995.
2. Kline, 1995, p. 159.
3. Davies, 1989b; Thorne, 1993; Alloway, 1995.
4. Connell, 1996a, p. 62.
5. Australian Sports Commission, 1991.
6. Australian Sports Commission, 1991, p. 56.
7. For details of this study, see chapter 5.
8. Angus, 1993.
9. See further discussion of this in chapter 8.
10. Messner, 1990.
11. Whitson, 1990.
12. Messner, 1990, p. 103.
13. Hargreaves, 1992; Schact, 1996. While it is customary to relate misogyny in sport with the locker room, it is by no means restricted to team or field sports. See Maloney, 1994.
14. Whannel, 1992, p. 144.
15. White, Young and McTeer, 1995.
16. Sabo, 1989, p. 185.
17. Whitson, 1990, p. 23.
18. *Courier-Mail*, 20 September 1993. Quoted in MacLennan and Yeates, 1995, p. 23.
19. Sabo, 1989, p. 186.
20. Yeates, 1995.
21. Vamplew, 1991; Miedzian, 1991.
22. 'Brawl fallout widens', *Townsville Daily Bulletin*, 24 April 1997, p. 16.
23. 'ARL chief slams bank for dumping Cup', *Townsville Daily Bulletin*, 23 April 1997, p. 30.

24. Wolf-Light, 1992/3. See also Kidd, 1987.
25. Dyer, 1982.
26. Chandler, 1996.
27. Scraton, 1992.
28. Australian Sports Commission, 1991, p. 56.
29. Australian Sports Commission, 1991, p. 58.
30. See, for example, Senate Select Committee on Community Standards Relevant to the Supply of Services Utilizing Electronic Technologies, 1993.
31. National Committee on Violence, 1990, p. 82.
32. Edgar, 1991.
33. Alloway and Gilbert, 1997/in press.
34. See Cunningham, 1995.
35. Buckingham and Sefton-Green, 1994.
36. Durkin, 1995.
37. Braun and Giroux, 1989.
38. Alloway and Gilbert, 1998/in press.
39. Alloway and Gilbert, 1998/in press.
40. This example comes from *GamePro*, June 1994, p. 127, and has been cited in Alloway and Gilbert, 1998/in press.
41. Giroux, 1995, p. 301.
42. Giroux, 1995, p. 302.
43. Cunningham, 1995, p. 200.
44. From *Megazone*, July 1995, p. 37, quoted in Alloway and Gilbert, 1998/in press.
45. Alloway and Gilbert, 1998/in press.
46. Alloway and Gilbert, 1998/in press.
47. Quoted in Alloway and Gilbert, 1998/in press.
48. Quoted in Alloway and Gilbert, 1998/in press.

Chapter 4

1. Phillips, 1993, p. 11.
2. Cameron, 1997.
3. Cameron, 1997, p. 49.
4. Butler, 1990, p. 33.
5. Cameron, 1997, p. 49.
6. Cameron, 1997, p. 49.
7. Coates, 1993, p. 166.
8. Smith, 1995.
9. Phillips, 1993.
10. Silverstein and Rashbaum, 1994.
11. Kewley and Lewis (eds), 1993.
12. Elium and Elium 1992.
13. See, for instance, Miedzian, 1991.
14. Biddulph, 1994: Biddulph, 1997.
15. Hawley, 1993.
16. Elium and Elium, 1992.
17. Stoltenberg, 1990.

18. Quoted in Smith, 1995, p. 19.
19. Smith, 1995, p. 3.
20. Elium and Elium, 1992.
21. Elium and Elium, 1992, pp. 26, 28.
22. Elium and Elium, 1992, p. 84.
23. Lareau, 1992, p. 208.
24. Lareau, 1992, p. 209.
25. See also Freebody, Ludwig, and Gunn, 1995.
26. Phillips, 1993, Silverstein and Rashbaum, 1994, and Smith, 1995, all provide evidence of this.
27. Stoltenberg, 1990, p. 63.
28. Dinnerstein, 1976.
29. Chodorow, 1978.
30. Segal, 1990, p. 79.
31. Rowland and Thomas (eds), 1996.
32. Rowland and Thomas (eds), 1996, p. 93.
33. Smith, 1995.
34. Smith, 1995, p. ix.
35. Smith, 1995, p. x.
36. Bittman, 1991. Phillips (1993, pp. 15–16) provides details of British studies.
37. Phillips 1993 is an exception here.
38. Elium and Elium, 1992; Hawley, 1993.
39. Smith, 1995, p. ix.
40. Elium and Elium, 1992, pp. 91–2.
41. Biddulph, 1994, pp. 12–13.
42. Bly, 1991.
43. Biddulph, 1994.
44. Biddulph, 1994, p. 99.
45. Biddulph, 1994, p. 3.
46. Biddulph, 1994, pp. 105–6.
47. See Biddulph, 1994, pp. 70, 108, 111.
48. See Biddulph, 1994, pp. 103, 106, 87, 76.
49. Elium and Elium, 1992.
50. Hawley, 1993.
51. Kewley and Lewis, 1993. In the Australian context, see West, 1996.
52. Biddulph, 1994, p. 87.
53. O'Connor, 1992. Findings from a 1997 study in South Australia indicate similar findings. See Golding and Friedman, 1997.
54. Gilbert, Gilbert and McGinty, 1995, p. 42.
55. Szirom, 1988, p. 50.
56. Kelly, 1992, p. 29.
57. Szirom, 1988, p. 91.
58. Szirom, 1988, p. 88.
59. Kelly, 1992, p. 29.
60. In Kelly, 1992, p. 29.
61. Stoltenberg, 1990, p. 59.
62. Seidler, 1987, p. 82.
63. Seidler, 1987, p. 96.

64. Seidler, 1987, p. 96.
65. Pleck, Sonenstein, and Ku, 1993, p. 21.
66. Chodorow, 1978, pp. 43–4.
67. See, for example, Szirom, 1988; Davidson, 1990; Kelly, 1992 and Whatley, 1992.
68. Davidson, 1990, p. 6.
69. Referenced in Szirom, 1988, p. 67.
70. Kelly, 1992, p. 21.
71. Klein (ed.), 1992, p. 3.
72. National Health and Medical Research Council, 1992.
73. Gilbert and Gilbert, 1995, p. 46.
74. Pleck, Sonenstein and Ku, 1993.
75. Whatley, 1992; Fine, 1988.
76. Cited in Kelly, 1992, p. 31.
77. Epstein (ed.), 1995.
78. Kelly, 1992, p. 27.

Chapter 5

1. Cited in Mac An Ghaill, 1994, p. 122.
2. See for example, Willis, 1977; Walker, 1988; Beynon, 1989.
3. See Skeggs, 1991; McRobbie, 1991.
4. See, for example, Connell, et al., 1982; Mac An Ghaill, 1994; Thorne, 1993.
5. Mac An Ghaill, 1994, p. 61.
6. Jordan, 1995, p. 72.
7. Jordan, 1995, p. 73.
8. Johnson, 1997, p. 22.
9. Angus's study of a Catholic boys' school is an excellent illustration of the pervasiveness of gender relations in schools. See Angus, 1993.
10. Davies, 1992, p. 128.
11. Davies, 1996, p. 8.
12. Mac An Ghaill, 1994.
13. Mac An Ghaill, 1994, p. 30.
14. Thorne, 1993, p. 34.
15. Alloway, 1995.
16. Walkerdine, 1989.
17. Carli, 1997.
18. Mac An Ghaill, 1995, p. 49.
19. Kenway, et al., 1997, pp. 26–7.
20. Wolpe, 1988.
21. Mac An Ghaill, 1995, p. 49.
22. Beynon, 1989 p. 194.
23. Askew and Ross, 1988 pp. 58–9.
24. Baker and Davies, 1989.
25. Haywood and Mac An Ghaill, 1996, p. 54.
26. See Brabek and Larned, 1997; Goldberger, 1997.
27. Brittan, 1989.
28. White, 1996.

29. Seidler, 1989, p. 3.
30. Davies, 1996, p. 214.
31. Martino, 1995a.
32. Willis, 1977.
33. Mac An Ghaill, 1994.
34. Ainley, et al., 1994.
35. Board of Senior Secondary School Studies, Queensland, 1997.
36. Gilbert and Gilbert, 1996.
37. Redman and Mac An Ghaill, 1996 p. 245.
38. Mac An Ghaill, 1994, p. 93.
39. Beynon, 1989; Connell, et al., 1982; Mac An Ghaill, 1994; Thorne, 1993; Walker, 1988; Willis, 1977; Eckert, 1989.
40. Mac An Ghaill, 1994.
41. Willis, 1977. Criticisms appear in Skeggs, 1991, and Walker, 1986.
42. Willis, 1977, p. 149.
43. Mac An Ghaill, 1994, pp. 56–7.
44. Mac An Ghaill, 1994, p. 58.
45. Walker, 1988, p. 3.
46. Walker, 1988, p. 39.
47. Walker, 1988, p. 46.
48. Walker, 1988, p. 46.
49. Thorne, 1993.
50. Mac An Ghaill, 1994, p. 60.
51. Walker, 1988, p. 54.
52. Walker, 1988, p. 61.
53. Mac An Ghaill, 1994, p. 61.
54. Mac An Ghaill, 1994, p. 67.
55. Abraham, 1989.
56. Haywood and Mac An Ghaill, 1996, pp. 55–6.
57. Denborough, 1996, p. 92.
58. Redman and Mac An Ghaill, 1996.
59. Denborough, 1996, p. 114.
60. Majors, 1989.
61. Majors, 1989, p. 85.
62. Connell et al., 1982, p. 73.
63. Eckert, 1989, p. 5.
64. Wight, 1994.
65. Connell 1989, p. 297.
66. Adler, Kless, and Adler, 1992.

Chapter 6

1. Gerschik and Miller, 1994, p. 28.
2. Shakespeare, 1996.
3. Seymour, 1997.
4. Clements, Clare and Ezelle, 1995.
5. McCarthy and Crichlow, 1993, p. xx.
6. Wetherell and Edley, 1995.
7. Mackay, 1996; Cuneen and Luke, 1995. A typical example of the

implicit equation of youth with male is in Beresford and Omaji, 1996.

8. Beresford and Omaji, 1996; National Review of Education for Aboriginal and Torres Strait Islander Peoples, 1994.
9. Groome and Hamilton, 1995. Note that girls' attendance rates tend to be even lower than those of boys.
10. Palmer and Collard, 1993; Nakata, 1995.
11. Johnston, 1991, p. 92.
12. The use of terms needs to be clarified here. We are aware of the need to recognise the cultural distinctiveness of the various black minorities in Australia, and to avoid grouping them into some single category where these differences are important. When we use the term Aboriginal and Islander, we are referring to people of Aboriginal, Torres Strait Islander and Pacific Islander descent, all of whom are affected by the distinctions and discrimination derived from the concept of 'race'. When the reference is to one or other of these groups, the more specific term is used.
13. Groome and Hamilton, 1995, p. xi. Groome and Hamilton studied Aboriginal students in schools where there were significant numbers of such students, and point out that their observations do not necessarily apply to Aboriginal students who are isolated from groups of peers.
14. Palmer and Collard, 1993, p. 119.
15. Delgado and Stefancic, 1995, p. 211.
16. Franklin, 1993, p. 151.
17. Wetherell and Edley, 1995, p. 151.
18. Delgado and Stefancic, 1995, p. 213.
19. Marriott, 1996.
20. Groome and Hamilton, 1995, p. 15.
21. Johnston, 1991, p. 86; Malin, 1994.
22. Folds, 1987; Groome and Hamilton, 1995.
23. Groome and Hamilton, 1995, p. 32.
24. See Walker, 1988, for illustration of this.
25. Groome and Hamilton, 1995.
26. Malin, 1994.
27. Groome and Hamilton, 1995; Groome, 1995; Folds, 1987. For evidence of these tensions, see Dawes, 1995.
28. Groome and Hamilton, 1995, p. 34.
29. Beresford and Omaji, 1996, p. 127.
30. Hunter, 1990.
31. Beresford and Omaji, 1996, p. 45. See also Folds, 1987. Chapter 7 discusses further these issues of violence and masculinity among Aboriginal and Islander people, and of the emasculation thesis as an explanation of violence.
32. Martin, quoted in Johnston, 1991, pp. 95, 97.
33. Groome and Hamilton, 1995, p. 33.
34. Dawes, 1995, p. 224.
35. Gibbs and Merighi, 1994; Hannerz, 1969; Sewell, 1995. For a discussion of violence and Aboriginal boys, see chapter 6.

36. Beresford and Omaji, 1996; Dawes, 1995.
37. Beresford and Omaji, 1996.
38. Beresford and Omaji, 1996, p. 143.
39. Select Committee on Youth Affairs, 1992, p. 143.
40. Franklin, 1993.
41. Folds, 1987; Groome and Hamilton, 1995.
42. Folds, 1987.
43. Dawes' 1995 study provides interesting illustration of differences among Aboriginal and Torres Strait Islander subcultures.
44. Though even here discrimination can produce inequality, such as the view in schools that Pacific Islanders are more to be admired than Aboriginal students. See Groome and Hamilton, 1995, p. 19.
45. Dawes, 1988.
46. Burbank, 1980, quoted in Johnston, 1991, p. 87.
47. Beresford and Omaji, 1996, p. 59.
48. Connolly, 1994, p. 199.
49. Recent Australian experience of racism in sport is a good example of this.
50. Moore, 1994.
51. Jetnikoff, 1997/in press.
52. Rizvi, 1993.
53. Walker, 1988, p. 39.
54. Luke, 1997, p. 32.
55. Cheng, 1996.
56. Walker, 1988, p. 52.
57. Walker, 1988, p. 51.
58. Walker, 1988, p. 89.
59. Hughes makes this point about gender issues in Aboriginal education. This may well account for the lack of research noted earlier on the construction of gender for Aboriginal boys. See Hughes, 1995.
60. Thorne, 1993, p. 118.
61. Mac An Ghaill, 1994, p. 160.
62. Federation of Parents' and Citizens' Associations of New South Wales, 1993.
63. Mason, 1996, p. 31.
64. Hatton and Swinson, 1994, p. 286.
65. Beckett and Denborough, 1995, p. 403.
66. Glascott, 1997.
67. Mac An Ghaill, 1994, p. 166.
68. Dawes, 1995, p. 226.
69. Redman and Mac An Ghaill, 1996, p. 248.
70. Hatton and Swinson, 1994, p. 285.
71. Taylor, 1996; Emslie, 1996.
72. Mason, 1996.
73. Bibby, 1992, p. 32.
74. Epstein and Johnson, 1994, p. 204.
75. Ward, 1995.
76. Epstein, 1996; Epstein and Johnston, 1994.
77. Hatton and Swinson, 1994, p. 214.

78. Epstein, 1997, p. 109. See also Epstein and Johnson, 1994, and Mac An Ghaill, 1994.
79. Epstein and Johnson, 1994, p. 204.
80. Rutherford, 1990, quoted in Mac An Ghaill, 1994, p. 94.
81. Ward, 1995, p. 85
82. Beckett and Denborough, 1995, p. 392.
83. Mason, 1996, p. 31.
84. Frank, 1992–3.
85. Epstein, 1997; Mason, 1996.
86. Mac An Ghaill, 1995.

Chapter 7

1. Willis, 1977.
2. Collins, et al., 1996.
3. Connell, 1996b, p. 220.
4. Connell, et al., 1982, p. 88.
5. Pellegrini, 1993.
6. Thorne, 1993, p. 93.
7. Pellegrini, 1993.
8. Boulton, 1994.
9. Wood, 1984.
10. Haywood and Mac An Ghaill, 1996.
11. Mac An Ghaill, 1994, p. 92.
12. Skeggs, 1991.
13. Alloway, 1995; Walkerdine, 1986.
14. Walkerdine, 1986; Connolly, 1995.
15. Dixon, 1997.
16. Kenway and Fitzclarence, 1997, p. 120.
17. Alloway, 1995; Thorne, 1993, p. 47.
18. Gilbert, 1989a.
19. Wight, 1994.
20. Gilbert, Gilbert and McGinty, 1995.
21. Olweus, 1993, p. 9.
22. Collins et al., 1996.
23. Collins et al., 1996, p. 53.
24. Olweus, 1993, p. 34.
25. Rigby, 1996.
26. Muehlenhard and Falcon, 1990, cited in Hinson, 1995a.
27. Olweus, 1993, p. 10.
28. Rigby, 1996, p. 21.
29. Rigby, 1996.
30. Rigby, 1996, p. 80.
31. Standing Committee on Social Issues, Legislative Council, Parliament of New South Wales, 1995, p. 258.
32. Collins et al., 1996.
33. Willis, 1977, p. 32.
34. Kenway and Fitzclarence, 1997, p. 119.
35. Kenway and Fitzclarence, 1997, p. 121.

36. Willis, 1977, p. 35.
37. Willis, 1977, p. 36.
38. Polk, 1995, p. 61.
39. Bessant and Watts, 1995.
40. It is estimated that domestic violence affects 90 per cent of Aboriginal families living in trust areas. On this and related matters, see Atkinson, 1990a, Atkinson, 1990b, Beresford and Omaji, 1996, Wilson, 1982.
41. Atkinson, 1990a, p. 16.
42. Beresford and Omaji, 1996, p. 44.
43. Atkinson, 1990b, p. 6.
44. See Beresford and Omaji, 1996, p. 80.
45. Moon, 1992, p. 195.
46. Moon, 1992, p. 201.
47. Egger, 1995.
48. Braithwaite and Daly, 1995, p. 222.

Chapter 8

1. From 1995 to 1997, we have worked with colleagues at James Cook University on two projects funded by the Australian government on boys and literacy. Much of our thinking and conceptualising of this issue has arisen from that work. Relevant and associated publications include: a professional development kit for schools, published from the first 1995–6 project (Alloway, Davies, Gilbert, Gilbert and King, 1996); a refined and extended version of this kit published from the second phase of the project 1996–7 (Alloway and Gilbert (eds) 1997a; Alloway and Gilbert (eds) 1997b); a paper arising from this second project (Alloway and Gilbert, 1997).
2. New South Wales Government Advisory Committee on Education, Training and Tourism (Chair: S. O'Doherty), 1994, p. 18.
3. Teese, et al., 1995.
4. Australian Council for Educational Research, 1997, p. 4.
5. See, for instance, Freebody, 1992.
6. Sheridan (ed.), 1983.
7. See, for example, Nichols, 1995.
8. See Anderson and Yip, 1987; Children's Rights Workshop, 1976.
9. Frith, 1981; Gilbert, 1994.
10. Patterson and Lee, 1993; Fox, 1993.
11. Martino, 1995a.
12. Benton, 1995a; Benton, 1995b.
13. See the discussion in chapter 1, for instance, of the data about links between reading and numeracy and average weekly wages for young men and women, in Australian Council for Educational Research, 1997, p. 9.
14. See chapter 3 for a discussion of these terms in relation to electronic gaming culture.
15. See, for example, Coates, 1993.
16. Nichols, 1994.
17. Nichols, 1994, p. 303.

18. Lareau, 1992.
19. This reliance upon women workers is also noted in an Australian study of working class communities (Freebody, Ludwig, and Gunn, 1995).
20. See discussion of these in chapter 4.
21. See Thorne, 1993.
22. Luke, 1992.
23. Phillips, 1993, p. 231.
24. See description in chapter 5 of the study we conducted with boys in North Queensland schools.
25. Stanworth, 1984; Clarricoates, 1978; Evans, 1982; Currie, 1990.
26. Flynn, 1994.
27. Gottlieb, et al., 1994.
28. Nichols, 1995.
29. Flynn, 1994, p. 66. The gendered link between reading difficulty and behaviour problems is also noted in an Australian study by Prior, et al., 1995, p. 36.
30. Currie, 1990, p. 149.
31. Nichols, 1995, p. 4.
32. Nichols, 1995, p. 4.
33. Freebody, Ludwig, and Gunn, 1995, p. 173.
34. See discussion in Eagleton, 1983.
35. See Thomas, 1991.
36. See discussion in Gilbert, 1989b.
37. Hunter, 1988; Patterson, 1995.
38. Patterson, 1995, p. 110.
39. See discussion of this issue in Gilbert and Gilbert, 1996b.
40. This is discussed more fully in Alloway and Gilbert, 1997. See also Hunter, 1988; Gilbert, 1989b; Patterson, 1995.
41. See Patterson and Lee, 1993
42. See discussion in Freebody, 1992 and 1993.
43. See Freebody, Luke, and Gilbert, 1991.
44. See discussion in Gilbert, P. 1988.
45. See discussion of boys' writing in Poynton, 1985; Gilbert, 1993; Buckingham and Sefton-Green, 1994.
46. Kenworthy, 1994, p. 75.
47. Kenworthy, 1994, p. 91.
48. Alloway and Gilbert, 1997, p. 55.
49. See Alloway and Gilbert, 1997, pp. 55–6.
50. Mac An Ghaill, 1994.
51. Martino, 1995a, p. 354.
52. Nichols, 1994, p. 303.
53. Nichols, 1994, p. 305.
54. Nichols, 1994, p. 307.
55. See discussion of boys as readers in Sanderson, 1995.
56. Browne and Fletcher (eds), 1995.
57. White, 1986.
58. See, for example, arguments made in texts like Showalter, 1977 and Spender, 1980.
59. See discussion in Davies, 1989a.

60. As in Moss, 1989; Gilbert and Taylor, 1991; Christian-Smith (ed.), 1993.
61. See, for example, Gee, 1990; Lankshear and McLaren, 1993.
62. See Alloway and Gilbert (eds) 1997a and Alloway and Gilbert (eds) 1997b—books developed specifically for working with boys and literacy issues, using a framework from critical literacy discourses. See also Davies, 1997 and Martino, 1995b.

Chapter 9

1. Browne and Fletcher (eds), 1995.
2. Gilbert and Gilbert, 1996b. A similar list appears in the O'Doherty Report, the New South Wales government report into the education of boys. See New South Wales Government Advisory Committee on Education, Training and Tourism (O'Dohery Report), 1994.
3. Clarke, 1995.
4. Moran, 1995.
5. Griffiths, 1995.
6. Carosi and Tindale, 1995.
7. Kokori, 1995.
8. Hill, 1991; Kenway and Willis, 1990; Kenway, et al., 1997.
9. Gilbert and Gilbert, 1996b.
10. See Olweus, 1993 and Rigby, 1996.
11. New South Wales Government Advisory Committee on Education, Training and Tourism (O'Doherty Report), 1994.
12. Collins et al., 1996, pp. 173–5.
13. Redman, 1996. On 'protest masculinities', see Connell, 1995, pp. 109–12.
14. Askew and Ross, 1988.
15. Keira Technology High, 1994.
16. Collins et al., 1996, p. 143.
17. Kenway and Fitzclarence, 1997, p. 127.
18. New South Wales Government Advisory Committee on Education, Training and Tourism (O'Doherty Report), 1994, pp. 31–2.
19. Collins et al., 1996, p. 176. See the earlier discussion of this point in chapter 1.
20. Collins et al., 1996, p. 60.
21. Redman, 1996, p. 172.
22. Hinson, 1995a, p. 141.
23. Hinson, 1995a, p. 144.
24. O'Donoghue, 1995.
25. Katz, 1995.
26. Collins et al., 1996, p. 60.
27. Kenway, 1995, p. 44.
28. Kenway and Fitclarence, 1997.
29. Hinson, 1995a.
30. Olweus, 1993.
31. McLean, 1996, p. 68.
32. Kenway, 1995, p. 44.

33. Herbert, 1992.
34. Forsey, 1994.
35. See also Hinson, 1995b; Department of Employment, Education and Training, 1995.
36. Friedman, 1996. See also Denborough, 1996; Forsey, 1990; Forsey, 1989; Salisbury and Jackson, 1996.
37. Alloway, et al., (eds) 1996. A revised and expanded version of this project is: Alloway and Gilbert, (eds), 1997a and Alloway and Gilbert (eds), 1997b.
38. Queitsch, 1997.
39. Coleman and Skeen, 1987.
40. Salisbury and Jackson, 1996.
41. Alloway, 1995; Alloway and Gilbert (eds), 1997b.
42. Collins et al., 1996, p. 85.
43. Connell, 1994.
44. Collins et al., 1996, p. 173.
45. Martinez, 1994.
46. Kenway, et al., 1997.
47. Dunn, 1995, p. 321.
48. Kenway and Fitzclarence, 1997, p. 120.
49. Collins et al., 1996, p. 119.
50. Allard, 1995. See the *Stages* project by Allard et al., 1995.
51. Phillips, 1993.
52. Clyde, 1989.
53. Clyde, 1989, p. 96.
54. McLean, 1995 p. 299.
55. Askew and Ross, 1988, p. 57.
56. An instance of this was outlined in chapter 8, where boys reacted against a critical reading of masculinity in an English lesson.
57. McLean, 1995, p. 299.
58. For a recent addition to the long list of excellent resources here, see Allard, et al., 1995.
59. See note 36.
60. Kruse, 1992, p. 100.
61. Connell, 1995, p. 79.
62. Connell, 1983, p. 22.
63. Dunn, 1995.
64. Connell, 1994, p. 19.
65. Mills, 1997.
66. Kenway and Fitzclarence, 1997, p. 127.
67. Denborough, 1996, p. 100.
68. Denborough, 1996; Clark, 1996.
69. Jordan, 1995, p. 81.
70. Standing Committee on Social Issues, 1995.
71. Salisbury and Jackson, 1996.
72. Kruse, 1992.
73. Cohen, 1987, quoted in Redman, 1996, p. 177.
74. Dunn, 1995, p. 323.

Bibliography

Abraham, J. (1989) 'Gender differences and anti-school boys', *The Sociological Review*, 37, 1, 65–87

Adler, P., Kless, S. and Adler, P. (1992) 'Socialisation to gender roles: Popularity among elementary school boys and girls', *Sociology of Education*, 65, 3, 169–187

Ainley, J., Robinson, L., Harvey-Beavis, A., Elsworth, G., Fleming, M. (1994) *Subject Choice in Years 11 and 12*. Canberra: Australian Government Publishing Service

Allard, A., Cooper, M., Hildebrand, G. and Wealands, E. (1995) *Stages: Steps Towards Addressing Gender in Educational Settings*. Carlton, Vic.: Curriculum Corporation

Alloway, N. (1995) *Foundation Stones: The Construction of Gender in Early Childhood*. Carlton, Vic.: Curriculum Corporation

——and Gilbert, P. (1997) 'Boys and literacy: Lessons from Australia', *Gender and Education*, 9, 1, 49–58

——and Gilbert, P. (1998/in press) 'Video game culture: Playing with masculinity, violence and pleasure', In S. Howard (ed.) *Wired Up: Young People and the Electronic Media*. London: Taylor and Francis

——and Gilbert, P. (eds) (1997a) *Boys and Literacy: Professional Development Units*. Carlton, Vic.: Curriculum Corporation

——and Gilbert, P. (eds) (1997b) *Boys and Literacy: Teaching Units*. Carlton, Vic.: Curriculum Corporation

——, Davies, B., Gilbert, P., Gilbert, R. and King, D. (eds) (1996) *Boys and Literacy: Meeting the Challenge. Books 1, 2 and 3*. Townsville: James Cook University of North Queensland/ Department of Employment, Education, Training and Youth Affairs

Anderson, J. and Yip, L. (1987) 'Are sex roles represented fairly in children's books? A content analysis of old and new readers', *Unicorn*, 13, 3, 155–61

Angus, L. (1993) 'Women in a male domain: Gender and organisational culture in a Christian Brothers College', in L. Angus, (ed.) *Education, Inequality and Social Identity*. Washington D.C.: Falmer Press

Askew, S. and Ross, C. (1988) *Boys Don't Cry: Boys and Sexism in Education*. Milton Keynes: Open University Press

Atkinson, J. (1990a) 'Violence in Aboriginal Australia: Colonisation and gender', *The Aboriginal and Islander Health Worker*, 14, 2, 5–21

——(1990b) 'Violence in Aboriginal Australia. Part Two', *The Aboriginal and Islander Health Worker*, 14, 3, 4–27

Australian Bureau of Statistics (1990–1) *Law and Order, Queensland*, Canberra: Australian Government Publishing Service

Australian Council for Educational Research (1997) *Reading and Numeracy in Junior Secondary School: Trends, Patterns and Consequences*. Melbourne: Australian Council for Educational Research

Australian Education Council (1993) *National Action Plan for the Education of Girls 1993–7*. Carlton, Vic.: Curriculum Corporation

Australian Institute of Criminology (1995) *Australian Prison Trends*. Canberra: Australian Institute of Criminology

Australian Sports Commission (1991) *Sport for Young Australians: Widening the Gateways to Participation*. Canberra: Australian Sports Commission

Baker, C. and Davies, B. (1989) 'A lesson on sex roles', *Gender and Education*, 1, 1, 59–75

Baker, C.D. and Freebody, P. (1989) 'Talk around text: Constructions of textual and teacher authority in classroom discourse', in S. de Castell, A. Luke and C. Luke (eds) *Language, Authority and Criticism: Readings on the School Textbook*. London/Philadelphia: Falmer Press

Bazalgette, C. and Buckingham, D. (eds) 1995 *In Front of the Children: Screen Entertainment and Young Audiences*. London: British Film Institute

Beckett, L. and Denborough, D. (1995) 'Homophobia: Implications for mainstream policy and practice', in Ministerial Council for Education, Employment, Training and Youth Affairs (ed.) *Proceedings of the Promoting Gender Equity Conference*. Canberra: Australian Capital Territory Department of Education

Belsey, C. (1980) *Critical Practice*. London: Methuen

Benton, P. (1995a) 'Recipe fictions . . . Literary fast food? Reading interests in year 8', *Oxford Review of Education*, 21, 1, 99–109

——(1995b) 'Conflicting cultures: Reflections on the reading and viewing of secondary-school pupils', *Oxford Review of Education*, 21, 4, 457–69

Beresford, Q. and Omaji, P. (1996) *Rites of Passage: Aboriginal Youth, Crime and Justice*. Fremantle: Fremantle Arts Centre Press

Berger, M., Wallis, B. and Watson, S. (1995) *Constructing Masculinity*. New York: Routledge

Bessant, J. and Watts, R. (1995) 'Young people and violence: A focus on schools', in D. Chappell and S. Egger (eds) *Australian Violence: Contemporary Perspectives II*. Canberra: Australian Institute of Criminology

Bettencourt, B. and Miller, N. (1996) 'Gender differences in aggression as a function of provocation: A meta-analysis', *Psychological Bulletin*, 119, 3, 422–47

Beynon, J. (1989) 'A school for men: An ethnographic case study of routine violence in schooling', in S. Walker and L. Barton (eds) *Politics and the Processes of Schooling*. Milton Keynes: Open University Press

Bibby, M. (1992) 'Gay bashing: Implications for parents', *Parent and Citizen*, Autumn, 32

Biddulph, S. (1994) *Manhood: A Book about Setting Men Free*. Sydney: Finch Publishing

——(1995) 'Foreword', in R. Browne and R. Fletcher, (eds) *Boys in Schools: Addressing the Real Issues—Behaviour, Values and Relationships*. Sydney: Finch Publishing

——(1997) *Raising Boys: Why Boys are Different—and How to Help Them Become Happy and Well-balanced Men*. Sydney: Finch Publishing

Bittman, M. (1991) *Juggling Time: How Australian Families Use Time*. Canberra: Office of the Status of Women, Department of the Prime Minister and Cabinet

Bly, R. (1991) *Iron John: A Book About Men*. London: Element

Board of Senior Secondary School Studies, Queensland (1997) *Statistics Bulletin*. Brisbane

Boulton, M. (1994) 'The relationship between playful and aggressive fighting in children, adolescents and adults', in J. Archer (ed.), *Male Violence*. London: Routledge

Brabek, M. and Larned, A. (1997) 'What we do not know about women's ways of knowing', in M. Walsh (ed.) *Women, Men, and Gender: Ongoing Debates*. New Haven: Yale University Press

Braithwaite, J. and Daly, K. (1995) 'Masculinities, violence and communitarian control', in D. Chappell and S. Egger (eds) *Australian Violence: Contemporary Perspectives II*. Canberra: Australian Institute of Criminology

Braun, C. and Giroux, J. (1989) 'Arcade video games: Proxemic, cognitive and content analyses', *Journal of Leisure Research*, 21, 92–105

Brittan, A. (1989) *Masculinity and Power*. Oxford: Blackwell

Brooks-Gunn, J. (1992) 'The impact of puberty and sexual activity upon the health and education of adolescent girls and boys', in S.S. Klein (ed.) *Sex Equity and Sexuality in Education*. Albany: State University of New York Press

Browne, R. and Fletcher, R. (eds) (1995) *Boys in Schools: Addressing the Real Issues—Behaviour, Values and Relationships*. Sydney: Finch Publishing

Buckingham, D. and Sefton-Green, J. (1994) *Cultural Studies Goes to School: Reading and Teaching Popular Media*. London: Taylor and Francis

Butler, J. (1990) *Gender Trouble: Feminism and the Subversion of Identity*. New York: Routledge

Cameron, D. (1997) 'Performing gender identity: Young men's talk and the construction of heterosexual masculinity', in S. Johnson and U.H. Meinhof (eds) *Language and Masculinity*. Oxford: Blackwell Publishers

Carli, L. (1997) 'Biology does not create gender differences in personality', in M. Walsh (ed.) *Women, Men and Gender: Ongoing Debates*. New Haven: Yale University Press

Carosi, F. and Tindale, R. (1995) 'Give me a helmet', in R. Browne and R. Fletcher (eds) *Boys in Schools: Addressing the Real Issues—Behaviour, Values and Relationships*. Sydney: Finch Publishing

Chandler, T. (1996) 'The structuring of manliness and the development of rugby football at the public schools and Oxbridge, 1830–1880', in J. Nauright and T. Chandler (eds) *Making Men: Rugby and Masculine Identity*. London: Frank Cass

Cheng, C. (1996) '"We choose not to compete": The "merit" discourse in the selection process, and Asian and Asian American men and their masculinity', in C. Cheng (ed.) *Masculinities in Organisations*. Thousand Oaks, Cal.: Sage

Children's Rights Workshop (1976) *Sexism in Children's Books: Facts, Figures and Guidelines*. London: Writers and Readers Publishing Cooperative

Chodorow, N. (1978) *The Reproduction of Mothering*. Berkeley, California: University of California Press

Christian-Smith, L. (ed.) (1993) *Texts of Desire*. London: The Falmer Press

Clark, M. (1996) Gender as an educational issue. Unpublished paper Social Justice Section. Australian Department of Immigration and Ethnic Affairs

Clarke, P. (1995) 'I'll get you at lunch', in R. Browne and R. Fletcher (eds) *Boys in Schools: Addressing the Real Issues—Behaviour, Values and Relationships*. Sydney: Finch Publishing

Clarricoates, K. (1978) 'Dinosaurs in the classroom', *Women's Studies International Quarterly*, 1, 4, 353–64

Clements, J., Clare, I. and Ezelle, L. (1995) 'Real men, real women, real lives? Gender issues in learning disabilities and challenging behaviour', *Disability and Society*, 10, 4, 425–35

Close, A. (1996) 'Homeless in the heart', *Weekend Australian Review*, 9–10 March, 1, 4

Clyde, M. (1989) 'Who is the odd man out: men in early childhood settings?' *Early Child Development and Care*, 52, 93–99

Coates, J. (1993) (2nd edition) *Women, Men and Language: A Sociolinguistic Account of Gender Differences in Language*. London: Longman

Coleman, M. and Skeen, P. (1987) 'Nontraditional boys: A review of research and theories with suggestions for teachers', *Early Child Development and Care*, 28, 115–28

Collaer, M. and Hines, M. (1995) 'Human behavioral sex differences: A role for gonadal hormones during early development?', *Psychological Bulletin*, 118, 1, 55–107

Collins, C., Batten, M., Ainley, J. and Getty, C. (1996) *Gender and*

School Education. Canberra: Australian Government Publishing Service
Commonwealth Department of Human Services and Health (1995) *Youth Suicide in Australia—a Background Monograph*. Canberra: Australian Government Publishing Service
Connell, R. (1983) *Which Way Is Up? Essays on Class, Sex and Culture*. Sydney: Allen & Unwin
——(1989) 'Cool guys, swots and wimps: The inter-play of masculinity and education', *Oxford Review of Education*, 15, 3, 291–303
——(1994) 'Knowing about masculinity, teaching boys and men', in J. Lemaire (ed.) *Girls, Boys and Equity: A Practical Resource for Use in Schools*. Sydney: New South Wales Teachers Federation
——(1995) *Masculinities*. Sydney: Allen & Unwin
——(1996a) 'Politics of changing men', *Arena*, 6, 53–72
——(1996b) 'Teaching the boys: new research on masculinity, and gender strategies for schools', *Teachers College Record*, 98, 2, 206–35
——, Ashenden, D., Kessler, S. and Dowsett, G. (1982) *Making the Difference: Schools, Families and Social Division*. Sydney: Allen & Unwin
Connolly, P. (1994) 'All lads together?: Racism, masculinity and multi-cultural/anti-racist strategies in a primary school', *International Studies in Sociology of Education*, 4, 2, 191–211
——(1995) 'Boys will be boys? Racism, sexuality and the construction of masculine identities amongs infant boys', in J. Holland, M. Blair and S. Sheldon (eds) *Debates and Issues in Feminist Research and Pedagogy*. Clevedon: Multilingual Matters
Cuneen, C. and Luke, G. (1995) 'Discretionary decisions in juvenile justice and the criminalisation of indigenous young people', *Youth Studies Australia*, 14, 4, 38–46
Cunningham, H. (1995) 'Mortal Kombat and computer game girls', in C. Bazalgette and D. Buckingham (eds) *Not in Front of the Children*. London: British Film Institute
Currie, Y. H. (1990) 'Do boys really need more help? An examination of why so many more boys than girls get special help in Berkshire's mainstream schools', *International Journal of Adolescence and Youth*, 2, 143–50
Davidson, N. (1990) *Boys will be . . . ? Sex Education and Young Men*. London: Bedford Square Press
Davies, B. (1989a) 'Education for sexism: A theoretical analysis of the sex/gender bias in education', *Educational Philosophy and Theory*, 21, 1, 1–19
——(1989b) *Frogs and Snails and Feminist Tales: Preschool Children and Gender*. Sydney: Allen & Unwin
——(1993) *Shards of Glass: Children Reading and Writing Beyond Gendered Identities*. Sydney: Allen & Unwin
——(1996) *Power, Knowledge, Desire: Changing School Organisation and Management Practices*. Canberra: Department of Employment, Education, Training and Youth Affairs

——(1997) 'Constructing and deconstructing masculinities through critical literacy', *Gender and Education*, 9, 1, 9–30

Davies, L. (1992) 'School power cultures under economic constraint', *Educational Review*, 43, 2, 127–36

Dawes, G. (1988) White road, black failure: An ethnographic study of an Aboriginal and Islander school dropout, unpublished Master of Education dissertation, James Cook University of North Queensland

——(1995) To be somebody: The transition from school to life after school for a cohort of urban Aboriginal and Torres Strait Islander youth, unpublished Doctor of Philosophy thesis, James Cook University of North Queensland, Townsville

Dawson, G. (1991) 'The blond Bedouin: Lawrence of Arabia, imperial adventure and the imagining of English-British masculinity', in M. Roper and J. Tosh (eds) *Manful Assertions: Masculinities in Britain since 1800*. London: Routledge

Delgado, R. and Stefancic, J. (1995) 'Minority men, misery, and the marketplace of ideas', in M. Berger, B. Wallis and S. Watson (eds) *Constructing Masculinity*. New York: Routledge

Denborough, D. (1996) 'Step by step: Developing respectful and effective ways of working with young men to reduce violence', in C. McLean, M. Carey and C. White (eds) *Men's Ways of Being*. Boulder: Westview Press

Department of Employment, Education and Training (1991) *Retention and Participation in Australian Schools, 1967–1990*. Canberra: AGPS

——(1995) *No Fear: A Kit Addressing Gender Based Violence*. Canberra

Dinnerstein, M. (1976) *The Mermaid and the Minotaur: Sexual Arrangements and Human Malaise*. New York: Harper and Row

Dixon, C. (1997) 'Pete's tool: Identity and sex-play in the design and technology classroom', *Gender and Education*, 9, 1, 89–104

Dunn, J. (1995) 'Addressing gender equity through boys' programs', in Gender Equity Taskforce of the Ministerial Council for Education, Employment, Training and Youth Affairs (Ed.) *Proceedings of the Gender Equity Conference*. Canberra: Australian Capital Territory Department of Education and Training

Durkin, K. (1995) *Computer Games: Their Effects on Young People. A Review*. Sydney: Office of Film and Literature Classification

Dwyer, B. (1992) The Construction of narrative within one year three classroom, unpublished M. Ed. thesis, School of Education, James Cook University of North Queensland

Dyer, K. (1982) *Challenging the Men: The Social Biology of Female Sporting Achievement*. St Lucia: University of Queensland Press

Eagleton, T. (1983) *Literary Theory: An Introduction*. Oxford: Blackwell

Eckert, P. (1989) *Jocks and Burnouts: Social Categories and Identity in the High School*. New York: Teachers College Press

Edgar, P. (1991) *Australian Broadcasting Tribunal's Inquiry into TV Violence in Australia*. Transcript of speech delivered to the Catholic Education Office's Media Concerns Seminar, Melbourne, June

Edley, N. and Wetherell, M. (1995) *Men in Perspective: Practice, Power and Identity*. London: Prentice Hall

Egger, S. (1995) 'Violence and masculinity: A commentary', in D. Chappell and S. Egger (eds) *Australian Violence: Contemporary Perspectives II.* Canberra: Australian Institute of Criminology

Elium, D. and Elium, J. (1992) *Raising a Son: Parenting and the Making of a Healthy Man.* Stroud, UK: Hawthorn Press

Emslie, M. (1996) 'Ignored to death: Representations of young gay men, lesbians and bisexuals in Australian youth suicide policy and programs', *Youth Studies Australia*, 15, 4, 38–42

Epstein, D. (1996) 'Keeping them in their place: Hetero/sexist harassment, gender and the enforcement of heterosexuality', in J. Holland and L. Adkins (eds) *Sex, Sensibility and the Gendered Body.* London: Macmillan

——(1997) 'Boyz' own stories: Masculinities and sexualities in schools', *Gender and Education*, 9, 1, 105–15

——(ed.) (1995) *Challenging Lesbian and Gay Inequalities in Education.* Buckingham: Open University Press

——and Johnston, R. (1994) 'On the straight and narrow: The heterosexual presumption, homophobias and schools', in D. Epstein (ed.) *Challenging Lesbian and Gay Inequalities in Education.* Buckingham: Open University Press

Evans, T. (1982) 'Being and becoming: teachers' perceptions of sex-roles and actions towards their male and female pupils', *British Journal of Sociology of Education*, 3, 2, 127–43

Federation of Parents' and Citizens' Associations of New South Wales (1993) *1993 Annual Conference Discussion Paper: Homophobia.* Sydney

Fine, M. (1988) 'Sexuality, schooling, and adolescent females: The missing discourse of desire', *Harvard Educational Review*, 58, 1, 29–55

Fisher, S. (1994) 'What about the boys?', *xy: men, sex and politics*, Spring

Fletcher, R. (1993) *Australian Men and Boys . . . A Picture of Health? Graphs of Health Indicators for Australian Males.* Newcastle: University of Newcastle

——(1994) *Boys' Education Strategy 1995?* Newcastle: University of Newcastle

Flynn, J. (1994) 'Prevalence of reading failure in boys compared with girls', *Psychology in the Schools*, 31, January, 66–71

Folds, R. (1987) *Whitefella School: Education and Aboriginal resistance.* Sydney: Allen & Unwin

Foley, D. (1990) 'The great American football ritual: Reproducing race, class and gender inequality', *Sociology of Sport Journal*, 7, 111–35

Formaini, H. (1990) *Men: The Darker Continent.* London: Mandarin

Forsey, C. (1989) *'Taking the Rap' . . . a Series of Classroom Activities.* Footscray, Vic.: West Education Centre

——(1990) *The Making of Men: Guidelines for Working with Boys to Counter the Male Sex-role.* Footscray, Vic.: West Education Centre

——(1994) *Hands Off! The Anti-violence Guide to Developing Positive Relationships.* Footscray, Vic.: West Education Centre

Foucault, M. (1984) *The History of Sexuality: An Introduction.* Harmondsworth: Penguin
——(1988) 'Technologies of the self', in L. Martin, H. Gutman and P. Hutton (eds) *Technologies of the Self: A Seminar with Michel Foucault.* London: Tavistock
Fox, M. (1993) 'Men who weep, boys who dance: The gender agenda between the lines in children's literature', *Language Arts,* 70, 2, 84–8
Frank, B. (1992–3) 'Straight/strait jackets for masculinity: Educating for "real men"', *Atlantis,* 18, 1 and 2, 47–59
Franklin, C. (1993) 'Ain't I a man?: The efficacy of black masculinities for the men's studies in the 1990s', in R. Major and J. Gordon (eds) *The American Black Male: His Present Status and his Future.* Chicago: Nelson Hall
Freebody, P. (1992) 'Inventing cultural-capitalist distinctions in the assessment of HSC papers: Coping with inflation in an era of "Literacy Crisis"', in F. Christie (ed.) *Literacy in Social Processes.* Darwin: Northern Territory University Press
——(1993) 'Social class and reading', in A. Luke & P. Gilbert (eds) *Literacy in Contexts: Australian Perspectives and Issues.* Sydney: Allen & Unwin
——and Baker, C.D. (1987) 'The construction and operation of gender in children's first school books', in A. Pauwels (ed.) *Women and Language in Australian and New Zealand Society.* Sydney: Australian Professional Publications
——, Luke, A. and Gilbert, P. (1991) 'Reading instruction and discourse critique: Rethinking the politics of literacy', *Curriculum Inquiry* 21, 235–57
——, Ludwig, C. and Gunn, S. (1995) *Everyday Literacy Practices in and Out of Schools in Low Socio-economic Urban Communities.* Report to the Curriculum Corporation, Commonwealth Department of Employment, Education and Training, Canberra, published by the Centre for Literacy Education Research, Griffith University, Queensland
Friedman, B. (1996) *Boys-Talk: A Program for Young Men about Masculinity, Non-violence and Relationships.* Adelaide: Men Against Sexual Assault
Frith, G. (1981) 'Little women, good wives: is English good for girls?', in A. McRobbie and T. McCabe (eds) *Feminism for Girls: An Adventure Story.* London: Routledge and Kegan Paul
Gee, James (1990) *Social Linguistics and Literacies.* London: The Falmer Press
Gerschik, T. and Miller, A. (1994) 'Manhood and physical disability', *Changing Men,* 27, Winter, 25–30
Gibbons, A. (1991) 'The brain as "sexual organ"', *Science,* 5023, 957–59
Gibbs, J. and Merighi, J. (1994) 'Young black males: Marginality, masculinity and criminality', in T. Newburn and E. Stanko (eds) *Just Boys Doing Business? Men, Masculinities and Crime.* London: Routledge
Gilbert, P. (1988) 'Student text as pedagogical text', in S. De Castell,

A. Luke, and C. Luke (eds) *Language Authority and Criticism: Readings on the School Textbook*, Lewes/Philadelphia: Falmer Press, 195–202

——(1989a) *Gender, Literacy and the Classroom*. Melbourne: Australian Reading Association

——(1989b) *Writing, Schooling and Deconstruction: From Voice to Text in the Classroom*. London: Routledge

Gilbert, P. (1993) *Gender Stories and the Language Classroom*. Geelong, Vic.: Deakin University Press

——(1994) *Divided by a Common Language? Gender and the English Classroom*. Carlton, Vic.: Curriculum Corporation

——(1996) *Talking About Gender: Terminology Used in the Education of Girls Policy Area and Implications for Policy Priorities and Programs*. A Women's Employment, Education and Training Advisory Group Project: Department of employment, Education Training and Youth Affairs, Canberra

——and Gilbert, R. (1995) *What's Going On? Girls' Experiences of Educational Disadvantage*. Sydney: J.S. McMillan

——and Taylor, S. (1991) *Fashioning the Feminine: Girls, Popular Culture and Schooling*. Sydney: Allen & Unwin

——Gilbert, R. and McGinty, S. (1995) 'Girls talk', in P. Gilbert and R. Gilbert (1995) *What's Going On? Girls' Experiences of Educational Disadvantage*. Sydney: J.S. McMillan

Gilbert, R. and Gilbert, P. (1996a) 'Gender perspectives on society and environment', in R. Gilbert, R. (ed.) *Studying Society and Environment: A Handbook for Teachers*. Melbourne: Macmillan Educational

——and Gilbert, P. (1996b) 'Technologies of schooling and the education of boys', in N. Alloway, B. Davies, P. Gilbert, R. Gilbert and D. King (eds) (1996) *Boys and Literacy: Meeting the Challenge. Book 3*. Townsville: James Cook University of North Queensland/Department of Employment, Education, Training and Youth Affairs

Gilligan, J. (1996) *Violence: Our Deadly Epidemic and its Causes*. New York: G. P. Putnam

Giroux, H. (1995) 'Pulp fiction and the culture of violence', *Harvard Educational Review*, 65, 2, 299–314

Glanville, J. (1995) 'Australian Youth Policy and Action Coalition: Indigenous Youth Project identifies issues of concern', *Youth Studies Australia*, 14, 4, 14–15

Glascott, K. (1997) 'Student's harsh lesson in sex education', *Australian*, 3 April, 9

Goldberger, N. (1997) 'Ways of knowing: Does gender matter?', in M. Walsh (ed.) *Women, Men, and Gender: Ongoing Debates*. New Haven: Yale University Press

Golding, S. and Friedman, B. (1997) *Guys Talk Too: Improving Yong Men's Sexual Health. Report of the Young Men and Acquaintance Rape Survey*. Adelaide: Family Planning, South Australia

Goldstein, J. (1989) 'Beliefs about human aggression', in J. Groebel and R. Hinde (eds) *Aggression and War: Their Biological and Social Bases*. Cambridge: Cambridge University Press

Gottlieb, J., Alter, M., Gottlieb, B. and Wishner, J. (1994) 'Special education in urban America: It's not justifiable for many', *Journal of Special Education*, 27, 4, 453–65

Graham, D. (1994) 'Adolescent suicide in the Australian rural recession', *Australian Journal of Social Issues*, 29, 4, 407–11

Gray, B. (1995) 'Education for life: Homosexuality, AIDS and education', *Education Australia*, 29, 19–21

Greenstein, B. (1993) *The Fragile Male*. London: Boxtree

Griffiths, C. (1995) 'Cowering behind the bushes', in R. Browne and R. Fletcher (eds) *Boys in Schools: Addressing the Real Issues—Behaviour, Values and Relationships*. Sydney: Finch Publishing

Groome, H. (1995) 'Towards improved understandings of Aboriginal young people', *Youth Studies Australia*, 14, 4, 17–21

——and Hamilton, A. (1995) *Meeting the Educational Needs of Aboriginal Adolescents*. Commissioned Report No. 35 of the National Board of Employment, Education and Training, Canberra: Australian Government Publishing Service

Halpern, D. (1994) 'Stereotypes, science, censorship, and the study of sex differences', *Feminism and Psychology*, 4, 4, 523–30

Hannerz, U. (1969) *Soulside: Inquiries into Ghetto Culture and Community*. New York: Columbia University Press

Hargreaves, J. (1992) 'Sex, gender and the body in sport and leisure: Has there been a civilizing process?' in E. Dunning and C. Rojek (eds) *Sport and Leisure in the Civilizing Process: Critique and Counter-critique*. London: Macmillan

Hatton, E. and Swinson, S. (1994) 'Sexual orientation, policy and teaching', in E. Hatton (Ed.) *Understanding Teaching: Curriculum and the Social Context of Schooling*. Sydney: Harcourt Brace

Hawley, R. (1993) *Boys will be Men: Masculinity in Troubled Times*. Middlebury, Vermont: Paul S. Eriksson

Haywood, C. and Mac An Ghaill, M. (1996) 'Schooling masculinities', in M. Mac An Ghaill (Ed.) *Understanding Masculinities: Social Relations and Cultural Arenas*. Buckingham: Open University Press

Healy, D. and Croce, C. (1995) *Adolescent Health in Australia*. Australian Youth Policy and Action Coalition

Herbert, C. (1992) *Sexual Harassment in Schools: A Guide for Teachers*. London: David Fulton

Hill, B. (1991) *Values Education for Australian Schools*. Hawthorn: Australian Council for Educational Research

Hinson, S. (1995a) 'Rethinking sex-based harassment in Australian schools: A practice-focused approach', in Gender Equity Taskforce of the Ministerial Council for Education, Employment, Training and Youth Affairs (ed.) *Proceedings of the Gender Equity Conference*. Canberra: Australian Capital Territory Department of Education and Training

——(1995b) 'The need for a practice-focused approach to policy, curriculum, professional development and whole school programs addressing sex-based harassment in Australian schools', in Ministerial Advisory Committee on Gender Equity *Girls and Boys:*

Challenging Perspectives, Building Partnerships. Brisbane: Department of Education, Queensland

Hoptman, M. and Davidson, R. (1994) 'How and why do the two cerebral hemispheres interact?', *Psychological Bulletin*, 116, 2, 195–219

Hudson, B. (1984) 'Femininity and adolescence', in A. McRobbie and M. Nava (Eds) *Gender and Generation*. London: Macmillan

Hughes, P. (1995) 'Gender and issues for Aboriginal and Torres Strait Islander education', in Ministerial Council for Education, Employment, Training and Youth Affairs (ed.) *Proceedings of the Promoting Gender Equity Conference*. Canberra: Australian Capital Territory Department of Education

Hunter, E. (1990) 'Using a socio-historical frame to analyse Aboriginal self-destructive behaviour', *Australian and New Zealand Journal of Psychiatry*, 24, 191–98

Hunter, I. (1988) *Culture and Government: The Emergence of Literary Education*. London: Macmillan

——(1994) *Rethinking the School*. Sydney: Allen & Unwin

Hyde, J., Fennema, E. and Lamon, S. (1990) 'Gender differences in mathematics performance: A meta-analysis', *Psychological Bulletin*, 107, 2, 139–55

Jetnikoff, A. (1997/in press) 'Concealing and revealing: Boys, literacy and biculturalism', in N. Alloway and P. Gilbert (eds) *Boys and Literacy: Teaching Units*. Carlton, Vic: Curriculum Corporation

Johnson, S. (1997) 'Theorizing language and masculinity: A feminist perspective', in S. Johnson and U. Meinhof (eds) *Language and Masculinity*. Oxford: Blackwell

Johnston, E. (1991) *Royal Commission into Aboriginal Deaths in Custody. National Report: Volume 2*. Canberra: Australian Government Publishing Service

Jones, S. (1993) *The Language of Genes: Biology, History and the Evolutionary Future*. London: HarperCollins

Jordan, E. (1995) 'Fighting boys and fantasy play: the construction of masculinity in the early years of school,' *Gender and Education*, 7, 1, 69–85

Kaplan, G. and Rogers, L. (1990) 'The definition of male and female: Biological reductionism and the sanction of normality' in Gunew, S. (ed.) *Feminist Knowledge: Critique and Construct*. London: Routledge

Katz, J. (1995) 'Reconstructing masculinity in the locker room: The mentors in violence prevention project', *Harvard Educational Review*, 65, 2, 163–74

Keira Technology High (1994) 'Dealing with sex based harassment', in J. Lemaire, (ed.) *New Agendas: Girls, Boys and Equity. A Practical Resource for Use in Schools*. Sydney: Centre for Teaching and Learning, New South Wales Teachers Federation

Kelly, L. (1992) 'Not in front of the children', in M. Arnot and L. Barton (eds) *Voicing Concerns: Sociological Perspectives on Contemporary Education Reforms*. Wallingford, Oxfordshire: Triangle Books

Kenway, J. (1995) 'Taking stock of gender reform in Australian schools: Past, present and future', in Ministerial Council for Education, Employment, Training and Youth Affairs (MCEETYA) *Proceedings of the Promoting Gender Equity Conference*. Canberra: ACT Department of Education and Training

——and Fitzclarence, L. (1997) 'Masculinity, violence and schooling: Challenging "poisonous pedagogies"', *Gender and Education*, 9, 1, 117–133

——and Willis, S. (eds) (1990) *Hearts and Minds: Self-esteem and the Schooling of Girls*. Lewes: Falmer Press

——, Willis, S., Blackmore, J. and Rennie, L. (1997) *Answering Back: Girls, Boys and Feminism*. Sydney: Allen & Unwin, 26–7

Kenworthy, C. (1994) '"We want to resist your resistant readings": Masculinity and discourse in the English classroom', *Interpretations*, 27, 2, 74–95

Kessler, S., Ashenden, D., Connell, R., and Dowsett, G. (1985) 'Gender relations in secondary schooling', *Sociology of Education*, 58, 34–48

Kewley, J. and Lewis, H. (eds) (1993) *Fathers*. Ringwood, Vic.: McPhee Gribble

Kidd, B. (1987) 'Sports and masculinity', in M. Kaufman, (ed.) *Beyond Patriarchy: Essays by Men on Pleasure, Power, and Change*. Toronto: Oxford University Press

Kimura, D. (1992) 'Sex differences in the brain', *Scientific American*, 267, 3, 81–7

Klama, J. (1988) *Aggression: Conflict in Animals and Humans Reconsidered*. Harlow: Longman

Klein, S.S. (ed) (1992) *Sex Equity and Sexuality in Education*. Albany, NY: State University of New York Press

Kline, S. (1995) 'The empire of play: Emergent genres of product-base animations', in C. Bazalgette and D. Buckingham (eds) *In Front of the Children: Screen Entertainment and Young Audiences*. London: British Film Institute

Kohn, M. (1992) 'Sex and the brain', *New Statesman and Society*, 5, 230, 31–2

Kokori, K. (1995) 'Breaking the rules', in R. Browne and R. Fletcher (eds) *Boys in Schools: Addressing the Real Issues—Behaviour, Values and Relationships*. Sydney: Finch Publishing

Kristeva, J. (1986) 'Women's time', in T. Moi (ed.) *The Kristeva Reader*. Oxford: Basil Blackwell. 187–213.

Kruse, A. (1992) '". . . We have learnt not just to sit back, twiddle our thumbs and let *them* take over". Single-sex settings and the development of a pedagogy for girls and pedagogy for boys in Danish schools', *Gender and Education*, 4, 81–104

Lankshear, C. and McLaren, P. (1993) *Critical Literacy: Politics, Praxis and the Postmodern*. Albany, NY: State University of New York Press

Lareau, A. (1992) 'Gender differences in parent involvement in schooling', in J. Wrigley (ed.) *Education and Gender Equality*. London: The Falmer Press, 207–24

Laursen, B. and Collins, W. (1994) 'Interpersonal conflict during adolescence', *Psychological Bulletin*, 115, 2, 197–209

Lemaire, J. (1994) New South Wales Teachers' Federation: Submission to Government Advisory Committee on Education, Training and Youth Affairs on Gender Equity and Boys Education Strategies, Unpublished document

Luke, A. (1992) 'The body literate: discourse and inscription in early literacy instruction', *Linguistics and Education*, 4, 107–29

——(1997) 'Representing and reconstructing Asian masculinities: This is not a movie review', *Social Alternatives*, 16, 3, 32–4

Lydeamore, J. et al. (1993) Gender Equity in Senior Secondary School Assessment (ESSA) Project, unpublished Final Report, Senior Secondary Assessment Board of South Australia (SSABSA): Adelaide

Lynn, R. (1994) 'Sex differences in intelligence and brain size: A paradox resolved', *Personality and Individual Differences*, 17, 2, 257–71

Mac An Ghaill, M. (1994) *The Making of Men: Masculinities, Sexualities and Schooling*. Buckingham: Open University Press

——(1995) '(In)visibility: Sexuality, race and masculinity in the school context', in D. Epstein (ed.) *Challenging Lesbian and Gay Inequalities in Education*. Buckingham: Open University Press

McCarthy, C. and Crichlow, W. (1993) 'Introduction', in C. McCarthy and W. Crichlow (eds) *Race, Identity and Representation in Education*. Routledge: New York, xiii–xxix

Mackay, M. (1996) 'Aboriginal juveniles and the criminal justice system: The case of Victoria', *Children Australia*, 21, 3, 11–22

McLean, C. (1995) 'The costs of masculinity: Placing men's pain in the context of male power', in Ministerial Council for Education, Employment, Training and Youth Affairs (MCEETYA) *Proceedings of the Promoting Gender Equity Conference*. Canberra: ACT Department of Education and Training

——(1996) 'Boys and education in Australia', in C. McLean, M. Carey and C. White (eds) *Men's Ways of Being*. Boulder, Col.: Westview Press

MacLennan, G. and Yeates, H. (1995) 'Masculinity, class and sport in the nineties', *XY: Men, Sex, Politics*, 5, 3, 22–23

McMahon, A. (1993) 'Male readings of feminist theory: the psychologisation of sexual politics in the masculinity literature', *Theory and Society*, 22, 5, 675–96

McNay, L. (1992) *Foucault and Feminism: Power, Gender and the Self*. Cambridge: Polity Press

McRobbie, A. (1991) *Feminism and Youth Culture: From 'Jackie' to 'Just Seventeen'*. London: Macmillan

Majors, R. (1989) 'Cool Pose: The proud signature of black survival', in M. Kimmel and M. Messner (eds) *Men's Lives*. New York: Macmillan

Malin, M. (1994) 'Why is life so hard for Aboriginal students in urban classrooms?', *The Aboriginal Child at School*, 22, 2, 141–53

Maloney, E. (1994) 'Why surfers dump on sex', *The Bulletin*, 2 August, 93–5

Marriott, D. (1996) 'Reading black masculinities', in Mac An Ghaill, M. (ed.) *Understanding Masculinities: Social Relations and Cultural Arenas*. Buckingham: Open University Press

Martinez, L. (1994) 'Boyswork: Whose work?', *Redress. Association of Women Educators' Journal*, 3, 2, 3–12

Martino, W. (1995a) 'Gendered learning practices: Exploring the costs of hegemonic masculinity for girls and boys in schools', in Ministerial Council for Education, Employment, Training and Youth Affairs (MCEETYA) (1995) *Proceedings of the Promoting Gender Equity Conference*. Canberra: ACT Department of Education and Training, 343–64

——(1995b) 'Critical literacy for boys', *Interpretations*, 28 2, 18–32

Maslen, G. (1997) 'Who is heeding the cry for help?', *The Australian Higher Education Supplement*, 5 February

Mason, G. (1996) 'Violence against lesbians and gay men', in K. Healey (ed.) *A Culture of Violence? Issues for the Nineties*. Balmain, NSW: The Spinney Press

Messner, M. (1989) 'Sports and the politics of inequality', in M. Kimmel and M. Messner (eds) *Men's Lives*. New York: Macmillan

——(1990) 'Masculinities and athletic careers: Bonding and status differences', in M. Messner and D. Sabo (eds) *Sport, Men and the Gender Order: Critical Feminist Perspectives*. Champaign, Ill.: Human Kinetics Books

Miedzian, M. (1991) *Boys will be Boys: Breaking the Link Between Masculinity and Violence*. New York: Anchor Books

Miles, R. (1991) *The Rites of Man: Love, Sex and Death in the Making of the Male*. London: Paladin

Mills, M. (1997) 'Boys and masculinities in schools', *Education Links*, 54, 22–4

Moir, A. and Jessel, D. (1991) *Brainsex: The Real Difference Between Men and Women*. London: Mandarin

Moon, B. (1992) 'Theorising violence in the discourse of masculinities', *Southern Review*, 25, 2, 194–204

Moore, D. (1994) *The Lads in Action: Social Process in an Urban Youth Subculture*. Aldershot: Arena

Moran, M. (1995) 'Young and powerful', in R. Browne and R. Fletcher (eds) *Boys in Schools: Addressing the Real Issues—Behaviour, Values and Relationships*. Sydney: Finch Publishing

Moss, G. (1989) *Un/Popular Fictions*. London: Virago Education Series

Muehlenhard, C. and Falcon, P. (1990) 'Men's heterosocial skill and attitudes towards women as predictors of verbal sexual coercion and forceful rape', *Sex Roles*, 23, 241–59

Nakata, M. (1995) 'Cutting a better deal for Torres Strait Islanders', *Youth Studies Australia*, 14, 4, 29–33

National Committee on Violence (1990) *Violence: Directions for Australia*. Canberra: Australian Institute of Criminology

National Health and Medical Research Council (1992) *Breaking Out—*

Challenges in Adolescent and Mental Health in Australia. Canberra: Australian Government Publishing Service

National Review of Education for Aboriginal and Torres Strait Islander Peoples (1994) *Statistical Annex.* Canberra: Australian Government Publishing Service

New South Wales Government Advisory Committee on Education, Training and Tourism (O'Dohery Report) (1994) *A Report to the Minister for Education, Training and Youth Affairs on the Inquiry into Boys' Education 1994.* Sydney

New South Wales Government Advisory Committee on Education, Training and Tourism (Chair: S.O'Doherty) (1994) *A Report to the Minister for Education, Training and Youth Affairs on the Inquiry into Boys' Education. Challenges and Opportunities: A Discussion Paper.* Sydney: Ministry of Education and Youth Affairs

Nichols, S. (1994) 'Fathers and literacy', *Australian Journal of Language and Literacy,* 17, 4, 301–12

——(1995) 'Learning difficulties and gender: Examining some key assumptions', in Ministerial Council for Education, Employment, Training and Youth Affairs (MCEETYA) (1995) *Proceedings of the Promoting Gender Equity Conference.* Canberra: ACT Department of Education and Training, 365–80

O'Brien, N. (1997) 'Drop in suicides since gun buy-back', *Australian,* 9 May, 5

O'Connor, M. (1992) *Boys will be . . . A Report on the Survey of Year Nine Males and their Attitudes to Forced Sex.* Brisbane: Domestic Violence Resource Centre

O'Donoghue, J. (1995) 'Violence in schools', in L. Adler and F. Denmark (eds) *Violence and the Prevention of Violence.* Westport, Conn.: Praeger

O'Moore, A. (1995) 'Bullying in children and adolescents in Ireland', *Children and Society,* 9, 2, 54–72

Ollis, D. and Tomaszewski, I. (1993) *Gender and Violence Project: Position Paper.* Canberra: Department of Employment, Education and Training, Australian Government Publishing Service

Olweus, D. (1993) *Bullying at School: What We Know and What We Can Do.* Oxford: Blackwell

Palmer, D. and Collard, L. (1993) 'Aboriginal young people and youth subcultures', in R. White (ed.) *Youth Subcultures: Theory, History and the Australian Experience.* Hobart: National Clearinghouse for Youth Studies

Patterson, A. (1995) 'Supervising freedom: The English profile; English curriculum; and English pedagogy', *Australian Journal of Language and Literacy,* 18, 2

——and Lee, A. (1993) *Reading Disadvantage: Girls' Reading Boys' Coming-of-Age Novels in Secondary English Classrooms.* Report from a Gender Equity in Curriculum Reform Project, Canberra: Department of Employment, Education and Training

Pellegrini, A. (1993) 'Boys' rough-and-tumble play, social competence and group composition', *British Journal of Developmental Psychology*, 11, 237–48

Peters, M. (1991) 'Sex differences in human brain size and the general meaning of differences in brain size', *Canadian Journal of Psychology*, 45, 4, 507–22

Phillips, A. (1993) *The Trouble with Boys: Parenting the Men of the Future*. London: Pandora

Pleck, J., Sonenstein, F. and Ku, L. (1993) 'Masculinity ideology: Its impact on adolescent males' heterosexual relationships', *Journal of Social Issues*, 49, 3, 11–29

Polk, K. (1991) 'A scenario of masculine violence: Confrontational homicide', in H. Strang and S. Gerull (eds) *Homicide: Patterns, Prevention and Control*. Conference Proceedings No. 17. Canberra: Australian Institute of Criminology

——(1995) 'Youth violence: Myth and reality', in D. Chappell and S. Egger (eds) *Australian Violence: Contemporary Perspectives II*. Canberra: Australian Institute of Criminology

Poynton, C. (1985) *Language and Gender: Making the Difference*. Geelong, Vic.: Deakin University Press

Prentky, R. (1985) 'The neurochemistry and neuroendocrinology of sexual aggression', in D. Farrington and J. Gunn (eds) *Aggression and Dangerousness*. Chichester: Wiley

Prior, M., Sanson, A., Smart, D., and Oberklaid, F. (1995) 'Reading disability in an Australian community sample', *Australian Journal of Psychology*, 47, 1, 32–7

Queitsch, A. (1997) 'Disrupting discourses in media texts: The lives of Djakapurra', in N. Alloway and P. Gilbert (eds) *Boys and Literacy: Teaching Units*. Carlton, Vic.: Curriculum Corporation

Redman, P. (1996) '"Empowering men to disempower themselves": heterosexual masculinities, HIV and the contradictions of anti-oppressive education', in Mac An Ghaill, M. (ed.) *Understanding Masculinities: Social Relations and Cultural Arenas*. Buckingham: Open University Press

——and Mac An Ghaill, M. (1996) 'Schooling sexualities: heterosexual masculinities, schooling and the unconscious', *Discourse: Studies in the Cultural Politics of Education*, 17, 2, 243–56

Ridley, M. (1994) *The Red Queen*. London: Penguin

Rigby, K. (1996) *Bullying in Schools: And What to Do About It*. Melbourne: Australian Council for Educational Research

Rizvi, F. (1993) 'Children and the grammar of popular racism', in C. McCarthy and W. Crichlow (eds) *Race, Identity and Representation in Education*. New York: Routledge, 126–39

Rose, S. (1992) *The Making of Memory: From Molecules to Mind*. Toronto: Bantam Books

Rowland, R. and Thomas, A. (eds) (1996) 'Mothering sons: A crucial feminist challenge', Special Feature, *Feminism and Psychology*, 6, 1, 93–154

Rutherford, J. (1990) 'A place called home: Identity and the cultural politics of difference', in J. Rutherford (ed.) *Identity: Community, Culture and Difference*. London: Lawrence and Wishart

Sabo, D. (1989) 'Pigskin, patriarchy and pain', in M. Kimmel and M. Messner (eds) *Men's Lives*. New York: Macmillan

——and Panepinto, J. (1990) 'Football ritual and the social reproduction of masculinity', in M. Messner and D. Sabo (eds) *Sport, Men, and the Gender Order: Critical Feminist Perspectives*. Champaign, Ill.: Human Kinetics Books

Salisbury, J. and Jackson, D. (1996) *Challenging Macho Values: Practical Ways of Working with Adolescent Boys*. London: Falmer

Sanderson, G. (1995) 'Being "cool" and a reader', in R. Browne and R. Fletcher (eds) *Boys in Schools: Addressing the Real Issues— Behaviour, Values and Relationships*. Sydney: Finch Publishing

Schact, S. (1996) 'Misogyny on and off the "pitch"', *Gender and Society*, 10, 5, 550–65

Scraton, S. (1992) *Shaping Up to Womanhood: Gender and Girls' Physical Education*. Buckingham: Open University Press

Segal, L. (1990) *Slow Motion: Changing Masculinities, Changing Men*. London: Virago

Seidler, V. (1985) 'Fear and intimacy', in A. Metcalf and M. Humphries *The Sexuality of Men*. London: Pluto Press

——(1987) 'Reason, desire, and male sexuality', in P. Caplan (ed.) *The Cultural Construction of Sexuality*. London: Routledge, 82–112

——(1989) *Rediscovering Masculinity: Reason, language and sexuality*. London: Routledge

Select Committee on Youth Affairs (1992) *Youth and the Law: Discussion Paper No. 3* Legislative Assembly, Perth

Senate Select Committee on Community Standards Relevant to the Supply of Services Utilizing Electronic Technologies (1993) *Report on Video and Computer Games and Classification Issues*. Canberra: Parliament of the Commonwealth of Australia

Sewell, T. (1995) 'A phallic response to schooling: Black masculinity and race in an inner-city comprehensive', in M. Griffiths and B. Troyna (eds) *Antiracism, Culture and Social Justice in Education*. Stoke-on-Trent: Trentham Books

Seymour, W. (1997) 'The body: Physicality and rehabilitation', in M. Caltabiano, R. Hil and R. Frangos (eds) *Achieving Inclusion: Exploring Issues in Disability*. Townsville: Centre for Social and Welfare Research, James Cook University of North Queensland

Shakespeare, T. (1996) 'Power and prejudice: Issues of gender, sexuality and disability', in Barton, L. (ed.) *Disability and Society: Emerging Issues and Insights*. London: Longman

Shaywitz, B., Shaywitz, S., Pugh, D., Constable, R., Skudlarski, P., Fulbright, R., Bronen, R., Fletcher, J., Shankweller, D., Katz, L. and Gore, J. (1995) 'Sex differences in the functional organisation of the brain for language', *Nature*, 373, 6515, pp. 607–9

Sheridan, E.M. (ed) (1983) *Sex Stereotypes and Reading*. Newark, NJ: International Reading Association

Showalter, E. (1977) *A Literature of Their Own: British Women Novelists from Bronte to Lessing*. Princeton, NJ: Princeton University Press

Silverstein, O. and Rashbaum, B. (1994) *The Courage to Raise Good Men*. New York: Viking

Skeggs, B. (1991) 'Challenging masculinity and using sexuality', *British Journal of Sociology of Education*, 12, 1, 127–40

Smith, B. (1995) *Mothers and Sons: The Truth About Mother-Son Relationships*. Sydney: Allen & Unwin

Smith, G. (1996) 'Dichotomies in the making of men', in C. McLean, M. Carey and C. White (eds) *Men's Ways of Being*. Boulder, Col.: Westview Press

Spender, D. (1980) *Man-made Language*. London: Routledge and Kegan Paul

Standing Committee on Social Issues, Legislative Council, Parliament of New South Wales (1995) *A Report into Youth Violence in New South Wales*. Sydney

Stanworth, M. (1984) 'Girls on the margins: a study of gender divisions in the classroom', in A. Hargreaves and P. Woods (eds) *Classrooms and Staffrooms*. Milton Keynes: Open University Press, 147–58

Star, S. (1991) 'The politics of right and left: Sex differences in hemispheric brain asymmetry', in S. Gunew (ed.) *A Reader in Feminist Knowledge*. London: Routledge

Stoltenberg, J. (1990) *Refusing to Be a Man: Essays on Sex and Justice*. New York: Meridian Books (Penguin)

Swann, J. (1992) *Girls, Boys and Language*. Oxford: Blackwell Publishers

Szirom, T. (1988) *Teaching Gender? Sex Education and Sexual Stereotypes*. Sydney: Allen & Unwin

Tavris, C. (1992) *The Mismeasure of Woman*. New York: Touchstone Books

Taylor, D. (1996) 'Letting young people die', *Arena Magazine*, 22, 12–13

Teese, R., Davies, M. Charlton, M., and Polesel, J. (1995) *Who Wins at School? Boys and Girls in Australian Secondary Education*. Department of Education Policy and Management, The University of Melbourne: J.S. McMillan

——, McLean, G. and Polesel, J. (1993) *Equity Outcomes: A Report to the Schools Council's Task Force on a Broadbanded Equity Program for Schools*. Canberra: Australian Government Publishing Service

'The trouble with men' (1996) *The Economist*, 340, 7985, 28 September, 17–18

Thomas, K. (1991) 'Notions of gender in the construction of English', *Gender and Education*, 3, 2, 117–35

Thorne, B. (1993) *Gender Play: Girls and Boys at School*. Buckingham: Open University Press

Turner, A. (1994) 'Genetic and hormonal influences on male violence', in J. Archer (ed.) *Male Violence*. London: Routledge

Vamplew, W. (1991) *Sports Violence in Australia: Its Extent and Control*. Canberra: Australian Sports Commission

Vance, C. (1995) 'Social construction theory and sexuality', in

M. Berger, B. Wallis and S. Watson (eds) *Constructing Masculinity.* New York: Routledge

Vincent, S. (1996) 'It's not size that counts after all', *HQ*, September–October, 22–4

Walker, J. (1986) 'Romanticising resistance, romanticising culture: A critique of Willis' theory of cultural production', *British Journal of Sociology of Education*, 7, 1, 59–80

——(1988) *Louts and Legends: Male Youth Culture in an Inner-city School.* Sydney: Allen & Unwin

Walkerdine, V. (1986) 'Post-structuralist theory and everyday practices: The family and the school', in S. Wilkinson (ed) *Feminist Social Psychology.* Milton Keynes: Open University Press

——(1989) 'Femininity as performance', *Oxford Review of Education*, 15, 3, 267–79

——(1990) *Schoolgirl Fictions.* London: Verso

Ward, N. (1995) '"Pooftah", "wanker", "girl": Homophobic harassment and violence in schools', in Ministerial Advisory Committee on Gender Equity (ed.) *Girls and Boys: Challenging Perspectives, Building Relationships. Proceedings of the Third Conference of the Ministerial Advisory Committee on Gender Equity.* Brisbane: Department of Education, Queensland

West, P. (1996) *Fathers, Sons and Lovers.* Sydney: Finch Publishing

Wetherell, M. and Edley, N. (1995) *Men in Perspective: Practice, Power and Identity.* London: Prentice Hall/Harvester Wheatsheaf

Whannel, G. (1992) *Fields of Vision: Television Sport and Cultural Transformation.* London: Routledge

Whatley, M. (1992) 'Goals for sex-equitable sexuality education', in S. S. Klein (ed.) *Sex Equity and Sexuality in Education.* Albany, NY: State University of New York Press

White, J. (1986) 'The writing on the wall: Beginning or end of a girl's career?' *Women's Studies International Forum*, 9, 5, 561–74

White, M. (1996) 'Men's culture, the men's movement, and the constitution of men's lives', in C. McLean, M. Carey and C. White (eds) *Men's Ways of Being.* Boulder, Col.: Westview Press

White, P., Young, K. and McTeer, W. (1995) 'Sport, masculinity and the injured body', in D. Sabo and D. Gordon (eds) *Men's Health and Illness: Gender, Power and the Body.* Thousand Oaks: Sage

Whitson, D. (1990) 'Sport and the social construction of masculinity', in M. Messner and D. Sabo (eds) *Sport, Men and the Gender Order: Critical Feminist Perspectives.* Champaign, Ill.: Human Kinetics Books

Wight, D. (1994) 'Boys' thoughts and talk about sex in a working class locality of Glasgow', *Sociological Review*, 42, 4, 703–37

Willis, P. (1977) *Learning to Labour: How Working-class Kids get Working-Class Jobs.* Aldershot: Saxon House

Wilson, P. (1982) *Black Death, White Hands*, Sydney: Allen & Unwin

Wolf-Light, P. (1992/3) 'Win some. Lose some', *Achilles Heel*, Winter, 28–9

Wolpe, A. (1988) *Within School Walls: The Role of Discipline, Sexuality and the Curriculum.* Routledge: London

Wood, J. (1984) 'Groping towards sexism: Boys' sex talk', in A. McRobbie and M. Nava (eds) *Gender and Generation*. London: Macmillan

Wylie, P. (1955) *A Generation of Vipers*. London: Frederick Muller Ltd

Yates, L. (1997) 'Gender equity and the boys debate: What sort of challenge is it?' *British Journal of Sociology of Education*, 18, 3, 337–47

Yeates, H. (1995) 'The league of men: Masculinity, the media and rugby league football', *Media Information Australia*, 75, 35–45

Yunupingu, M. (1994) *National Review of Education for Aboriginal and Torres Strait Islander People. A Discussion Paper*. Canberra: Australian Government Publishing Service

Index

Masculinity goes to school